OXFORD MONOGRAPHS ON
LABOUR LAW

General Editors: Paul Davies,
Keith Ewing, Mark Freedland

THE RIGHT TO STRIKE

Oxford Monographs on Labour Law

General Editors: Paul Davies, Fellow of Balliol College, Oxford and Reader in Law at Oxford University; Keith Ewing, Professor of Public Law at King's College, London, and Fellow of Trinity College, Cambridge; and Mark Freedland, Fellow and Tutor in Law at St. John's College, Oxford.

This series is the first new development in the literature dealing with labour law for many years. The series recognizes the arrival not only of a renewed interest in labour law generally, but also the need for a fresh approach to the study of labour law following a decade of momentous change in the UK and Europe. The series is concerned with all aspects of labour law, including traditional subjects of study such as industrial relations law and individual employment law, but it will also include books which examine the law and economics of the labour market and the impact of social security law upon patterns of employment and the employment contract.

Forthcoming titles in this series

Legislating for Conflict
SIMON AUERBACH

The Law Relating to Dismissal from Employment
HUGH COLLINS

The Right to Strike

K. D. EWING

CLARENDON PRESS · OXFORD
1991

Oxford University Press, Walton Street, Oxford OX2 6DP

Oxford New York Toronto
Delhi Bombay Calcutta Madras Karachi
Petaling Jaya Singapore Hong Kong Tokyo
Nairobi Dar es Salaam Cape Town
Melbourne Auckland

and associated companies in
Berlin Ibadan

Oxford is a trade mark of Oxford University Press

Published in the United States
by Oxford University Press, New York

Library of Congress Cataloging in Publication Data

Ewing, K. D. (Keith D.)
The right to strike / K.D. Ewing.
(Oxford monographs on labour law)
Includes bibliographical references (p. 170) and index.
1. Strikes and lockouts—Law and legislation—Great Britain.
I. Title. II. Series.
KD3076.E95 1990   344.41'01892–dc20   [344.1041892]   90–7842
ISBN 0–19–825439–3

Typeset by Hope Services (Abingdon) Ltd.
Printed in Great Britain by
Biddles Ltd.,
Guildford and King's Lynn

To
Kate and Lucy

Editor's Preface

It is our aim as editors of this new series to promote the publication of books which will make a distinctive contribution to the study of labour law. For this purpose we have adopted a deliberately open-ended view of the subject. Consequently we expect to deal with topics which straddle the frontiers between labour law and other areas of law, whether it be social security law, pensions law, or company law. We expect also that books in the series will not necessarily adopt a formal or legalistic approach, for we would wish to encourage authors to draw upon the contributions made by other disciplines, whether it be industrial relations, political science, or economics. And we would expect, finally, that books in the series will not concentrate exclusively on legal developments in Britain. We are conscious of the importance of EEC law, and aware of the growing interest in the labour laws of EEC member states, as well as in comparative labour law generally.

This preface is written by two of the editors, because the third editor is the author of this second title in the series, and therefore cannot join in our commendation of his book to our readers. It has, indeed, required some advocacy on our part to persuade Keith Ewing to publish this book in our series, and we have had to be able to show convincingly that standards of at least ordinary rigour have been applied to the decision whether the book was suitable for inclusion. Our conviction that this decision was fully justified is based upon the view that this text manages, in a particularly useful way, to show how the impact of the law upon those taking or considering industrial action is a complex and cumulative one, depending as much upon social security law and the law of the individual employment relationship as upon the law of economic torts and statutory immunities or trade union law. In the course of doing that, he makes a significant contribution to the continuing debate as to whether the law relating to industrial action should be constructed around the idea of a right to strike. Its interest can be expected to transcend any short-term changes to the current state of the law of industrial conflict.

13 November 1990   P.L.D.
                                                                          M.R.F.

Preface

There is much already written on the right to strike in Britain. But most of this is concerned with the liability of trade unions and their officials with very little attention being devoted to the individual worker. Trade unions have been content, it seems, with a legal regime which protects their funds but which leaves their members exposed to a range of sanctions. Labour law has been written for trade union bureaucracies rather than for trade union members.

The purpose of this study is to consider the position of the individual worker who engages in a strike or industrial action, described as one of the 'fundamental human liberties'[1] which is protected by international law. Following the introduction in Chapter 1 we move in Chapter 2 to consider the status of industrial action under the contract of employment. In Chapter 3 attention is directed to the recently controversial question of the payment of wages during industrial action short of a strike. Chapter 4 deals with the relevant provisions of the law of unfair dismissal for those engaged in a strike or other industrial action.

It ought perhaps to be said at this point that this is not a textbook designed to deal with all the ways in which labour law affects the striker. The concern is with the central questions such as the contract of employment, the payment of wages, and unfair dismissal. The most notable feature of the law in these areas is the extraordinary vulnerability of the workers involved. Not only does British law fall far short of international standards and the ideals they embrace, it also compares very unfavourably with the position in other developed economies.

But it is not only the labour law regime that continues to confer on employers an enormous power over workers engaged in a dispute. These powers are reinforced by social security law which denies both unemployment benefit and income support to strikers, and in the latter case penalizes their dependants by reducing the amount of benefit that would otherwise be payable. These issues are dealt with in Chapters 5 and 6, while Chapter 7 deals with an important initiative in Ireland to underline the fact that there is no inevitability about the British system and to demonstrate that other options are available. Again no attempt is made to deal with social security law exhaustively. The concern is with the principal features of the system.

The different themes emerging in the book are drawn together in Chapter 8 where a number of proposals for reform are made. It is suggested that an effective solution to the problems identified in the study requires a wide-

[1] *Stapleton* v. *Mitchell* 60 F. Supp. 51, at p. 61 (1945).

ranging response. It is not enough to provide for the suspension of the contracts of employment of those on strike without also legislating to protect strikers from dismissal which, in turn, would be ineffective without a guarantee of reinstatement. It is also suggested that there is no justification for the blanket disqualification of strikers from unemployment benefit and that there are no convincing reasons in principle to justify the withholding of income support from those in dispute, to say nothing of the penalties imposed on dependants. In addressing these questions reference is freely made to important developments in a number of other jurisdictions both inside and outside the European Community.

I am happy to record my deep gratitude to a large number of people who have helped in many ways to enable me to complete this study. I should mention first Tim Christian, Dean of the Faculty of Law at the University of Alberta, for having me there in the 1987/8 academic year. The faculty, the library, and the facilities generally, provided a wonderful environment for research and writing. I should also mention a number of other friends and colleagues whose insights and knowledge have been invaluable. This is true particularly of Douglas Brodie, Breen Creighton, Ted DeCoste, Paul Davies, Mark Freedland, Reuben Hasson, Ron McCallum, Kenneth Miller, Richard Mitchell, Brian Napier, Graham Smith, Andrew Stewart, Nick Wikeley and Frank Wilkinson. The work on the Irish Social Welfare Tribunal in Chapter 7 would not have been possible without the help in different ways of Conor Gearty, Tony Kerr, Declan Madden, and Gerry Whyte. I am grateful to Mr Michael Mongey, Secretary to the Social Welfare Tribunal, for his generous help in the preparation of this chapter. He shares no responsibility for any of the views expressed which are the result of my own observations. I also owe a special debt to a number of exceptional students, namely James Carlson and Simon Renouf at the University of Alberta, and Suzanne Bailey at the University of Cambridge. But perhaps my greatest debt is to Valerie Chuter and Mary Whiting for their quite extraordinary professional support.

K. D. E.
29 March 1990

Contents

Abbreviations

AEU	Amalgamated Engineering Union
APEX	Association of Professional, Executive, Clerical and Computer Staffs
ASLEF	Associated Society of Locomotive Engineers and Firemen
ASTMS	Association of Scientific, Technical and Managerial Staffs
ATGWU	Amalgamated Transport and General Workers' Union
AUEW	Amalgamated Union of Engineering Workers
AUEW-TASS	Amalgamated Union of Engineering Workers (Technical, Administrative and Supervisory Section)
BRB	British Railways Board
CBI	Confederation of British Industry
COHSE	Confederation of Health Service Employees
DHSS	Department of Health and Social Security
EAT	Employment Appeal Tribunal
EETPU	Electrical Electronic Telecommunication and Plumbing Union
EPCA	Employment Protection (Consolidation) Act 1978
ETU	Electrical Trades' Union
ILO	International Labour Organization
IPCS	Institution of Professional Civil Servants
ISTC	Iron and Steel Trades' Confederation
ITGWU	Irish Transport and General Workers' Union
MFGB	Miners' Federation of Great Britain
NACODS	National Association of Colliery Overmen, Shot-firers and Deputies
NALGO	National and Local Government Officers' Association
NCB	National Coal Board
NEETU	National Engineering and Electrical Trades' Union
NGA	National Graphical Association
NUT	National Union of Teachers
NUVB	National Union of Vehicle Builders
SOGAT	Society of Graphical and Allied Trades
STUC	Scottish Trades' Union Congress
TGWU	Transport and General Workers' Union
TUC	Trades' Union Congress
TULRA	Trade Union and Labour Relations Act 1974
USDAW	Union of Shop, Distributive and Allied Workers

Table of Cases

Table of Statutes

CANADIAN STATUTES

UNITED STATES STATUTES

Table of Statutory Instruments

[1]

Introduction

In 1985 Mr Rupert Murdoch's News International was negotiating with a number of trade unions about the launch of a new title, the *London Post*, which was to be produced at Wapping in London's docklands. If satisfactory arrangements could be made for the *Post*, steps would also be taken to transfer existing titles from their production sites in central London to the Wapping plant. But among the detailed proposals presented by the company were controversial demands for the abolition of the closed shop, the introduction of new technology and flexible working arrangements, a no-strike clause, and a provision that collective agreements should be legally enforceable. As could easily have been predicted, these proposals were rejected by the unions which in turn made counter-proposals designed to protect the job security of existing employees in the event of the titles being moved to Wapping. The union proposals were accompanied by a threat that if the company was not prepared to guarantee job security, there would be no option but to take industrial action. Tension mounted when the employers failed to respond positively to the union demands but indicated that the Wapping plant would be brought into readiness for the *London Post* and other group requirements, whether or not agreement was reached with the unions. SOGAT 82 and the NGA then ballotted their members with a view to taking industrial action, and following substantial majority votes in favour, members of both unions began an ill-fated strike at 7.30 a.m. on 24 January 1984.

The employers responded to the strike by dismissing some 5,500 workers involved, and by moving newspaper production to the new plant at Wapping. Although there was some initial disruption of production, this was short-lived, with replacement labour having being recruited to do the work of those on strike. The bitterness caused by the dismissals was fuelled considerably by claims that the replacement staff had been recruited secretly with the active assistance of the electrical union (the EETPU) at the same time as the company was negotiating with the print unions. The hostility towards the electricians which was thereby provoked no doubt contributed to the subsequent expulsion of that union from the TUC. This, however, was a sideshow (albeit an important one) to the main events, the most significant feature of which was the dismissal of the 5,500 workers engaged in what they regarded as a defensive strike, which had been called only after a ballot had been held. The company made it clear that the strikers would not be reinstated, though they subsequently made an offer which they considered 'to be generous and in excess of any possible moral or legal obligation'. Each dismissed employee was offered about £620 for each year of employment, with a minimum of £2,000, the total cost to the company being £50 million. The company also offered to transfer the premises and plant at Gray's Inn Road—the site at which *The Times* had been published—to the unions. These offers were, however, rejected, even though in the meantime the company had been successfully closing down the different campaigns of the unions designed to force them into submission.

Although it was not the first time that striking workers had been dismissed by their employer, the Wapping dispute clearly demonstrated the powerlessness of workers faced with an aggressive management determined to introduce change into the workplace. In so doing the drama vividly highlighted a central weakness of British labour law. For the fact is that the most striking feature of management's response is not that what they did was 'extremely rare' (Scarman 1977: 20) when judged by past industrial practice. More significant is that their conduct was perfectly lawful, with British law taking a most uncompromising line on the employer's power to dismiss strikers and to hire either temporary or permanent replacements. This is despite the fact that such a position would appear to be contrary to both the spirit and the letter of various international legal obligations, including the (original) European Social Charter, which serve to protect the right to strike. It is also despite legal standards operating elsewhere in the world, where the protection of the freedom to strike does enjoy a much greater legal recognition. It would come as a great shock to workers in France, West Germany, Spain, Italy, and parts of Canada to learn that they could be so treated for exercising what is regarded on the streets as a basic human right. In Britain, however, the balance of legality in a dispute lies with the employer at every turn, even where the purpose of the strike is to resist what are in effect the unlawful demands of the employer. Thus, as we shall discover in the following chapters of this book, at common law a strike or other forms of industrial action will almost certainly be a breach of contract by the workers involved. This will empower the employer to take a number of steps, including dismissal, for which there will be no right to complain provided the employer manages the termination efficiently, as the employers in the Wapping dispute appeared to do.

In the past the legal position has generated at best only a complacent response from workers' leaders. Perhaps this is because in practice dismissed workers were generally rehired at the end of the dispute. This, however, was not always the case, with the confrontation in 1977 between Mr George Ward and staff employed at his Grunwick photographic processing works leading to the dismissal of 137 strikers. They were never reinstated despite a recommendation that some of them should be by a Court of Inquiry (Scarman 1977: 23). And although the Labour governments of 1974 to 1979 had the opportunity to introduce legislation to provide adequate protection for those engaged in a dispute, they declined to do so, and did not appear to be under pressure to make proper use of the opportunity. But times have changed, with Wapping having demonstrated clearly that there is now a serious problem in need of urgent attention. It is significant that this was a dispute which involved members of previously strong, powerful and well-established unions. What chance has the fledgling organization struggling to survive in an anti-union firm? It is also significant that so many skilled people could be fired and be replaced so easily. If 5,500 could be discarded in this way, what hope has a handful of unskilled workers in a small workshop? And it is significant, too, that this was ultimately a defensive dispute with workers taking action to protect their jobs, and their terms and conditions of employment. It was not a dispute in which employers were presented with unreasonable demands to change existing terms and conditions of employment. We return in Chapter 8 to consider what measures ought to be taken to protect workers in this situation. But first we must examine in some detail the legal position relating to strikes and other industrial action as it affects workers and their organizations. We begin this enquiry by considering the effect of strike action on the contract of employment.

[2]
Strikes and the Common Law

I. INTRODUCTORY

There is in English law no comprehensive legal definition of a strike or industrial action. Perhaps the closest we come is Lord Denning's attempt in the Court of Appeal in 1975 when he said that a strike 'is a concerted stoppage of work by men [*sic*] done with a view to improving their wages or conditions, or giving vent to a grievance or making a protest about something or other, or supporting or sympathising with other workmen in such endeavour'.[1] Nor is there a statutory definition of a strike used for general purposes. Perhaps the closest we come here is to be found in the deepest corner of the Employment Protection (Consolidation) Act 1978. Schedule 13, paragraph 24 defines a strike for the purpose of determining continuity of employment in the following terms:

'strike' means the cessation of work by a body of persons employed acting in combination, or a concerted refusal or a refusal under a common understanding of any number of persons employed to continue to work for an employer in consequence of a dispute, done as a means of compelling their employer or any person or body of persons employed, or to aid other employees in compelling their employer or any person or body of persons employed, to accept or not to accept terms or conditions of or affecting employment.[2]

But strikes are not of course the only forms of industrial action that workers may take in order to exert pressure on an employer in a dispute. As Lord Templeman pointed out in *Miles* v. *Wakefield Metropolitan District Council*,[3] industrial action 'has many manifestations'. A review of the case-law alone reveals a rich variety of conduct, which includes working to rule; overtime bans; go-slows; boycotting (or blacking) certain work or certain posts; and in the case of the judges, who in 1989 were opposed to the Lord Chancellor's proposals to reform the legal profession, the threat to hold a meeting during office hours, thereby closing the courts. This action was eventually not taken because of the fierce public hostility to it.

---

[1] *Tramp Shipping Corporation* v. *Greenwich Marine Inc.* [1975] ICR 261, at p. 266. See also *Miles* v. *Wakefield Metropolitan District Council* [1987] 1 All ER 1081, at p. 1097.
[2] See also Trade Union Act 1984, and Employment Act 1988, s. 1: 'strike' means 'any concerted stoppage of work'.
[3] [1987] 1 All ER 1089, at p. 1097.

II. STRIKES AND THE CONTRACT OF EMPLOYMENT

It seems to be fairly clear that at common law a strike amounts to a breach of the contract of employment by those involved. So much was recognized by Donovan L.J. in *Rookes* v. *Barnard*[4] where he said that 'There can be few strikes which do not involve a breach of contract by the strikers'.[5] Put simply, so far as an employee is concerned, 'if he refuses to work he is in breach of the contract'.[6] This will be particularly true in the case of what might be called an 'offensive' strike, that is to say, one in which the intent is to change or modify an express term of the contract or one in which the intent is to limit or constrain the wide discretionary power under the contract which the common law confers on the employer. But the same may be true where the purpose of the strike is the defensive one of resisting conduct of the employer which is or which may be unlawful in the sense that the employer is acting in breach of contract. The point is illustrated by *Parkin* v. *South Hetton Coal Company*[7] where a colliery employee alleged that he had not been paid his proper amount and complained to an under-manager, who 'took no notice, but passed on'. In the course of litigation arising out of a resulting strike, Darling J. said that the men's refusal to work was 'repugnant to the very contract of service itself' while A. T. Lawrence J. said that the refusal to work was 'a breach of contract going to the whole consideration'. And to the argument that a strike to defend workers with a grievance was the equivalent of the employer's right to 'lay the pit by' sometimes, A. T. Lawrence J. replied that this was 'an extraordinary contention'.

An attempt to modify the rather uncompromising position of the common law was made by Lord Denning in *Morgan* v. *Fry*[8] where he said:

The truth is that neither employer nor workmen wish to take the drastic action of termination if it can be avoided. The men do not wish to leave their work for ever. The employers do not wish to scatter their labour force to the four winds. Each side is, therefore, content to accept a 'strike notice' of proper length as lawful. It is an implication read into the contract by the modern law as to trade disputes. If a strike takes place, the contract of employment is not terminated. It is suspended during the strike: and revives again when the strike is over.[9]

In other words, the effect of a strike preceded by proper strike notice is not to terminate the contract, but to suspend it. At first sight this seems monumentally significant, the doctrine being applicable apparently to all strikes regardless of their cause or function. In reality, however, it is unlikely that the courts would take the view that the giving of strike notice disables the employer from terminating the contract. At best this is likely to result in the contract being

---

[4] [1963] 1 QB 623.   [5] At p. 682.
[6] *Canadian Pacific Railway Company* v. *Zambri* [1962] SCR 609, at p. 617 per Cartwright J.
[7] (1907) 97 LT 98.   [8] [1968] 2 QB 710.   [9] At p. 728.

suspended during the course of a strike, but with the employer always remaining free to terminate the contract by giving lawful notice. In other words, strike notice is likely only to prevent the employer from lawfully dismissing the employees instantly. But these matters have never been fully canvassed, for even this modest limitation of the power of the employer has failed to win any acceptance, with the Employment Appeal Tribunal in *Simmons* v. *Hoover Ltd.*[10] declining to follow *Morgan* v. *Fry*,[11] holding that while 'there is no doubt' that Lord Denning in the Court of Appeal had introduced into the law the concept of suspension, 'it is only in embryonic form' with none of the consequences having been worked out.

Although it has since been followed by Walsh J. in the Supreme Court of the Republic of Ireland,[12] *Morgan* v. *Fry*[13] was nevertheless a truly unusual case. It was concerned with whether the defendant union official had committed the tort of intimidation by threatening to call members out on strike. The tort of intimidation (which consists of a threat by the defendant to commit an unlawful act against a third party unless the latter takes steps prejudicial to the plaintiff) had been reinvented by the House of Lords (after having been dormant for more than 150 years) in *Rookes* v. *Barnard*[14] but had been excluded from industrial conflict by the Trade Disputes Act 1965. *Morgan* v. *Fry*[15] related to events which had taken place before the 1965 Act came into force and it is clear that the Court of Appeal 'not unnaturally, was reluctant to apply the reasoning in *Rookes* v. *Barnard* to the facts in the case before them'.[16] This may help to explain why Lord Denning concluded that a threat to strike, accompanied by strike notice, is a suspension rather than a breach of the contract, thereby avoiding a characterization that the defendants' threat to strike amounted to unlawful conduct for the purposes of the tort. But quite apart from the special circumstances of *Morgan* v. *Fry*, the EAT sought to justify its rather cautious approach to that decision on a number of other grounds, it being pointed out for example that the doctrine of suspension was contrary to the large volume of authority, which included the following dictum of Lord Denning delivered only three years earlier in *J. T. Stratford & Son Ltd.* v. *Lindley*:[17]

it seems to me that the trade union officer, by giving the 'strike notice', issues a threat to the employer. He *threatens to induce the men to break* their contracts of employment unless the employer complies with the demand. That is a threat to commit a tort. It is clear intimidation unless it is protected by statute.[18]

But although *Simmons* v. *Hoover Ltd.*[19] appeared to reject the suspension theory as one way of modifying the stark common law rule, in that case Phillips

---

[10] [1977] ICR 61.
[11] [1968] 2 QB 710.
[12] *Becton, Dickinson & Co.* v. *Lee* [1973] IR 1.
[13] [1968] 2 QB 710.
[14] [1964] AC 1129.
[15] [1968] 2 QB 710.
[16] [1977] ICR 61, at p. 73.
[17] [1965] AC 269.
[18] At p. 285. Emphasis in original.
[19] [1977] ICR 61.

J. proposed another, suggesting that not 'all strikes are necessarily repudiatory', even if 'usually they will be'. Thus, 'it could hardly be said that a strike of employees in opposition to demands by an employer in breach of contract by him would be repudiatory'. But although this seems sensible and reasonable, even if difficult to reconcile with decisions such as *Parkin* v. *South Hetton Coal Company*,[20] it is controversial, at least as far as English law is concerned, and was not supported by a different division of the EAT in *Wilkins* v. *Cantrell and Cochrane (GB) Ltd.*[21] There it was said that where the employer repudiates the contract, the employee must 'make it plain that he is treating the contract not only as capable of being repudiatory [*sic*], but one which has been broken and which he therefore regards as at an end'. But the act of going on strike is not sufficient evidence that the employees have accepted the employer's repudiation by terminating the contract. Indeed, 'it would be a disaster' if going on strike were to be construed as a termination of the contract. So if the employees strike even in response to the employer's repudiatory conduct, the balance of legal advantage reverts to the employer. According to the EAT in *Wilkins*, 'the conduct of the employees then gives the employer a right to regard the conduct of the employee as a breach of the contract'. He may then decide 'whether or not to put an end to the contract by issuing notices of dismissal'.[22]

Apart from *Simmons*, there does not appear to be any other recent authority in English law to suggest that a strike may not be repudiatory. There is, however, authority to this effect in Australia, which indeed goes even further than Phillips J. appeared prepared to go. Although *Re Federated Storemen and Packers' Union of Australia, NSW Branch*[23] is a decision of the New South Wales Industrial Commission, the views expressed clearly bear upon the Commission's appreciation of the common law. In a quite remarkable passage, Macken J. said that it 'is trite law that strikes do not usually give rise to the exercise of an employer's right to summarily dismiss for misconduct'. And he continued by asserting that industrial action 'can rarely be held to evidence a firm and final determination on the part of an employee to abandon the employment contract'[24] not amounting to repudiation of a fundamental term of the contract. In the view of Macken J., only 'a repeated and serious breach of the employment contract will entitle an employer to dismiss an employee for misconduct', and in this case he held that the strike action by a 'small group of distribution employees'[25] would not 'amount to repudiation of their employment contract of sufficiently serious character as to end the relationship'. The contrast with the general rule (reinforced most recently by Lord Templeman in *Miles* v. *Wakefield Metropolitan District Council*[26] where he said that 'Any form of industrial action by a worker is a breach of contract'[27] is profound. Rather than seeing a strike as something which only exceptionally does not break the contract, Macken J. treats the exception as the rule. In reality,

---

[20] (1907) 97 LT 98. [21] [1978] IRLR 483. [22] At pp. 484–5.
[23] (1987) 22 I(ndustrial) R(eports) 198. [24] At p. 199.
[25] At p. 200. [26] [1987] 1 All ER 1089. [27] At p. 1097.

however, although this bold approach is welcome, it seems unlikely to gain general acceptance and is indeed difficult to reconcile with a leading case in the High Court of Australia[28] where it was said that 'a definite refusal of a general kind to pursue the employer's lawful policy of business' would be a breach of contract justifying dismissal.[29]

In view of the failure of either the Denning or the Phillips approaches to win wider support, that leaves a third possible modification of the common law position. This is the view that a strike *supported by proper strike notice* amounts to a termination rather than a breach of the contracts of employment of the employees concerned. But this too seems unpromising, for as Wedderburn (1986: 191) has argued, 'There is no belief more widespread, more reasonable, but legally more erroneous than that held by many managers and most workers that a strike notice, equivalent in length to that needed to end the contract, makes industrial action lawful'. In Wedderburn's view, 'most unions and workers do not regard a strike notice as equivalent to asking for the workers' cards. Nor do most employers. It is a notice announcing a withdrawal of labour—a strike—not a mass resignation.' Nevertheless, the argument has been raised by defendants in a recent case, *Boxfoldia Ltd*. v. *NGA (1982)*[30], where a national officer of the union wrote to the plaintiffs stating: 'I have been instructed to write giving the company 14 days' notice of withdrawal of all NGA members' labour from the company'. When the notice expired, thirty-nine employees of Boxfoldia failed to report for work, it being common ground that the reason for this was their participation in the official strike which had been called by the NGA. The company then sued the NGA in tort for inducing the employees to strike in breach of their contracts of employment, for which the union would be liable if only because the action was not supported by a strike ballot as required by the Trade Union Act 1984.

The union's defence in this case was that no tort had been committed because the employees had not been induced to break their contracts, but to terminate them, with the contracts of most of the employees involved being terminable by two weeks' notice. And it is interesting to note that the court accepted that in some cases strike notice could have the effect contended for, with Saville J. rejecting the view that there is some rule of law that strike notice must always be regarded as a notice of contractual breach rather than intended termination. The position in any given case depends on 'the meaning and effect of the words used in the context in which they were used'.[31] On the facts of this case, however, it was held that there had been a breach rather than a notice to terminate the contracts. It was not written by the union with authority from the individual members; it did not purport to communicate the decision of the employees to bring their contracts to an end; and it did not purport to give the appropriate termination notice stipulated in the contract. So although it is possible in principle to give a strike notice which terminates

---

[28] *Adami* v. *Maison De Luxe Ltd.* (1924) 35 CLR 143.
[29] At p. 153.   [30] [1988] IRLR 383.   [31] At p. 385.

the contract, in practice it may be difficult to do so. For such notice to be so construed, it would have to be much more carefully and clearly drafted to reflect an intention to terminate. But the advantages of such a course to individual strikers are at best marginal. It is true that employees would escape any liability in damages for breach of contract. Yet although actions in damages against employees are not unknown, they are very unusual. And it is also to be pointed out that employees who resign rather than be dismissed might 'lose certain [very limited] unfair dismissal rights',[32] though they may acquire others particularly where the action is defensive. We return to these matters in Chapter 3.

III. INDUSTRIAL ACTION SHORT OF A STRIKE

So much then for strikes. The position regarding industrial action by workers short of a strike will depend upon the terms of the contract. It can safely be assumed, however, that almost all forms of industrial action (with the possible exception in some cases of a refusal to work voluntary overtime) will be a breach of contract by the individuals concerned, for so wide will be the powers of the employer under the express and implied terms of the contract of employment. The first case illustrating this point, *Bowes and Partners Ltd.* v. *Press*,[33] concerned a concerted refusal by trade union members in a coal-mine to descend in the cage with non-unionists. They were, however, willing to descend together when the cage returned from the pit bottom, but management refused to permit them to do so. The Court of Appeal held the employees' conduct to be a breach of contract, with Lindley L.J. stating that the 'men had no right to take that course and to assert the power of dictating to the masters how the men should ascend or descend'.[34] More recently in *Cresswell* v. *Inland Revenue*,[35] it was held that a concerted refusal to operate new technology was a breach of contract. In that case tax officers engaged in the administration of the PAYE scheme performed their duties by using various manual techniques. The Inland Revenue wished to computerize the system, a proposal with which, following a dispute with the Inland Revenue Staff Federation, the plaintiffs refused to co-operate. The plaintiffs did, however, indicate that they were willing to continue operating under the existing conditions but the employers responded by making it clear that this was unacceptable and that the employees would not be paid while they refused to operate the new system. The dispute was referred ultimately for adjudication by the High Court, with the plaintiffs seeking a declaration that they were not bound under the terms of their contracts of employment to operate the new computerized system and that the defendants were acting in breach of contract in seeking to compel them to do so. It was argued for the plaintiffs that although the employer may within limits change the manner in which the employees do the work they are

---

[32] *Boxfoldia Ltd.* v. *NGA (1982)* [1988] IRLR 383, at p. 385.
[33] [1894] 1 QB 202.   [34] At p. 207.   [35] [1984] IRLR 190.

employed to do, they cannot do so if the change in the manner of performing the work has the effect of changing the nature of the job. To this Walton J. responded by saying that it was 'a very fine line' from such a submission 'to the submission that employees have a vested right to preserve their working obligations completely unchanged as from the moment when they first begin work', something which 'cannot surely, by any stretch of the imagination, be correct'.[36] On the other hand, it is not altogether clear why it should be so readily assumed and accepted that the employer has the right to change working obligations without consent or consultation. Nevertheless, it was held that employees were expected to adapt themselves 'to new methods and techniques' introduced in the course of their employment.[37] The only apparent qualification was that the employer must offer retraining and may not require the employee to acquire esoteric skills. But it is not clear what the position would be if the employee were unable to adapt, or if the change imposed by the employer had the effect of reducing job satisfaction. The crucial point, however, is that a concerted refusal to work under contractual conditions, whether for offensive or defensive reasons, is likely to be a breach of contract.

But in addition to refusals to work with non-unionists or to perform the job in the manner dictated by management, it is also likely to be a breach of contract for workers taking concerted action to refuse to perform some ancillary duties of their employment, while continuing to perform the others. The decision in *Sim* v. *Rotherham Metropolitan Borough Council*[38] would suggest the need for caution even before employees withdraw what they consider to be non-contractual services, for so wide and open-ended are the implied terms of the contract of employment and the duties imposed thereby. The case concerned the extent of the contractual obligations of schoolteachers who were engaged in a dispute over pay. In the course of the dispute the teachers took action of various kinds, including a refusal to cover for absent colleagues when so assigned by the principal of the school in question; refusing to supervise pupils during lunch breaks; refusing to participate in any sporting, musical or dramatic events at lunch times; refusing to undertake any administrative duties in connection with school meals; and refusing to attend any staff meetings or consultations with parents outside school hours. The issue in the case was whether the refusal to cover for absent colleagues in particular was a breach of contract by those involved, though the decision clearly had implications for the other sanctions which the employees had imposed. Scott J. began by noting that the contracts under which teachers are engaged were silent on the questions in dispute but rather than treat this as a cause for caution, the lack of specificity in the contracts as to what employees could be required to do was turned to the advantage of the employer. Teachers as professional people are 'employed to provide a particular service and have a contractual obligation to do so properly'. Scott J. continued by stating:

---

[36] At p. 194.   [37] At p. 195.   [38] [1986] 3 All ER 387.

All schools need a framework of administrative rules to regulate their orderly conduct. An example par excellence is the school timetable. No school could operate without one. Schools, like all institutions, require some sort of administrative hierarchy. In the case of schools, the administrative head is the head teacher. He or she is responsible to the education authority for the proper conduct of the school. He or she has the power and the duty within the school to give administrative directions for the proper running of the school. The school timetable derives its authority from the position of the head teacher. It is, in my view, a professional obligation of each teacher to co-operate in running the school during school hours in accordance with the timetable and other administrative regulations or directions from time to time made or given.[39]

It is true that Scott J. drew the line at 'unreasonable directions' but gave as an example the extreme case of a direction to discriminate against a pupil on racial grounds. And as if to emphasize the open-ended nature of the employer's power over employees, Scott J. continued by stating in a quite remarkable passage:

The conclusions I have reached do not depend in any way on the particular policy of the particular education authority regarding the use of supply teachers to provide cover. Whether a supply teacher may be called for after the first day of absence, the third day of absence or the fifth day of absence of a member of staff is a matter of policy for the authority in question. Similarly, the number of staff to be employed at a particular school is a matter of policy for the authority. In practice, the authorities no doubt consult with the teachers' unions before establishing a policy or changing an established policy. No doubt, also, the authorities should keep in mind in this regard the effect of their policy on the teachers. But the contracts of the teachers give them, in my view, no control over these policy matters. A change in policy by an authority may increase the burden on the teachers. It may require the teachers at a school to cover for an absent colleague for five days of absence rather than for three. A change in policy may, by reducing the number of teachers, increase the size of classes or increase the number of classes to be taken. But the teachers' professional and contractual obligations to comply with the reasonable administrative directions given by or under the authority of the head teacher for the purpose of organising the proper conduct of the school during school hours remain, in my judgment, unaltered.[40]

So under the guise of implied terms of the contract of employment, the employer may thus increase the burden on employees, increase the size of classes, or increase the number of classes which in turn will add to the time the employee must devote to the activities of the employer. Quite how wide the open-ended nature of the employment contract may be is thus difficult to fathom. Indeed, even the above dictum may not exhaust the burden on employees. Scott J. held that the exact ambit of professional duty is set by both the profession itself and by public expectation. In other words the legal obligations of employees may be set by the social expectations of third parties—a truly remarkable development. Nevertheless, given the principles expressed in *Sim*, it is hardly surprising that the Court found for the defendant

---

[39] At p. 405.   [40] At p. 407.

local education authorities. Although they were not up for decision it was strongly suggested that the failure to perform duties other than the cover arrangements would also amount to a breach of contract. (This is with the exception of the supervision of school meals which the employers accepted was beyond the professional obligations of the teacher—though remarkably an injunction was granted in another case to restrain such action on the basis that it was arguably a breach of contract.[41]) So teachers were held to have contractual obligations outside school hours, including obligations to prepare classes and mark schoolwork (though paradoxically it has been held that such duties do not count as contractual for computing continuity of service for the purposes of access to statutory employment rights in the case of those teachers whose classroom hours bring them just short of the prescribed statutory minima[42]). As far as other obligations are concerned, such as invigilation of examinations and meetings after school, these would be regarded as contractual if they could be regarded as part of the professional obligations of the teacher. There can be little doubt now how a court would decide on such matters should the matter arise for adjudication.

So non-performance of some contractual duties (even those assumed to be voluntary) will be a breach of contract as much as a refusal to perform contractual tasks in the manner prescribed by management. But what about working to rule where employees purport to perform contractual duties literally in such a way that the activity of the enterprise is disrupted? To explain to trade unionists that working according to the formal rules laid down by the employer is a breach of contract provokes only disbelief. Yet it seems to be fairly well established now that such is the position, having been decided in *Secretary of State for Employment* v. *ASLEF*.[43] This case was concerned with the emergency procedure of the Industrial Relations Act 1971, section 33(4) which applied where workers were engaged in a strike or irregular action short of a strike which would be gravely injurious to the national economy. One of the issues before the Court of Appeal was whether a work to rule by railway workers amounted to irregular action short of a strike, which was defined to mean any concerted course of conduct which in the case of all or some of the workers involved a breach of contract. In holding against the defendant unions the Court of Appeal examined the matter in some detail, with Lord Denning defining the principal issue before the Court in the following terms:

the principal discussion before us (and it is the most important discussion for the purposes of the case) was as to the general instruction to the men to 'work to rule', or, as it is put more fully in the instructions, 'Strictly observe all B.R.B. rules'. The meaning of that instruction is not in doubt. It is well known to every one in the land. The instruction was intended to mean, and it was understood to mean, 'Keep the rules of

---

[41] *Solihull Metropolitan Borough Council* v. *NUT* [1985] IRLR 211.
[42] *Lake* v. *Essex County Council* [1979] ICR 577
[43] [1972] 2 All ER 949.

your employment to the very letter, but, whilst doing so, do your very utmost to disrupt the undertaking'. Is that a breach of contract?[44]

In answering the question so posed in the affirmative, Lord Denning responded by saying:

Now I quite agree that a man is not bound positively to do more for his employer than his contract requires. He can withdraw his goodwill if he pleases. But what he must not do is wilfully to obstruct the employer as he goes about his business. That is plainly the case where a man is employed singly by a single employer. Take a homely instance, which I put in the course of argument. Suppose I employ a man to drive me to the station. I know there is sufficient time, so that I do not tell him to hurry. He drives me at a slower speed than he need, with the deliberate object of making me lose the train, and I do lose it. He may say that he has performed the letter of the contract; he has driven me to the station; but he has wilfully made me lose the train, and that is a breach of contract beyond all doubt. And what is more, he is not entitled to be paid for the journey. He has broken the contract in a way that goes to the very root of the consideration; so he can recover nothing.[45]

And, if it is a breach of contract for a single employee to act in a manner which is wilfully disruptive, then so must it be a breach of contract for a group of employees to take concerted action which is designed wilfully to disrupt. According to Lord Denning:

So much for the case when a man is employed singly. It is equally the case when he is employed 'as one of many' to work in an undertaking which needs the service of all. If he, with the others, takes steps wilfully to disrupt the undertaking, to produce chaos so that it will not run as it should, then each one who is a party to those steps is guilty of a breach of his contract. It is no answer for any one of them to say 'I am only obeying the rule book', or 'I am not bound to do more than a 40 hour week'. That would be all very well if done in good faith without any wilful disruption of services; but what makes it wrong is the object with which it is done. There are many branches of our law when an act which would otherwise be lawful is rendered unlawful by the motive or object with which it is done. So here it is the wilful disruption which is the breach. It means that the work of each man goes for naught. It is made of no effect. I ask: is a man to be entitled to wages for his work when he, with others, is doing his best to make it useless? Surely not. Wages are to be paid for services rendered, not for producing deliberate chaos. The breach goes to the whole of the consideration. . . .[46]

The interesting feature of this dictum is that a breach of contract will be created by the employee's unreasonable application of the employer's rule book. Also interesting is the suggestion that a refusal to work more than the contractual number of hours could amount to a breach of contract as well. In other words a refusal to work non-contractual overtime could be a breach of contract when done with a disruptive intent. Thus, the Court was referred to an instruction sent out by one of the rail unions to its members rostered for time in excess of eight hours to book off duty after the eight hours and thus

[44] At p. 966.   [45] Ibid.   [46] At p. 967.

not to work the remainder of the shift. According to Lord Denning, this instruction, if obeyed for example by signalmen, would be a breach of contract because of the trouble it could cause, even though overtime was not compulsory. It is not clear, however, how far this goes and in what circumstances a ban on voluntary overtime would be a breach of contract. It may be significant, however, that Lord Denning accepted that there would be no breach of contract by workers who refused to work voluntary overtime on Sunday (with Sunday working not being mandatory under the contracts of rail staff) or on their rostered rest days.

The point is, however, that a work-to-rule will almost certainly be regarded as a breach of contract, and depending on the circumstances, so may an overtime ban, even though as in the *ASLEF* case, overtime is not compulsory. This gives rise to the astonishing suggestion that workers may be in breach of contract not only by literally applying the terms of the contract, but also by refusing to accept additional obligations beyond those which the contract requires. It is, however, perhaps only exceptionally that a breach of contract will be established in the latter type of situation. (Indeed, in an industrial action context it will be exceptional to find a case where the employee's industrial action is not a breach of contract, so wide are the terms of the contract, as both *Cresswell* and *Sim* readily illustrate.) For apart from the important qualifying remarks of Lord Denning himself, one case in point is the decision of the New Zealand Supreme Court in *Elston* v. *State Services Commission (No. 3)*[47] which indicates that the last quoted dictum of Lord Denning will not generally authorize the employer to impose changes to the terms and conditions of employment with which workers must comply on pain of being in breach of contract. The issue in that case related to an attempt by the operator of a power station to convert the station from one which was fuelled by oil to one fuelled by natural gas. Workers who refused to operate the gas were suspended without pay, and in one of the several issues raised in the case it appears to have been accepted that they were under no legal obligation to undertake the new tasks. Nor could the *ASLEF* decision be used to compel them to do so, with Barker J. concluding that the remarks of Lord Denning were not in point. There was nothing in this case to show that the workers were 'producing deliberate chaos'. More importantly, perhaps, there was nothing to show that if the employers had chosen to operate on oil, the employees would have done other than their normal work.

IV.   COMMON LAW CONSEQUENCES OF STRIKES AND OTHER INDUSTRIAL ACTION

It thus being likely that strikes and other forms of industrial action will amount to a breach of contract, the next question to consider is the steps which may be

[47] [1979] 1 NZLR 218.

lawfully taken against workers who engage in such activity. A first response of the employer may be a desire to have the action stopped and the strikers return to work. But because of the rule against specific performance of personal contracts it will not be possible to obtain injunctions against the employees to restrain their breaches of contract. A further difficulty is section 16 of TULRA 1974 which prohibits a court from ordering specific performance of an employment contract or of granting an injunction which would have this effect. Yet although it may not be possible for an employer directly to obtain an injunction to restrain a strike in breach of contract, it may be possible to do so indirectly, and not in contract but in tort. Thus, since *Lumley* v. *Gye*[48] it has been tortious for one person to induce another to break a contract of service. So a union or a union official will be liable in tort to an employer for calling on members to strike or take other industrial action. The action is truly astonishing to the extent that it allows an employer to circumvent the rule against specific performance, which purports to exist lest contracts of service be turned into 'contracts of slavery'.[49] For although an injunction is generally not available directly against an employee, the employer may obtain an injunction against the union or its officials to restrain the inducement of the breaches of the employment contracts. This will have the effect of stopping the strike and will in practice lead to the workers being ordered back to work by the union. In fact, because of the rules governing the granting of injunctive relief, it is possible that an interlocutory injunction will be granted even though the industrial action complained of is not in fact in breach of contract, rare though this may be. Absent any statutory considerations, in order to obtain an interlocutory injunction, the employer need only show that there is a serious question to be tried and that the balance of convenience lies in favour of granting the relief sought. It does not have to be shown that there is a breach of contract.

But although injunctive relief is thus available in tort against the union and/ or its officials, thereby outflanking the rule against specific performance, it may not be available in all cases because of the immunity for acts done in contemplation or furtherance of a trade dispute. This tortious immunity is not the subject of the present enquiry, though it may be noted that the scope of the immunity has been significantly restricted since 1980 so that the role of the tort of inducing breach of employment contracts has greatly expanded. There is, for example, no immunity for strikes which are not supported by a secret ballot; which do not relate wholly or mainly to a trade purpose; or which are proscribed as secondary action. But tortious liability of those who induce the breach of contract may not be the only way by which the rule against specific performance of employment contracts can be outflanked. A very important recent development is *Barretts and Baird (Wholesale) Ltd.* v. *IPCS*[50] which

[48] (1853) 2 E & B 216.
[49] *De Francesco* v. *Barnum* (1890) 45 Ch.D. 430, at p. 438 (Fry L.J.).
[50] [1987] IRLR 3.

suggests that the breach of contract by the striking worker may also be the basis of liability in tort as well as contract against the worker concerned. This development has been facilitated by the emergence of the wider tort of unlawful interference with business, of which inducing breach of contract of employment is merely a species: it is merely one kind of unlawful means. In *Barretts and Baird (Wholesale) Ltd.* it was accepted by Henry J. that breach of the contract of employment could amount to unlawful means for the purposes of the genus tort, and workers could thus be sued personally as tortfeasors, whereas in the past only their union officials had been sued. Although the tort was not made out on the facts of that particular case—mainly because there had been no intention to injure the plaintiffs who were not the employers of the defendants in question—Henry J. was nevertheless correct to point out that the so-called right to strike will be much narrower than previously thought. For the fact is that the immunity for torts committed in the course of a dispute is limited to specific torts (including inducing breach of contract) which do not include breach of contract as the unlawful means in the tort of unlawful interference with business. This means that all industrial action in breach of contract will be tortious by the workers involved. It remains to be seen whether this means in turn that the employer can thus obtain injunctive relief in tort to restrain action in breach of contract. Although in *Barretts and Baird (Wholesale) Ltd.*, Henry J. held such relief to be ruled out by section 16 of TULRA 1974, he may not have the last word on the matter.

A second possible response of the employer may be to discharge the strikers and to hire replacements. But although a strike and other forms of industrial action will normally be regarded as a breach of contract, it is not every breach of contract which will justify the dismissal of an employee. In one leading case *Laws* v. *London Chronicle (Indicator Newspapers) Ltd.*[51] it was held that summary dismissal would be justified only if the employee has 'disregarded the essential conditions of the contract of service'. In the same case it was also held that 'one act of disobedience or misconduct can justify dismissal only if it is of such a nature which goes to show (in effect) that the servant is repudiating the contract, or one of its essential conditions'.[52] Yet it appears to be assumed without much equivocation that a strike will generally justify summary dismissal, a view taken, for example, in *Simmons* v. *Hoover Ltd.*[53] where the EAT endorsed the decision of the industrial tribunal which had held that 'so extreme a form of industrial action as a strike would certainly justify a summary dismissal as a matter of law'. (It will be recalled that in the same case Phillips J. suggested that exceptionally a strike would not necessarily be repudiatory in which case summary dismissal would not be justified.) The same view was most recently expressed by Lord Templeman in *Miles* v. *Wakefield Metropolitan District Council*[54] where he said that 'Any form of industrial action by a worker is a breach of contract which entitled [*sic*] the

---

[51] [1959] 1 WLR 698.   [52] At pp. 700–1.
[53] [1977] ICR 61.   [54] [1987] 1 All ER 1089.

employer at common law to dismiss the worker because no employer is contractually bound to retain a worker who is intentionally causing harm to the employer's business'.[55] This rule applies regardless of the circumstances of the strike, that is to say whether it is an offensive strike (seeking to change existing terms and conditions), or a defensive strike (seeking to preserve existing terms and conditions from attack by the employer). In the *Miles* case Lord Templeman explained, perhaps unconvincingly, that the 'courts are not competent to determine and are not concerned to determine whether a strike or other form of industrial action is justified or malicious, wise or foolish, provoked or exploited, beneficial or damaging; history has proved that any such determination is speculative and liable to be unsound'.[56]

It is in fact difficult to find authority for the view that a strike would not justify summary dismissal. A rare example perhaps is the Australian case, *Hall* v. *General Motors–Holden's Ltd.*[57] where the claimant was dismissed for taking industrial action in support of shop stewards who had been dismissed. He then applied for a penalty to be imposed upon the respondent company for an alleged breach of an Award which provided for the termination of employment by a week's notice, but also that the company could dismiss an employee without notice 'for malingering, inefficiency, neglect of duty or misconduct'. The question in *Hall*'s case was whether his conduct was such that the company was entitled to dismiss him without notice, a question answered by reference to common law principles. Hence the relevance of this case for wider common law liabilities. After referring to several common law authorities, Keely J. dismissed the application, and in so doing said that '(1) the claimant had "disregarded the essential conditions of the contract of service"; and (2) his conduct was "inconsistent with the fulfilment of the express or implied conditions of service"; and again (3) his conduct was "inconsistent with the relation established"'.[58] But despite this decision, the Court nevertheless suggested that a strike would not always justify instant dismissal. Thus Keely J. said that factors 'may exist of such a nature that in all the circumstances the right to summarily dismiss does not arise'.[59] And he gave as possible examples 'a bona fide belief of danger to life arising from the proposed work', and a strike for a very short time, though surely the latter will depend very much on the circumstances of a given case. If a strike for a short time is designed to inflict maximum damage on the employer then arguably the principles expressed by Lord Templeman in *Miles* would apply to permit the employer instantly to dismiss in response to repudiatory conduct. That seems, however, to be of academic interest only, there being no other credible authority to support the position adopted by Keely J. But if this notion were to gain general acceptance, it would not prevent employers from dismissing striking workers even where

---

[55] At p. 1097.   [56] Ibid.   [57] (1979) 45 FLR 272.
[58] At p. 278. See also *Re New Zealand Engineering, Coachbuilding, Aircraft, Motor and Related Trades Industrial Union of Workers and Shortland Freezing Company* [1973] 1 NZLR 326, at p. 332.
[59] *Hall* v. *General Motors–Holden's Ltd.* (1979) 45 FLR 272, at p. 279.

the circumstances were such as not to permit summary dismissal. It would always be open to the employer in such cases to dismiss with notice or with wages in lieu of notice, with the length of notice required depending to a large extent on the length of service of each striking employee.

A third possible response available to the employer may be to seek damages for any loss suffered as a result of the strike. Although it is rarely done, it would be possible for the employer to sue the employees who have taken industrial action in breach of contract. Perhaps because it is a rare course of action, the principles governing this situation are very unclear. But presumably the extent of the damages recoverable by the employer will be confined to damage suffered during the contractual notice period, which by statute shall be not less than one week. Presumably also the damages recoverable within this period will be subject to the employer's duty to mitigate his loss. But the problem which arises is this: for what loss may the employer recover? One interesting case is *Ebbw Vale Steel, Iron & Coal Co.* v. *Tew*[60] where a number of miners stopped work because the work in a certain area had become too difficult. A further stoppage had occurred after a fatal accident, when the defendants claimed to be entitled by custom and practice to leave work automatically. In an action by the employers for damages for breach of contract, it was held that there had been a breach, but a question arose as to how the damages were to be calculated. In ordering a retrial the Court of Appeal directed that the County Court judge 'should ascertain the workman's probable output during the time of default, find its selling value, deduct the expenses which would have been incurred had the workman performed his contract, and which were not incurred when he failed to produce it, and award that amount to the employers'. The employer was thus entitled to the commercial value of the coal which the worker would have produced less any costs including wages. It is perhaps difficult to find a starker example in the Law Reports of the Marxist concept of surplus value. It must certainly be difficult to find anything more galling for workers.

A more recent decision awarding damages in contract to an employer for workers' breach during a strike is *NCB* v. *Galley*[61] where a number of pit deputies imposed an overtime ban in breach of their contracts of employment, the relevant terms of which were included in a collective agreement between the Board and NACODS, the men's union. The effect of the ban was that no productive work was possible on Saturdays until substitute pit deputies were brought in to work the Saturday shifts some two months later. In the meantime the loss of profit suffered by the employer on at least one Saturday (16 June 1956) was £535 and it was argued that all shot-firers and deputies were liable to the plaintiffs for a share of this loss. It appears to have been accepted by the Court of Appeal that the amount of damages for which production workers

---

[60] (1935) 79 Sol. Jo. 593.
[61] [1958] 1 WLR 16.

could be assessed would be the net value of their labour to the employers—as in the *Tew* case. Pearce L.J. (delivering the opinion of the Court) continued:

Suppose that no question of supervision entered into the matter and that five face-workers were obliged by the terms of their contracts of service to work a special shift. Suppose further that if they did work it they would produce between them coal of the net value to their employers of £500, each contributing equally to the total. Suppose further that one of these face-workers failed, in breach of his contract, to work the special shift. The damages resulting from the breach would, we should have thought, be £100, whether or not the other four face-workers intended, to his knowledge, to absent themselves as well. There would be no question of charging him with the whole loss of £500.[62]

So far it seems clear enough—a production worker is liable for a portion of the loss suffered by the employer as a result of his breach of contract. But he is liable as an individual and not as a member of a group for loss caused by him as an individual. Approaching the matter in this way the Court then went on to ask what loss had been suffered by the employer as a result of the breach of contract by this individual worker. And although the Court accepted that the breach of contract by a supervisory worker would cause a far greater loss of output than the breach by a production worker, nevertheless in this case it could not be shown that the breach of contract by this individual defendant contributed to the plaintiff's loss. He would have been engaged on safety work rather than production work. How then, asked the Court, 'can it be said that the loss of output is any measure of his liability?'.[63]

To say the least, the reasoning of the Court, which is very difficult to follow, is perverse, even though it may not be unwelcome. It means, for example, that the damages assessed against a production worker will be greater than those assessed against a supervisory worker, even though the actual loss suffered to the employers may, as in this case, be far greater where the industrial action is taken by members of the latter group because it causes a total closure of the enterprise. And apart from this rather paradoxical result, the reasoning appears to some extent to be illogical. Even though the test to be applied is the loss caused by the individual employee acting in breach *qua* individual and not as a member of a group, the Court could as easily have held that the total loss of profit caused by the dispute could be apportioned equally between those in breach of contract. In other words, to paraphrase Pearce L.J., the damages resulting from the breach were £535 (on 16 June 1956). The damages of each individual resulting from the collective breach would be £535 divided by the number of employees in breach, which would be assessable against the defendant whether or not the other deputies and shot-firers intended to absent themselves as well. Although it is reasonable that an individual employee in breach should not necessarily be liable for the full extent of the employer's loss, it does not follow from this, as the Court seems to imply, that if loss of profits

---

[62] At p. 29.   [63] Ibid.

are assessable as damages then this should be confined, in the case of a coal-miner, only to those who are directly involved in the production of the coal, particularly when action by non-production workers may be just as devastating. Yet the reasoning of the Court is not just paradoxical and illogical. The decision to assess damages at £3. 18s. 2d. as reflecting the cost of replacement labour, was bizarre. Not only had the cost not been incurred on the day in question, but it would surely have been appropriate to have deducted from this assessment the wages which would otherwise have been payable to *Galley* to determine the employer's true loss, if the cost of replacement was to be the basis for determining the extent of the damage.

V.   CONCLUSION

By way of conclusion it should now be clear that a strike as well as most other forms of industrial action will be a breach of contract by the workers involved. This leaves the employer with a number of possible remedies, including injunctive relief in some cases; the dismissal and replacement of the strikers; and damages, with the amount of damages appearing to depend on whether the strikers are production workers or not. Apart from damages against the individual workers, it may be possible also to sue the union organizing the action in tort for damages for inducing breach of contract. The union will be liable if the immunities do not apply and if the action has been authorized or endorsed by a 'responsible person'.[64] There is, however, a limit on the amount of damages recoverable from a trade union by any one plaintiff, with the limit depending upon the size of the union.[65] Workers engaged in industrial action are thus very exposed. Yet strangely, perhaps, there seems no great desire to modify the common law position—though some attempt has been made to address some of its consequences, such as the introduction of immunity in tort for inducing breach of contract, and such as the remedies for unfair dismissal which apply, albeit to a dismal extent, to dismissals for participating in a strike or other industrial action.

But so far as addressing the fundamental problem is concerned—the fact that industrial action is itself a breach of contract—that prospect was killed by the disproportionately influential views of the Donovan Royal Commission which reported in 1968. The Commission considered but rejected the notion that strikes should have the effect of suspending rather than terminating the contract, stating that:

The concept is not as simple as it sounds: and before any such new law could be formulated problems of some difficulty would have to be faced and solved. They include the following:

   (a) To what strikes would it apply? To unofficial and unconstitutional as well as to official strikes? How would strikes be defined for this purpose?

---

[64] Employment Act 1982, s. 15. See now Employment Bill 1990, clause 6.
[65] Employment Act 1982, s. 16.

(b) Would it also apply to other industrial action such as a ban on overtime in breach of contract or to a 'go-slow'?

(c) Would it apply to 'lightning strikes' or only to strikes where at least *some* notice was given, though less than the notice required for termination of the contract? If so, what length of notice should be required?

(d) Would the new law apply to the gas, water, and electricity industries, which at present are subject to the special provisions of s. 4 of the Conspiracy and Protection of Property Act 1875? What also would be the position under s. 5 of the same Act?

(e) Would the employer still be allowed instantly to dismiss an employee for grave misconduct during the course of the strike? (Note: this is the case under French law where strikes are treated as suspending the contract of employment.) If so, what kind of acts would constitute 'grave misconduct'?

(f) Would 'contracting out' of the new law be permissible, e.g. in collective bargains, or in individual contracts of employment?

(g) Would strikers be free to take up other employment while the contract was suspended? If so, would any obligations of secrecy in the suspended contract be suspended too?

(h) If all efforts to end the strike failed, upon what event would the suspensions of the contract cease and be replaced by termination? (Donovan 1968: 244)

These questions invite several responses. The first is that they appear from the vantage point of the 1990s to be hopelessly inflated concerns which by no stretch of the imagination are insuperable. The first three questions invite some policy decisions as to the forms of industrial action which are to be legally protected. Having made that decision, we could either confine the doctrine of suspension to those disputes, or apply it to all disputes but create alternative sanctions applicable to those who exceed what is to be permitted. The fourth question is no longer a problem, with both sections 4 and 5 of the 1875 Act having been repealed, while the fifth question seems silly if it is being raised as a serious obstacle. There seems no reason why an employer would not be free to terminate a suspended contract where the employee acts in a manner which, apart from the strike, would be a repudiation of a fundamental term of the contract. So violence directed towards the employer's property would justify termination of a suspended contract, as would any breach of the duty of fidelity, though this would not necessarily be compromised by taking up alternative employment until the strike is concluded. So far as the sixth question is concerned, a model is already provided by TULRA, s. 18(4). This provides that a no-strikes clause or a collective disputes procedure in a collective agreement is not to be incorporated into a contract of employment unless certain formalities are complied with. Presumably the same exception, or something similar, could qualify a statutory provision suspending contracts of employment during a strike.

It is of course the case that in practice most strikes do not end in dismissal. The employer–employee relationship survives during and after the strike, and in practice, if not in law, the contract of employment is in a state of suspension.

Yet there is no evidence of any difficulties caused by this *de facto* status and no reason to believe that there would be any difficulty if the *de facto* position was also the *de jure* position. Contracts of employment survive long periods of absence by employees—notably in the case of women on maternity leave. Yet this takes place without incident and certainly without any undermining of the concept of the contract of employment. This is not to deny, however, that there are problems with the concept of suspension. But they are different problems from the ones identified by Donovan. The major problem is touched upon by Donovan's last question which is posed in terms of when could the employer dismiss. The real problem, however, may be that a doctrine of suspension may not deal with perhaps one of the most important yet most neglected consequences of industrial action, namely the absence of any protection against dismissal. It is difficult to see how this would be significantly changed by a concept of suspension. If all that is done is to provide that the contract is suspended during a strike or other industrial action, it would presumably still be possible for the employer to terminate the contract either with or without notice. The effect of suspension would surely be to suspend the contract until it was lawfully terminated, but it would not prevent the contract from being terminated. The problem with suspension then is not the quixotic concerns of Donovan. Rather the problem is that the concept does not adequately confront one of the major consequences flowing from the fact that a strike and other industrial action is invariably a breach of contract.

[3]

Industrial Action and the Payment of Wages

I. INTRODUCTORY

In the last chapter we examined some of the legal consequences which flow from the fact that strikes and other forms of industrial action will invariably be a breach of contract by the workers involved. In this chapter we consider a related question which has given rise to a fair amount of litigation in recent years, particularly in cases of industrial action falling short of a strike. Perhaps one reason for taking such action rather than going on all-out strike is the belief that the right to wages and salaries will be preserved. But is this belief justified? In particular, is an employer required to submit to such pressure or may he decline to accept partial performance of the contract without dismissing those concerned? And if the employer does decide to accept partial performance by the labour force, is he obliged to pay for the work performed, and if so how much is to be paid? Before addressing these questions, we must say something about the statutory context in which they are tackled.

II. THE STATUTORY CONTEXT

A. *The Truck Acts 1831–1940*

Until 1986 the principal source of statutory regulation for the payment of wages was the Truck Acts 1831–1940. Several of the provisions of these Acts are relevant here, but it is to be noted that the fundamental provision was section 3 of the 1831 Act which provided that the entire amount of wages earned by or payable to any artificer shall be actually paid in the current coin of the realm. The Act of 1896 authorized deductions to be made from wages in respect of fines or damaged goods provided that the safeguards laid down in sections 1 and 2 of the Act were complied with. These provided, for example, that the terms of the contract authorizing a fine should be posted up at the work-place, that the contract specified the conduct in respect of which the fine was imposed, and that the amount of the fine was fair and reasonable. Breach of the Truck Acts was a criminal offence by the employer concerned, though it was possible for an employee to obtain injunctive relief to prevent a breach of the Acts, and to bring an action for the recovery of wages wrongly withheld.

Valuable though the Acts were for the protection of workers, they were limited by the fact that they applied only to those engaged in manual labour (with the exception of the 1896 Act which applied also to shop assistants), a qualification which gave rise to some bizarre problems of scope. But in a sense it made very little difference just how widely the protection of the Acts extended, so far as our current enquiry is concerned, for in practice they were never likely to present a serious problem to employers wishing to discipline employees taking defensive action. Three cases are of particular significance.

The first is an Irish case, *Deane* v. *Wilson*,[1] where the employer was charged with a violation for withholding a bonus payment from an absent employee. The employee was absent for part of a day as a result of which an amount was deducted from the sum which would otherwise have been payable to her. In fact, the total bonus was withheld. The case against the employer was that this deduction was in fact a fine which had been imposed in breach of the requirements of section 1 of the 1896 Act. The case failed, with Andrews J. being:

unable to hold that the non-payment of the [bonus], which was not earned, and never became due, was a *deduction* from the *sum contracted to be paid* to the worker. There was no contract to pay it unless it was earned. If she had not worked at all during the week, though the contract for service remained, she would not have been entitled to any payment; and could it be said that when, being entitled to nothing, she was paid nothing, the non-payment was an offence under the Act? Further, even if this non-payment of the [bonus] which she did not earn could be possibly held to be a deduction from the sum contracted to be paid to her, it could not, in my opinion, be held to be a deduction for, or in respect of, a *fine*. The non-payment took nothing from her to which, in any view, she had become entitled, or to which, when the week ended, she could have ever become entitled. It was simply withholding payment of what she had not earned, and never could earn.[2]

Andrews J. continued by contending that to hold that non-payment of the bonus, when not earned, was an offence, would deprive the employer of a fair and reasonable means of securing uninterrupted work. For his part Kenny J. held that non-payment of the bonus was 'simply the contractual result of the woman's failure to work for a certain stipulated period'.[3] It is true that this case does not deal directly with the withholding of wages from those engaged in industrial action. It does, however, indicate that those who are absent from work because of industrial action need not be paid without any violation of the Truck Acts. And it also indicates that any contractual terms (express or implied) for the non-payment of wages to those who do not provide full performance of the contract would not amount to a violation of the Acts.

The second case is *Williams* v. *North's Navigation Collieries (1889) Ltd.*[4] where employees in the service of the defendants were ordered by magistrates (exercising power under the Employers and Workmen Act 1875) to pay 30

---

[1] [1906] 2 IR 405.   [2] At p. 409. Emphasis in original.
[3] At p. 413.   [4] [1906] AC 136.

shillings to the employer (in three instalments) for breach of contract. The employer responded by proposing to deduct the first instalment of 10 shillings from the wages of the employees concerned and to pay the balance. The employees sought damages and a declaration and injunction against the employer on the ground that he had violated the Truck Acts. The plaintiffs succeeded at first instance, but the decision of Bucknill J. was reversed by the Court of Appeal[5] which concluded that the Act did not make it an offence 'to withhold money due for wages on account of a legal set-off' (save that by section 5 in an action brought for wages no set-off was allowed for any goods supplied by the employer). The House of Lords, however, restored the decision of Bucknill J. In so holding the Lord Chancellor contended that the approach of the Court of Appeal could not be supported by the express language of the 1831 Act albeit the position was very anomalous in the sense that if the employer did not pay any wages at all and was sued 'he would be entitled then to set off in the action anything due to him except such sums as fall within the prohibition of s[ection] 5'.[6] Lord Atkinson justified the anomaly in the following terms:

The whole principle upon which this legislation is based is that the workman requires protection, that if not protected he may be over-reached; and it is quite consistent with that principle to hold that in any such action brought by him to recover his wages, he may be liable to have the sum found on investigation before the legal tribunal to be due to him by his master diminished by the sum found by the same tribunal on the same occasion to be due by him to his master, and yet at the same time to prohibit the master from, as it were, substituting himself for the legal tribunal, investigating his own claim against his workman in his own office and deciding in his own favour.[7]

Although no set-off of a judgment debt was allowed in *Williams*, the case did not necessarily present a serious hurdle to employers faced with partial performance by employees. First the Truck Acts applied only to wages earned, as indeed they had been in *Williams*. It would still be open to the employer to argue that someone who partially performs has not earned the agreed wages, so that any withholding of monies would fail to cross this initial hurdle. Alternatively the employer could simply refuse to pay any wages, leaving the worker to take the trouble and expense of suing for recovery, in which case it seems the employer could set off any damages caused by the industrial action from the wages of the employee. Paradoxically, perhaps the protection of workers in this context could serve to increase their misery. But lest there be any doubt about the potentially limited impact of the Truck Acts for the problem under discussion, the third of the significant decisions would conclusively resolve the matter. In *Hart* v. *Riversdale Mill Co.*[8] a Lancashire weaver complained that her employer had made a deduction from her wages for bad workmanship. Both the Divisional Court (by a majority) and the Court of Appeal held that

---

[5] [1904] 2 KB 44.   [6] [1906] AC 136, at p. 140.
[7] At p. 146.   [8] [1928] 1 KB 176.

there was nothing in the Truck Act 1831 which prohibited a deduction for bad work in the calculation of wages. Lord Hanworth M.R. expressed the position thus:

Is this deduction or the sum of which the workman has been deprived a sum she has been deprived of in calculating the real amount of her wages; or is it a sum which, after the wages have been ascertained, has been used by the employer to discharge himself pro tanto of the wages which ought to be paid in their entirety to the workman?[9]

The Court held that what had been lost was not a sum deducted from the worker's wages but a loss sustained in ascertaining what these wages would be. By the same token a deduction for participating in industrial action could doubtless be explained on the basis that any deduction was made in the process of determining what wages were actually due rather than from wages the amount of which had already been ascertained or earned.

B. *The New Statutory Regime*

Whatever the position under the Truck Acts, the matter is of course now of rather historical interest only. The Truck Acts were repealed in 1986 to be replaced by the new deregulatory regime set out in the Wages Act of that year. Section 1 of the Wages Act prohibits an employer from making any deduction from any wages of any worker employed by him unless the deduction is authorized by any 'relevant provision' of the worker's contract or the worker has previously signified in writing his agreement or consent to the making of the deduction.[10] A relevant provision in an employment contract is defined to mean a written term of the contract of which the employer gave the worker a copy at some time before the deduction was made. Alternatively, it could be an express or implied term of the contract whose existence and effect the employer had notified to the worker in writing at some time before the deduction was made. So the worker must either be given written notice of the terms of the contract authorizing deductions to be made or must have consented to such deductions in writing. Presumably notification could take place in the statutory written statement which should be issued under section 1 of the Employment Protection (Consolidation) Act 1978.[11] As it is the statement should in any event contain a note specifying the disciplinary rules and procedures applicable to the employee in question.

Unlike the Truck Acts which extended a much broader protection to manual workers, the Wages Act applies a very narrow protection across the board. Unusually for modern employment protection legislation (but setting a standard which could usefully be extended to the EPCA in response to the threshold problems arising thereunder) the Wages Act applies to workers, who are

---

[9] At p. 184.   [10] See *Pename Ltd.* v. *Paterson* [1989] ICR 12.
[11] See especially section 1(4)(a), though see now Employment Act 1989, s. 13 (Deakin 1990: 14).

defined to mean those employed under a contract of service, a contract of apprenticeship, or 'any other contract whereby the individual undertakes to do or perform personally any work or services for another party to the contract whose status is not by virtue of the contract that of a client or customer of any profession or business undertaking carried on by the individual'.[12] Any worker who falls within this wide definition may make a complaint to an industrial tribunal that the employer has made a deduction in contravention of section 1. If the complaint is well founded the tribunal must make a declaration to that effect and order the employer to pay to the worker the amount of any deduction made in contravention of section 1. In reality, however, these arrangements promise to offer very little protection to employees. All they seek to ensure is that the worker is notified of the disciplinary and other rules authorizing deductions. They do not purport to regulate the content of these rules. So a deduction may be made, whether or not it is reasonable, whether or not the employee is blameworthy, provided that the employee has been notified in advance. The Act thus reflects and projects the fiction of the common law. The employee enters freely into such contractual arrangements and agrees to be bound by them. If he disapproves then presumably the contract would not have been made in the first place. And if the employee ceases to approve these terms he can seek to change them by renegotiating with the employer, failing which the employee may resign (with due notice) and look for suitable employment elsewhere.

But there are exceptions even to the very limited protection which the Act provides. One of the six situations to which section 1 does not apply is 'any deduction from a worker's wages made by his employer, or any payment received from a worker by his employer, where the worker has taken part in a strike or other industrial action and the deduction is made, or the payment has been required, by the employer on account of the worker's having taken part in that strike or other action'.[13] This does not mean, of course, that workers whose wages are withheld in a dispute are totally without a remedy. They are still free to rely upon any common law remedies which they may have. But it does mean that they have no statutory remedy if the employer fails to comply with the procedures in the 1986 Act. The measure was introduced as a government amendment in Standing Committee with the Minister drawing parallels with section 62 of the Employment Protection (Consolidation) Act 1978, which, as we shall see, at that time denied industrial tribunals jurisdiction to deal with the fairness or otherwise of dismissals in the course of a dispute unless the employer was selective in dismissals or re-hiring after the dispute. The government's ostensible reasoning for the 1986 Act qualification was similar to that sometimes used to justify section 62, that is to say, that tribunals will not want to be drawn into making decisions on the difficult and contentious subjects that could arise.[14] Perhaps another reason is a desire to

[12] 1986 Act, s. 8.   [13] 1986 Act, s. 1(5)(e).
[14] Official Report, Standing Committee K, 27 Feb. 1986, cols. 123–37.

ensure that employers are not trapped into paying wages during a dispute, which they might be if they failed to notify their employees that deductions could be made for participation in industrial action.

III.   THE COMMON LAW RESPONSE

Parliament thus having abdicated responsibility to the judges, it becomes crucial to find out what the relevant common law rules are. Here we find that the legal position is still very unsettled in a number of key respects, with some of the basic ground rules still to be determined. Essentially, however, an employer faced with a group of workers taking industrial action short of a strike may respond either by refusing to accept, or by accepting, partial or limited performance of the contract, perhaps in the latter case because the employer has no choice but to do so due to pressing business needs or the existence of a duty to maintain a particular service. The question of the right of workers to wages in these situations has been considered by courts in several recent cases which have sown a fair amount of confusion. The general position, however, is that the employer is free to refuse to accept anything less than full performance of the contract, without at the same time having to terminate the contract. Equally, the employer is free to accept partial performance and to make only partial payment for the work provided.

A.   *Refusal to Accept Partial Performance*

1. *The Early Cases*   One possible response of the employer faced with concerted action short of a strike is to decline to accept any performance. Davies and Freedland (1984: 891) refer to this as the defensive lock-out. Such power has been acknowledged in several recent cases, the first being *Laurie* v. *British Steel Corporation*[15] where the employees were suspended for declining to work normally during an inter-union dispute. They were not paid for the period of the suspension and sought a declarator that they were entitled to such payment, arguing that the employer's only remedy in this situation was 'to rescind the contract with or without a claim for damages, or simply to claim damages', but that the employer could not refuse to pay wages unless he had in fact terminated the contract. The argument failed, with Lord Cowie applying the principle that 'a failure to perform any material or substantial part of the contract on the part of one will prevent him from suing the other for performance',[16] a principle which reflects 'the fundamental rule that if one party does not fulfil his part of the mutual contract he cannot turn round and demand performance by the other party of his part of the contract'.[17] And it did not follow that because the defenders elected not to exercise the rights of

---

[15]   1988 SLT 17.   [16]   *Turnbull* v. *McLean & Co.* (1874) 1R 730.
[17]   *Laurie* v. *British Steel Corporation*, 1988 SLT, at p. 19.

rescission referred to by the pursuers that the latter 'have the right to demand performance of the defenders' part of the contract when they have not carried out their own part'. Lord Cowie therefore held in favour of the defenders.

Laurie was decided in 1978, and although not reported until 1988, it nevertheless proved very influential in a number of subsequent cases, including *Cresswell* v. *Inland Revenue*[18] where, it will be recalled, Inland Revenue employees refused to operate the new computerized system for the administration of PAYE. They were told that they would not be permitted to operate the manual methods under which they had previously been engaged and that they would not be paid for the period during which they declined to operate the new arrangements.[19] Yet although it was accepted that the principle laid down in *Laurie* correctly stated the law of England, it was argued for the employees that what had actually happened here was that the employees had been suspended, that the suspension had taken place in breach of the contractual procedures for suspension, and that the employees were thus entitled to be paid during the period of the employer's breach. Support for this proposition was to be found in *Gorse* v. *Durham County Council*[20] where schoolteachers who refused to supervise school meals were notified that they had been 'suspended' in breach of a term of the disciplinary procedure that suspensions would not be imposed before giving the employees concerned an opportunity to be heard. The employees were held to be entitled to their salaries during the period of the suspension because it had been imposed in breach of the contractual procedures. But although this decision on its facts was approved in *Cresswell*,[21] it was distinguished, the Court taking the view that in this type of situation the employer has a choice of responses. He can choose to suspend the employees, as in *Gorse*, in which case any contractual procedures relating to suspension will operate. But, secondly, it was held that the employer is free to implement the obvious principle of 'no work, no pay', and that the argument that he is obliged to resort to suspension through the disciplinary procedure was 'shocking to commonsense'.[22] In this case the employer had been at pains to make it clear that he was not suspending the employees, and that they could attend at any time if they were willing to perform their contractual duties.

For Walton J. the matter was 'founded on the simplest consideration of what the plaintiff would have to prove in any action for recovery of pay in respect of any period where he was deliberately absent from work of his own accord'. But it was also recognized as 'of course true' that by applying the 'no work, no pay' principle 'the same result is achieved as a result of suspension'. That being so, the case must seriously undermine contractual disciplinary procedures for there must be many disciplinary situations—apart from those involving industrial action—where the employer could rely on these common law

[18] [1984] IRLR 190.
[19] For a similar case, see *McPherson* v. *London Borough of Lambeth* [1988] IRLR 470.
[20] [1971] 1 WLR 775.   [21] [1984] IRLR 190.
[22] See also *McPherson* v. *London Borough of Lambeth* [1988] IRLR 470.

powers rather than disciplinary procedures contractually agreed. It may well be that these procedures are ill-suited to the complications caused by the problem of partial performance. But it is not the function of the courts to come to the rescue of short-sighted employers by saying in effect that a disciplinary code will apply unless the employer needs more extensive powers, in which case they will be provided by the common law. Nor is it the function of the courts to facilitate the redundancy of carefully drafted disciplinary procedures in collective agreements. Section 18(4) of TULRA provides that terms in a collective agreement restricting the right to strike or to participate in other industrial action shall not impact upon the contract of employment unless the procedures laid down in the subsection are complied with should such arrangements operate. The effect of *Cresswell* will be to reduce them to naught. The employer may choose to comply with the contractual procedures, or he may not. To the extent that any such problems do arise, the Court in *Cresswell* would no doubt find comfort in consideration of equity. Thus, 'Why anybody should imagine that periods of deliberate abstention from work should count as if the service had continued during that period escapes me. It is quite plain that as a matter of equity they should not.'[23] But such considerations are rarely one-sided. So while it may be lawful for employers to wield great powers of direction and control over employees—as in *Cresswell*—it need not always be equitable to do so nor necessarily unreasonable to take defensive action to resist the use of such power.

2. *Miles and its Progeny*   Yet for all its difficulties this line of authority was effectively endorsed by the House of Lords in *Miles* v. *Wakefield Metropolitan District Council*,[24] a case relating to the refusal of a Registrar of Births, Deaths, and Marriages to perform marriage services on a Saturday morning, a typically busy period. This was done on the instruction of his union, NALGO, which was then engaged in a dispute with the defendant employer. The plaintiff was willing to work normally for the rest of his thirty-seven-hour week and indeed was willing to work on Saturdays but to perform duties other than weddings. For its part the Council notified him that if he was not prepared to perform the full range of duties on Saturdays he would not be paid. Adhering to the instruction from the union, the plaintiff did not in fact perform his normal duties on Saturday mornings. When the Council responded by paying him 34/37 of a week's pay, that is to say, it deducted the value of three hours from the salary, he sued to recover his full wages. A preliminary question for the courts in this case was that the employment of the plaintiff was governed by the Registration Service Act 1953, this giving rise to the question whether he as a statutory office-holder was subject to the same rules with regard to payment in the context of industrial action as regular employees. After some hesitation in the Court of Appeal, the House of Lords accepted that 'the plaintiff is in

---

[23] [1984] IRLR 190, at p.199.   [24] [1987] 1 All ER 1089.

no better position for present purposes than a worker under a contract of employment'. Having disposed of this matter, the courts were faced with a second question, whether in a case such as this the employer could withhold payment as well as either dismiss the employee concerned or sue for damages, if any damage was in fact suffered. This question was also answered in the affirmative with the earlier decisions in both *Laurie* and *Cresswell* being prominent in the Lords' judgment. According to Lord Bridge:

If an employee refuses to perform the full duties which can be required of him under his contract of service, the employer is entitled to refuse to accept any partial performance. The position then resulting, during any relevant period while these conditions obtain, is exactly as if the employee were refusing to work at all.[25]

Lord Brightman was equally forthright:

In an action by an employee to recover his pay it must be proved or admitted that the employee worked or was willing to work in accordance with his contract. . . . If an employee offers partial performance, as he does in some types of industrial conflict falling short of a strike, the employer . . . may decline to accept the partial performance that is offered, in which case the employee is entitled to no remuneration for his unwanted services, even if they are performed. That is the instant case.[26]

Miles was followed and applied in the rather more controversial circumstances of *Wiluszynski* v. *London Borough of Tower Hamlets*[27] which arose out of a dispute between the defendant local authority and NALGO over the grading and alleged victimization of two members of the union. The union had decided to take 'limited industrial action' which consisted of a refusal to respond to enquiries from members of the Council. The plaintiff complied with an instruction to this effect but performed the rest of his duties. Nevertheless, he was not paid for the period of the industrial action, the Council having informed employees engaged in the boycott that they would only be paid if they performed all of their duties, even though in the case of the plaintiff the responding to enquiries from Council members amounted to only a small part of his work. An action to recover the salary which had been withheld succeeded at first instance. Although the Court readily accepted that the plaintiff was in breach of contract, Michael Davies J. concluded that the breach 'was minimal, annoying to the members of course, but not affecting the conscientious performance of the plaintiff's duties in all respects save answering members' inquiries'.[28] Also relevant was the fact that the Council acquiesced in the plaintiff's conduct, and did nothing to exclude him from the premises, yet took the benefit of his work. But in upholding the employer's appeal, the Court

[25] At p. 1091.
[26] At p. 1092.
[27] [1989] ICR 493.
[28] [1988] IRLR 154, at p. 156. It was also stated, however, that the Council might have been entitled to make a small deduction from pay representing the time that would otherwise have been spent answering members' enquiries. But this point did not arise, not having been pleaded by the employers.

of Appeal took a rather different approach, with Fox L.J. relying on *Miles* as authority for the view that:

an employee is not entitled to remuneration under the contract of employment unless he is willing to perform that contract. That being so, the council in the present case was entitled to say to the plaintiff:
'If you will not perform the full range of your contractual duties, including the answering of members' inquiries, you will not be paid and you should not attend for work. If you do attend and do work, you will do so voluntarily.'[29]

So the employee was not entitled to be paid any wages or salary for the period of the partial performance, even though the employer had knowingly taken the benefit of the work actually done[30] and even though the work actually done represented virtually complete performance of the contract.[31]

But if the employer was permitting Wiluszynski to come to work and to do his work, had it not accepted or acquiesced in his partial performance, thereby undermining its position that the employee was working on a purely voluntary basis?[32] It seems not, for a distinction was drawn between passive conduct of the employer and conduct which facilitates or directs work to be done.[33] Having told employees that they will not be paid for partial performance, the employer is not required to 'accept that which is forced down his throat despite his objections'[34] and may sit back happily and take advantage of substantial performance of the contract without having to pay for it:

I do not think the council could be expected to take action physically to prevent those members of the staff who were refusing to comply with their contracts from entering the council's premises. A lock-out, apart from any other objections to it, was impractical

---

[29] [1989] ICR 493, at p. 499.

[30] See also *McPherson* v. *London Borough of Lambeth* [1988] IRLR 470.

[31] It should be noted that Fox L.J. did not regard the breach as 'insubstantial', asserting that it is 'constitutionally, in terms of the responsibility of councillors to their constituents and of the rights of constituents to be properly informed in relation to matters affecting them, a circumstance of considerable importance that councillors should be supplied with information by the officials of the council to enable them to answer the inquiries of constituents' ([1989] ICR 493, at p. 499).

[32] See the Supreme Court of Victoria in *Welbourn* v. *Australian Postal Commission* (1983) 52 ALR 669 where Fullager J. held that when faced with partial performance, an employer may either treat the contract as at an end, or treat it as still on foot, in which case 'no wages can be withheld if, in the pay period concerned, the employee has performed most of his duties in the knowledge that he would not be stopped from performing them and in the knowledge also that the employer intended to take the benefit of the work actually done, and if the employer has in fact taken the benefit of the work actually done'. The only exception to this which the court was prepared to permit was if there had been 'a total failure of consideration at the end of each period throughout which the refusal was carried into effect', in which case the employer 'could hold back the whole of the wages of the employee'.

[33] See also *Bond* v. *CAV Ltd.* [1983] IRLR 360 where an employee was held to be in breach of contract for refusing to operate a machine which was the subject of a dispute between the parties. It was held that he was entitled to full pay for his partial performance, despite having been warned that if he did not work normally he would not be paid. In the view of Peter Pain J. the employer had waived the breach 'by facilitating the plaintiff to work as he did', though he also held that if the employer's 'attitude had been merely passive' he might have had some doubt about whether there was a waiver.   [34] [1989] ICR 493, at p. 504 (Nicholls L.J.).

since some of the staff were working quite normally and in accordance with their contracts. Neither a policing system nor the obtaining of an injunction would be satisfactory. In the atmosphere of this dispute they were likely to worsen relations as indeed would a lock-out. It was, therefore, in my view, reasonable for the council to allow the staff in dispute to come and go as they wished.[35]

The only circumstances in which the employer would be deemed to have accepted the employee's partial performance (and then be under a duty to make full or partial payment) would be if he 'was in fact giving directions to the plaintiff as to the work which he did'.[36] Employees will, however, no doubt be fortified by the fact that the courts will be vigilant to determine whether the ostensibly passive employer is not in fact actively directing the work:

Where an employee continues to work, the court will be concerned to see that the employer's expression of attitude was genuine and not a charade, and that there was no question of the employee having reasonably been confused or misled about this when he continued to work. These are questions of fact in the particular case. But if the court is satisfied that the employer's pronouncements were genuine, that is, meant to be taken seriously, and that the employee could not reasonably have been confused or misled on this score as he carried on working, then there can be no question of waiver or estoppel or the like arising from the mere fact that the employer acquires the benefit of the work which the employee insists on performing. That is this case.[37]

B. *Partial Payment for Partial Performance*

A second possible response of the employer is to accept part performance but to make a deduction from the wages that are normally payable. The power to respond in this way was first recognized recently by Park J. in *Royle* v. *Trafford Borough Council*[38] where the local education authority proposed to reduce staffing levels. In response to an instruction from his union, the National Union of Schoolmasters, the plaintiff refused to take any additional pupils in his class. So when asked to increase his class size from thirty-one to thirty-six, the plaintiff refused and did so for a period of some six months, during which time he was not paid by the education authority even though he was permitted to attend and teach his class of thirty-one. The first question for the court in the claim for unpaid wages was 'whether the defendants elected to accept the plaintiff's defective performance of his obligations under his contract of employment and thereby affirmed that contract'.[39] Park J. responded in the affirmative, noting that the employers had never treated the employee's breach as a repudiation but had been prepared to accept from the employee such duties as he was willing to perform. By accepting imperfect performance, the

---

[35] At p. 500 (Fox L.J.). But note that during the dispute involving ambulance staff in 1989–90, a number of employers successfully secured injunctions to restrain the staff from providing a service on their terms rather than on those required by the employer. See Appendix 1.

[36] Ibid.   [37] At p. 505 (Nicholls L.J.).

[38] [1984] IRLR 184.   [39] At p. 189.

defendants were held to have implicitly affirmed the plaintiff's contract of employment. The second question, however, was how much of his salary was the plaintiff entitled to receive. Park J. concluded that the plaintiff was 'entitled to be paid his full salary only if he has properly and fully performed his duties under his contract of employment'.[40] In this case the employee had been in breach for six months by failing to teach five children. According to Park J., there was no reason why Royle should receive his full salary for the period and that a deduction should be made 'representing the notional value of the services' which were not provided, even though the authority had suffered no financial loss by reason of the defendant's breach. Without any explanation for so holding, in deciding to give judgment to the plaintiff, Park J. made a deduction of 5/36 from the total salary due.

This approach is clearly to be preferred to the rather extreme proposal suggested by *Henthorn* v. *CEGB*[41] that employees partially performing are not entitled to any wages. Nevertheless, it is by no means clear what, if any, the conceptual basis was for making a deduction from the salary of employees in circumstances where these employees were doing what they had always done and where the employer had suffered no economic loss as a result of the employees' conduct. Since the decision in *Royle*, however, developments have continued, with the courts now rationalizing the employer's right to make deductions on two quite different conceptual bases. The first of these cases is *Sim* v. *Rotherham Metropolitan Borough Council*,[42] another case arising out of the troubles in the schools in the mid-1980s. On this occasion four employees refused to 'cover' (i.e. stand in) for absent colleagues for a period of thirty-five minutes each. The employer responded by deducting between £2 and £3.37 from the monthly salary of these employees. As we have already seen, Scott J. held that the conduct of the teachers in this case was in breach of contract. So the second question which arose was whether the local education authority was entitled to make this deduction from pay. Again Scott J. held for the employer,

---

[40] At p. 190.

[41] [1980] IRLR 361. Note also *Buchanan* v. *Strathclyde Regional Council* (21 Oct. 1981, unreported) where a schoolteacher engaged in industrial action was absent from school for half a day as a result of which he had his entire pay for that day withheld. In proceedings by the teacher it was argued first that the employers were not entitled to withhold any payment for the day in question, and secondly that he should at the very least be paid for that part of the day during which he attended the school. The employers easily won on the first point, Lord Mayfield stating that 'where the pursuer has not carried out his obligation, that is to say to carry out work, he cannot sue for performance by the defenders, that is that they should pay him for no work'. The second point was more difficult, though this too was resolved in favour of the employer as a result of a very clear term of the employee's contract of employment that his wages accrued by the day. In a poorly reasoned passage Lord Mayfield held that because the contractual unit of pay was a day, the employer was entitled to withhold the entire unit for any non-performance on that day. The employer was thus under no obligation to pay for the services actually provided. It may, however, be a mistake to read too much into this case, Lord Mayfield concluding that although 'it is an implied term in a contract of employment that an employee shall be paid for his work . . . the specific terms in this contract prevail'. I am grateful to Dr Kenneth Miller, School of Law, Strathclyde University, for bringing this case to my attention.

[42] [1986] 3 All ER 387.

rejecting the plaintiffs' argument that even if they had acted in breach of contract, the defendant's only remedy was to bring an action for damages. In the view of the Court the doctrine of equitable set-off could be applied to permit an employer to reduce salaries payable under a contract of employment.

1. *The Equitable Set-off*   The application of the doctrine of equitable set-off to contracts of employment had never before been formally decided, though it was considered, albeit inconclusively, by both the Court of Appeal and the House of Lords in *Williams* v. *North's Navigation Collieries (1889) Ltd.*[43] It was perfectly legitimate then for the plaintiffs to argue that the doctrine should have no application to employment contracts. This they did on two grounds: first, because it would give an employer the power to make deductions from salary on account of supposed breaches of contract, thereby empowering him to be judge and jury in his own cause: and, second, because it would enable employers to frustrate disciplinary codes and circumvent grievance procedures contained in many contemporary contracts of employment. But these arguments were rejected on three grounds. The first was that they had 'sociological rather than legal weight',[44] whatever this means. If it means that they are based on considerations of policy, then they cannot be dismissed so casually, for policy is surely of some significance for the way in which the legal rules should develop. Indeed, it is, to say the least, paradoxical, that Scott J. had already recognized that there were exceptions to the right of equitable set-off 'attributable to reasons of public policy'. Is it not contradictory to accept 'commercial exigencies' as, surely, sociological factors legitimately influencing legal rules, but to dismiss industrial relations exigencies as sociological, and therefore irrelevant and of no consequence? And it is perhaps strange that sociological arguments of this kind could be accepted by the House of Lords in their interpretation of the open-textured Truck Acts but not by Scott J. in the creation of new common law rules. In *Williams* v. *North's Navigation (1889) Ltd.*[45] the House of Lords unanimously reversed a strong Court of Appeal decision and held that the Truck Acts prevented the employer from setting-off a judgment debt from wages, accepting the view that workers need protection to prevent them from being 'over-reached'.

The second basis for the decision was the claim that there was judicial authority which implicitly recognizes the propriety of set-offs against salaries, the authority being an *obiter* remark of Lord Hanworth in *Sagar* v. *Ridehalgh & Son Ltd.*,[46] and the decision of Park J. in *Royle*. At best, however, the authorities are evenly balanced. For the *obiter* remarks of Lord Hanworth in the Court of Appeal we can match the more recent comments by Parker L.J.,[47] and for the decision of Park J. we can match the decision of Peter Pain J. in

---

[43] [1904] 2 KB 44; [1906] AC 136.
[44] *Sim* v. *Rotherham Metropolitan Borough Council* [1986] 3 All ER 387, at p. 413.
[45] [1906] AC 136.
[46] [1931] 1 Ch. 310, at p. 316.   [47] [1985] 1 All ER 905, at p. 912.

Bond v. *CAV Ltd.*,[48] to say nothing of authorities in Australia and New Zealand. Admittedly, the decision of the New Zealand Supreme Court in *McCleneghan* v. *Bank of New Zealand*[49] was concerned with whether deductions from the pay of employees engaged in industrial action violated a statute (the Wages Protection Act 1964), the relevant provisions of which stated that 'the entire amount of wages payable to any worker shall be paid to the worker in money when they become payable'.[50] But the question for consideration was whether the amount deducted was 'wages payable', the answer to which 'must depend upon the contract of employment'.[51] So although it was an action brought under a statute, it was nevertheless one the outcome of which depended wholly on the application of common law principles. It is thus not a case which can be casually dismissed as turning on the provisions of the Wages Protection Act 1964 as Lord Oliver suggested in *Miles*.[52] The most significant issue in this context then was the submission for the bank that 'if an employee was absent without leave he was not entitled to payment for that period, either because of a failure of consideration or because the breach of contract justified an adjustment to the salary in respect of the days not worked'.[53] This was rejected by the Court which took the view that in 'the absence of a statutory or a contractual right to suspend pay the employer has a choice between two alternatives—to repudiate the contract and dismiss the worker or to affirm the contract and sue the worker for damages'.[54]

And what about the third argument? This was that 'the nature of equitable set-off makes it very difficult . . . to argue that employment contracts in general ought to be excluded from its application'.[55] Scott J. continued by asking rhetorically, 'Why should an equitable principle of this sort not apply to employment contracts? A fortiori, why should it not apply where the employee is suing for his contractual salary, but, in breach of contract, has failed to do all or some of the work required by his contract?' In his judgment 'no sufficient reason has been shown'.[56] Earlier in his judgment, however, Scott J. gave a very convincing justification why the doctrine should not apply. It will be recalled that the plaintiffs had argued that the doctrine would empower the employer to make deductions from salary on account of *supposed* breaches of contract, thereby empowering him to be judge and jury in his own cause. The argument continued with the claim that employees should not be put in a position in which, if they objected to the deductions, their only remedy would be to start an action in the courts. Remarkably in view of his subsequent comments, Scott J. said:

---

[48] [1983] IRLR 360.
[49] [1978] 2 NZLR 528.
[50] Wages Protection Act 1964, s. 4(1).
[51] [1978] 2 NZLR 528, at p. 534.
[52] [1987] 1 All ER 1089, at p. 1109.
[53] [1978] 2 NZLR 528, at p. 535.   [54] At p. 536.
[55] *Sim* v. *Rotherham Metropolitan Borough Council* [1986] 3 All ER 387, at p. 414.
[56] At p. 415.

I can see the force in that submission. It is true that employees whose salaries have been reduced by a purported application of equitable set-off may, in practice, find an effective remedy difficult to obtain. It may be that to allow equitable set-off to be used by employers so as to reduce the salaries paid to employees would open the door to abuse.[57]

What further justification is necessary to exclude the doctrine of equitable set-off from labour law? Is the prevention of abuse of employees less worthy of judicial concern than the commercial exigencies which have led to the exclusion of dishonoured bills of exchange and certain actions on bank guarantees? Although not mentioned, the scope of abuse is enormous. Quite apart from handing the employer a powerful weapon when workers refuse to obey lawful orders, it is a gift to an employer who requires employees to perform acts which are beyond the four corners of the contract.

2. *Quantum Meruit*   But if the approach in *Sim* is highly questionable, the alternative possible rationale is perhaps even more so. We have already encountered the decision of the House of Lords in *Miles*,[58] where the employer simply refused to accept part performance on Saturdays as a substitute for full performance. But in addition to dealing with this issue, several of their Lordships addressed some of the wider questions concerning the right to wages during industrial action short of a strike. The starting point in this respect is the speech of Lord Templeman who acknowledged that there may be circumstances where offered partial performance by the employee, 'the employer, in order to avoid greater damage, is obliged to accept the reduced work the worker is willing to perform'.[59] In those circumstances, said Lord Templeman, 'the worker cannot claim that he is entitled to his wages under the contract because he is deliberately working in a manner designed to harm the employer'. He continued, however, by asserting that the worker 'will be entitled to be paid on a *quantum meruit* basis for the amount and value of the reduced work performed and accepted'. And lest there be any doubt, his Lordship concluded by claiming that 'a worker who embarks on any form of industrial action designed to harm his employer gives up his right to wages under his contract of employment', and by suggesting that payment on the basis of *quantum meruit* was to be preferred to an analysis based on set-off. The latter presumes that the right to wages continues during the industrial action. The former, at least in Lord Templeman's view, presumes quite the contrary.

This approach was endorsed by Lord Brightman who preferred proceeding on the basis of *quantum meruit* rather than set-off in such circumstances for the following reason:

One has to start with the assumption that the employee sues for his pay; the employer is only bound to pay the employee that which the employee can recover by action. The

---

[57] At p. 413.   [58] [1987] 1 All ER 1089.   [59] At p. 1099.

employee cannot recover his contractual wages because he cannot prove that he has performed or ever intended to perform his contractual obligations. If wages and work are interdependent, it is difficult to suppose that an employee who has voluntarily declined to perform his contractual work can claim his contractual wages. The employee offers partial performance with the object of inflicting the maximum damage on the employer at the minimum inconvenience to himself. If, in breach of his contract, an employee works with the object of harming his employer, he can hardly claim that he is working under his contract and is therefore entitled to his contractual wages. But nevertheless in the case supposed the employee has provided *some* services, albeit less than the contract required, and the employer has received those (non-contractual) services; therefore the employer must clearly pay something, not the contractual wages because the contractual work has deliberately not been performed. What can he recover? Surely the value of the services which he gave and which the employer received, i.e. *quantum meruit*.[60]

Lord Brightman acknowledged that his remarks were *obiter*, but he felt undeterred, hoping that his thoughts may be 'of some assistance to those who seek a correct approach to the rights of the parties in the common case of industrial action which falls short of a withdrawal of labour'.[61] But perhaps fortunately, in view of the thoughts expressed, his remarks are of little help, and merely serve to confuse matters still further. Both Lords Brandon and Oliver expressly reserved their judgment on this issue, preferring not to 'comment about such a case until it arises'. In a similar vein, Lord Bridge of Harwich preferred not to express an opinion on cases where the employee partially performs but the employer nevertheless acquiesces in his breach of contract. He did say, however, that there 'may be no single, simple principle which can be applied in such cases irrespective of differences in circum-stances'.[62] And equally important, he cast doubt on the Templeman/Bright-man approach by saying that he found it 'difficult to understand the basis on which, in such a case, the employee in place of remuneration at the contractual rate would become entitled to a *quantum meruit*'.[63]

  If anything, *quantum meruit* is perhaps even more disadvantageous to employees than equitable set-off. It is true that like the equitable set-off it is a gift to the bully employer, now empowered with the right to threaten (and to carry out the threat) to withhold remuneration unless the employee undertakes to carry out instructions which may or may not be lawful under the contract. It is true too that it is another device available to the employer unilaterally to determine the amount of the deduction which will be made. If the matter comes to court (and the initiative to bring it here lies with the employee who can ill afford the cost), however, the disadvantage relative to set-off is that *quantum meruit* will place the burden of proof on the employee to show the value of the services provided whereas set-off imposes a duty on the employers to establish the extent of their loss. The value of the services provided may well be adjudged to be less than a payment based on a deduction for the employer's

[60] At p. 1092.   [61] At p. 1093.   [62] At pp. 1091–2.   [63] At p. 1092.

loss. But quite apart from the further difficulties placed upon employees, the doctrine of *quantum meruit* bears no relation to what happens in practice. As Lord Bridge pointed out in *Miles*,[64] its application 'would presuppose that the original contract of employment had in some way been superseded by a new agreement by which the employee undertook to work as requested by the employer for remuneration in a reasonable sum. This seems to me to be contrary to the realities of the situation'. Indeed, the whole point about the employer's acceptance of the employee's part performance of the contract is that the employer has chosen not to accept the employee's repudiation. That being so the employee is continuing to work under the existing contract through the choice of the employer, forced though that may be. How can it then be sensibly suggested, whether as a matter of principle or practice, that the existing contract has been displaced by some indeterminate and undefined substitute?

IV. CONCLUSION

It now seems clear that employers are free to withhold wages or unilaterally to make deductions from wages when faced with less than full performance by employees taking industrial action short of a strike. This is true regardless of the circumstances giving rise to the dispute, and in particular even where the legal status of the employee's conduct is unclear or where the employee's conduct is provoked by the unlawful or unreasonable behaviour of the employer. The position is all the more remarkable, first, for the fact that the employer may not only refuse to pay, but may also take advantage of the services provided, which as in *Wiluszynski* may be considerable; and, secondly, for the fact that the employer may elect to make a payment subject to a deduction the nature and size of which for all practical purposes he will determine.[65] The courts have thus given to employers a quite enormous power, particularly when we bear in mind the vulnerability of employees who take legal action to enforce rights under their contracts of employment. Workers who successfully sue to prevent unlawful conduct by the employer (such as the unilateral withholding of bonus payments) are liable to find that their resulting dismissals are not unfair[66]. Quite why the English (and Scottish) courts should find it necessary to reduce employees to a state of such submission, by the granting of powers so capable of abuse, is very unclear. We return to this question in Chapter 8. In the meantime we must consider the employer's power of dismissal over those engaged in a dispute.

---

[64] Ibid.

[65] For an example of the difficulties which can arise here, see *Jakeman* v. *South West Thames Regional Health Authority* [1990] IRLR 62 where ambulance staff were left without a remedy despite an allegedly excessive deduction from pay.

[66] See *Robertson* v. *British Gas Corporation* [1983] IRLR 304, and its sequel in *IDS Brief* 282, Aug. 1984, p. 8.

[4]
Industrial Action and Unfair Dismissal

I. INTRODUCTORY

As we saw in Chapter 2, workers who engage in industrial action in breach of contract may lawfully be dismissed by the employer without notice. This places the employer in an enormously powerful position, a position which, it has to be said, has not been significantly affected by the introduction of employment protection legislation. The first statute to regulate the manner of dismissal was the Contracts of Employment Act 1963 which laid down minimum periods of notice, with the length of notice required to dismiss an employee depending upon the length of continuous employment with the employer in question. The Act did not directly affect strike dismissals for it would still have been lawful to dismiss an employee without notice for participating in such action. Indirectly, however, workers who had been engaged in a strike or lock-out were penalized to the extent that any week during which the employee had been engaged in such action would not count as part of the period of continuous employment. This was followed by the Redundancy Payment Act 1965 which effectively provided that workers would cease to be eligible for a redundancy payment if they participated in a strike before redundancy notices were issued.[1] Eligibility was retained, however, if the strike took place after workers had been notified of their dismissal.[2]

II. THE STATUTORY FRAMEWORK

A. *The Industrial Relations Act 1971*

It might have been thought that the inequitable position of the employee in a strike would have been addressed by the introduction of the statutory protection against arbitrary dismissal. This measure, which was introduced in the Industrial Relations Act 1971, made it unfair for an employer to dismiss an employee save for specific reasons, and even then the employer was required to act in accordance with equity and the substantial merits of the case in treating

[1] See *Simmons* v. *Hoover Ltd.* [1977] ICR 61.
[2] See now EPCA 1978, ss. 49, 82, 92, and Sch. 13, as amended by the Employment Act 1982.

the reason as a ground for dismissal. An employee who is found to be unfairly dismissed by an industrial tribunal may be compensated or, exceptionally, reinstated or re-engaged in the employment. For reasons which need not be discussed here this provision has not been wholly effective in protecting job security. So far as protecting the rights of strikers is concerned, it has been wholly inadequate. The unfair dismissal law was introduced in 1971 by a Conservative government still pursuing monetarist economic policies. It was partly to implement international labour standards; partly to reduce the incidence of strikes about dismissal; but more especially to induce the unions to accept the more Draconian measures in the Industrial Relations Act in which it was contained. But whatever the purpose, the Act was not permitted to undermine the ultimate power of the employer in a labour dispute, with sections 25 and 26 expressly providing special rules for the dismissal of those taking part in a lock-out or a strike. In either case a dismissal would not be regarded as unfair unless it could be shown, first, that an employer had been selective in his dismissal or re-engagement of those taking part in the strike or lock-out; *and*, secondly, that those dismissed or not re-engaged had been selected because of their union membership or activities. The bottom line then was that a dismissal in the course of a strike was not unfair save for the victimization of union activists.

The function and values of the legislation were captured by Sir Hugh Griffiths in *Heath* v. *J. F. Longman (Meat Salesmen) Ltd.*[3] where he said:

It appears to this court that the manifest overall purpose of section 26 is to give a measure of protection to an employer if his business is faced with ruin by a strike. It enables him in those circumstances, if he cannot carry on the business without a labour force, to dismiss the labour force on strike; to take on another labour force without the stigma of its being an unfair dismissal.[4]

So the unequivocal function of the law, as understood and applied by the judges, was to preserve the economic power of the employer. Nowhere is there even a recognition of Lord Wright's comment that 'The right of workmen to strike is an essential element in the principle of collective bargaining'.[5] Without a right to strike, how can there be collective bargaining? The answer, it seems, is that collective bargaining could take place only on the employer's terms unless there were economic factors temporarily and fortuitously protecting the bargaining position of the union and its members. Yet although it is unsurprising that Heath's government should retain the power of employers in this way, it is frankly astonishing that this approach should be sustained by a Labour government in consultation with the TUC. Following the election of a Labour government in 1974, the Industrial Relations Act 1971 was repealed, though the provisions on unfair dismissal were retained, and indeed subsequently improved. The new legislation did little, however, to protect the

---

[3] [1973] ICR 407.   [4] At p. 410.
[5] *Crofter Hand Woven Harris Tweed* v. *Veitch* [1942] AC 435, at p. 463.

striker. In fact, initially the legislation was identical: that is to say, a dismissal of strikers (or as enacted in the Trade Union and Labour Relations Act 1974, Schedule 1, para. 8, those engaged in a lock-out) would not be unfair unless the employer selectively dismissed *and* selected for dismissal people because of their union membership or activities. There was nothing to stop the employer from dismissing all those engaged in the dispute or selectively to dismiss on other grounds. It is true that in 1975[6] these rules were modified—but only slightly. Under the new regime, since consolidated in the Employment Protection (Consolidation) Act 1978, s. 62, it was provided that an industrial tribunal would not have jurisdiction to hear a complaint of unfair dismissal of those taking part in a strike or any industrial action if all those taking part were dismissed and refused re-engagement. In other words, the employer had complete immunity against any complaint of unfair dismissal if he dismissed all those who participated in the strike or industrial action. It was only if the employer selectively dismissed or selectively re-engaged (for any reason— not just union membership or activities as before) any of those who had participated in the action that a complaint of unfair dismissal could be made. But even in such a case the dismissal would not necessarily be unfair for the complaint would have to be determined on established principles. And even if this were to lead to a holding of unfair dismissal, it is almost inconceivable that an employee would be successfully reinstated into his employment by a tribunal.

B. *A New Rationale for the Legislation*

So even under a Labour government there was no serious attempt to challenge the ultimate power of an employer in a dispute. He could lawfully discharge everyone who participated in a strike; he could perhaps lawfully victimize (in the sense that a discriminatory dismissal may be fair); and if he acted unlawfully he would be required to pay only a modest amount of compensation. As might be expected, the rationale of the legislation changed. The rhetoric was not now the need to protect the employer. Rather, it was one of state neutrality. Thus:

the whole policy of the law as enshrined in the Act of 1974 and the later enactments is to withdraw the law from the field of industrial disputes. There is a kind of legal laissez-faire or neutrality as soon as an industrial dispute breaks out. The continued provisions of paragraph 8 are in one sense the price of making that possible.[7]

But this argument is simplistic. First, it reflects an inconsistency of approach. The freedom to strike is frustrated both by the common law of tort and the common law of contract which vest considerable power in the employer—the law of tort to restrain a strike, and the law of contract to fire strikers. Yet it is recognized that in order to create the so-called neutrality in industrial disputes, the legislature must remove the tortious limits on the strike, otherwise there

---

[6] Employment Protection Act 1975, Sch. 16.
[7] *Gallacher* v. *Wragg* [1977] ICR 175, at pp. 178–9.

cannot be a fair fight. But the same argument must also apply to the law of contract. How is it consistent with a concept of state neutrality in a dispute to remove the employer's legal power over the union in a strike, but to retain the employer's legal power over union members?

Perhaps more importantly, the concept of neutrality is not only applied inconsistently, in this instance it is not even applied at all. Non-intervention is not neutrality if it sustains existing power structures. For the fact is that the contract of employment with its rights and duties is a form of intervention in work-place relations which vests absolute power in the employer. The failure to intervene to regulate or constrain that legal power is to sustain the employer by omission. It is naïve to suppose that because the government does not intervene to regulate a social and economic question that the state (or even the government) is neutral. In other words, in order to secure neutrality of the state in industrial conflict, the government has to intervene directly in the relationship between employer, union and worker. Under the present regime the government is neutrally unwilling to challenge the legal power of the employer. It is neutrally indifferent to that power. But this is not to suggest that a second rationale of the existing legislation is any more persuasive. Thus it is sometimes argued that the terms of the legislation can be justified in order to preserve judicial neutrality rather than state neutrality. In other words, the statutory provisions took the form they did in order to keep the courts out of industrial disputes and to prevent the judges from adjudicating on the merits of industrial disputes. This they would be required to do if called upon to determine whether or not a strike-related dismissal is unfair. And given the anti-labour attitude of the judges, no one could live happily with that. Or so it is said. Again, however, the argument is staggeringly simplistic.

In the first place the judges have already intervened in industrial conflict. They intervened by their development of the common law on the contract of employment which gives to the employer the power to dismiss those who take part in a strike. The legislation does not exclude the judges. Rather it invites them in to the extent that it provides for the legal regulation of the strike in accordance with common law doctrine. To deny a remedy for unfair dismissal does not achieve judicial neutrality—it is a vindication and triumph for the partisan qualities of the common law. And, even if it could be argued that it is necessary to prevent the judges from adjudicating on the reasonableness of dismissals in individual disputes, that goal is not secured by the legislation. The tribunals and courts are so excluded only if the employer dismisses everyone (or no one) and to that extent it could well be argued that in fact the legislation encourages the dismissal of strikers. But if the employer does discriminate, then the tribunals are seized of a duty to adjudicate on established principles whether or not a dismissal is fair. Inevitably that will involve some consideration of the conduct of the strikers and the merits of the strike. So the statute is only a qualified exclusion of the courts. It operates only so long as the employer does not discriminate. If the goal was to exclude the courts then there would be no jurisdiction over this type of case either. But not only is judicial neutrality illusory, and not only does the Act fail in the implementation of the stated goal. The fact is that if there was a serious concern to keep the judges out of industrial disputes in a manner which would not involve them in the adjudication of the merits of a dispute, there is only one way in which this could be done. This would be to provide that participation in a strike is not a ground for dismissal, and to override the rule against specific performance of employment contracts by providing expressly that a worker dismissed for this reason would be entitled automatically to be reinstated.

C. *Extending the Employer's Power*

1. *The 1982 Amendments* Section 62 of the EPCA 1978 thus vests considerable power in the employer. In the course of a strike he may dismiss all those who have taken part, and may do so with impunity. In a small enterprise with largely unskilled workers this is a very potent weapon indeed, particularly in a period of high unemployment, though the power is not confined to the small enterprise. It is a power which permits the employer to impose unlawful demands and to reinforce the demands with the threat of dismissal over those who refuse to comply. Even if the employer selectively dismisses or re-engages those participating in the dispute, the workers in question must run the gauntlet of the normal unfair dismissal proceedings, and even if they succeed there is no way in which the employer can be compelled to reinstate them into his employment. Yet despite the great social power thus conferred on an employer in the course of a dispute, the Conservative administration of Mrs Thatcher concluded that the legislation denied employers 'the ability to make a credible and legitimate response when they are faced with a strike'.[8] Three steps were taken to make matters even easier for employers than they were already under the 1978 Act. Until 1982, in order to benefit from the immunity, the employer was forbidden to retain or re-engage the services of any striking employee, the prohibition on re-engagement being a continuing one with no expiry period. If the employer did re-engage any of the striking employees at any future date, he would lose his immunity. The government was concerned about this 'completely open-ended obligation [whereby] employers could never take on sacked employees again without putting themselves at risk of placing the dismissals within the jurisdiction of the industrial tribunal'.[9] The first change then was the introduction in the Employment Act 1982, s. 9, of a measure enabling employers selectively to re-engage striking workers after a period of three months has elapsed from the dismissal of the workforce.

The second and perhaps more important change introduced by the 1982 amendments was to reverse the decision of the House of Lords in *Stock* v.

[8]   17 HC Debs. 743 (8 Feb. 1982).
[9]   Official Report, Standing Committee G, 24 Apr. 1982, col. 1112.

Frank Jones (Tipton) Ltd.[10] where it was held that in order to claim the protection of section 62, an employer must dismiss all the employees who had taken part in the strike, including those who may have returned to work before it ended. The government was thus concerned that the employer would find himself in a catch-22 situation, albeit 'the number of cases involving section 62 for which industrial tribunals have had jurisdiction to hear complaints is few':[11]

Some very strange situations could be created. An employer could allow strikers back to work in the belief that the action was ended without knowing, or having any means of knowing, that others who possibly could be based in a different part of the country proposed to continue the action even at a later date. If he accepted the return to work of the first group, he would risk complaints of unfair dismissal in the way described if he dismissed those who continued to strike. On the other hand, if he delayed their return until he was certain that none of his employees in other parts of the country intended to participate in the action, he would be ignoring the wish of the first group to remedy the fundamental breach of contract involved in taking industrial action and might be held to have locked out his employees, although he had been forced into that situation by the law as it now operated.[12]

In *Stock*, Viscount Dilhorne had concluded rather differently on the question of anomaly:

Much weight was sought to be placed on the anomalies which it was said would result from giving effect to the words used by Parliament. I am by no means satisfied that all the anomalies lie on one side, nor am I satisfied that dismissal of those allowed to return to work before the others engaged in industrial action were dismissed would necessarily render an employer liable to pay compensation, for [under the Act] a Tribunal can only make an award of compensation if it does not recommend reinstatement or re-engagement, or if it does so recommend and its recommendation is not complied with.[13]

Nevertheless the government proposed to deal with the issue by enabling employers to dismiss all employees still on strike after a detailed notice procedure had been completed. Employers would have been required to display at the work-place and send to each employee a notice warning him that he would be dismissed if he had not returned to work by a specified date. This, however, was rejected as 'unworkable' and 'administratively impossible'.[14] In its place was introduced a measure permitting an employer to dismiss only those who are on strike at the date of their dismissal: he need not dismiss employees who had returned to work during the strike.

This provision is subject to criticism for two reasons. First, it absolves the employer from any responsibility to notify employees that they will be dismissed unless they return to work by a particular date. So if the employer issues a notice which is received by only some employees those who fail to

[10] [1978] ICR 347.
[11] Official Report, Standing Committee G, 22 Apr. 1982, col. 1110.
[12] Ibid., cols. 1108–9.   [13] [1978] ICR 347, at p. 352.
[14] Official Report, Standing Committee G, 22 Apr. 1982, cols. 1110–11.

return to work by the deadline may be dismissed at no cost to the employer even though the individuals in question were never warned that they would be dismissed. Secondly, it is a charter for victimization and union-busting. The reality is that when an ultimatum of this kind is issued, the people who are likely to remain on strike are the activists. The employer is free to discard only these employees, again at no cost to himself. The amendment in fact makes the power of dismissal in a strike not only very potent, but also very desirable for the employer. This, however, is not the only change introduced in 1982. Until that year the employer's immunity applied only if he dismissed everyone who took part in the strike. The third amendment is one which enables the employer to retain the immunity by dismissing only those engaged at a particular 'establishment of the employer at or from which the employee works'. The effect of this is that a multi-site employer may retain the immunity by not dismissing all those engaged in a strike, but only those on strike at a particular site. This might be done in order to encourage strikers at other plants to return to work for fear of similar reprisals. Or it might be done to allow production to continue by dismissing those on strike and by hiring replacement workers. Remarkably, the word 'establishment' is not defined, and little guidance as to its meaning was offered to Parliament by government spokesmen. When asked what it meant from the Labour benches, the government spokesman confessed that he had once again been asked a question which he could not answer exactly.[15]

2. *Unofficial Action*   Although the 1982 amendments effectively introduced an employer's right to engage in discriminatory dismissals in trade disputes, the government had, by 1989, formed the view that these amendments had not gone far enough in this direction. A Green Paper published in that year drew attention to the incidence of unofficial industrial action:

our industrial relations system still suffers from a substantial amount of unofficial action—that is, industrial action taken by trade union members but not authorised or endorsed by their trade union. Unofficial strikes are a long-standing and deep-rooted feature of British industrial relations. The great majority of strikes in Great Britain have always been and still are unofficial. They are walkouts by groups of workers acting without the approval or sanction of their union, either on their own initiative or at the instigation of shop stewards or other union officials who have no authority under the union's rules to call strikes. By proceeding directly to industrial action, often without notice, they are bypassing the normal channels for settling problems peacefully. All too often this amounts to a form of industrial blackmail. (Department of Employment 1989: 1).

The Department continued by claiming that well over half a million working days were lost through unofficial action in 1987, with almost three times as many working days lost in the following year. This was in addition to

---

[15] Official Report, Standing Committee G, 24 Apr. 1982, cols. 1148–9.

'numerous small and unofficial strikes not included in available statistics'. These issues were also addressed by the Secretary of State, Mr Michael Howard, during the Second Reading debate when he claimed that some 75 per cent of strikes were unofficial, which 'means that they take place without being authorized in accordance with union rules and without being put to the test of a secret ballot'.[16] Concern was expressed, in particular, about the disruption in the public services by such action, attention being drawn to the fact that in the summer of 1989 'both British Rail and London Underground were particularly badly affected by unofficial action'. (Department of Employment 1989: 2). Indeed these disputes are widely believed to be the precipitating cause of the government's proposals.

The first proposal, now contained in clause 6 of the Bill, was to extend the vicarious liability of trade unions to include legal responsibility for the acts of shop stewards and other lay officials unless the union repudiated their actions.[17] If the action is not repudiated the employer may sue the union for an injunction and damages unless those organizing the strike comply with the balloting and other requirements which now regulate tortious immunity.[18] The government's second proposal, now contained in clause 9 of the 1990 Bill, dealt chiefly with the situation where the local action had been repudiated by the union. In that case an employee may be dismissed and is denied the right to complain of unfair dismissal even though other people who have participated in the strike and who are participating in the strike at the date of dismissal have not been dismissed.[19] Unions are thus placed in the horrible position of having to either repudiate local action to protect their funds, or passively endorse the action to protect their members. According to the government, the existing law stood in the way of employers effectively tackling the problem of unofficial strikes. An employer could not 'without risk of a complaint of unfair dismissal, dismiss individual employees who may have repeatedly organized unofficial action which has damaged his business' (Department of Employment 1989: 8) because as matters then stood 'the law on unfair dismissal means that, if an employer is to avoid risk of complaints of unfair dismissal, he must dismiss all of his employees who go on strike or none at all'. (ibid.: 7). It is as if the 1982 amendments had never been introduced! It is, of course, not the case that the employer had to dismiss everyone who had gone on strike in order to escape liability. The obligation to dismiss only those on strike at the date of dismissal permitted discriminatory action against the hard-core activist. If this was insufficient and there was a need to pin-point action more precisely against specific officials such a dismissal (even if others on strike at the date of dismissal

---

[16] 166 HC Debs. 46–7 (29 Jan. 1990).

[17] This was done by extending s. 15 of the Employment Act 1982 which deals with the circumstances in which a trade union is liable for the acts of its officials.

[18] And the 'repudiation will have to be unequivocal': Mr M. Howard, 166 HC Debs. 47 (29 Jan. 1990). See Employment Act 1982, s. 15(5) and (5A), as amended by the Employment Bill 1990, cl. 6.

[19] EPCA, s. 62 A(1), as inserted by Employment Bill 1990, cl. 9.

are not also dismissed) would almost certainly have been fair if provoked by repeated conduct causing 'damage to business'.

Clause 9 of the 1990 Bill thus sharpens up the power of selective dismissal which had been 'a reality'[20] of labour law at least since 1982. Nevertheless the Opposition were right to find this particular clause to be 'more objectionable than any other in the Bill',[21] for two reasons. First, it encourages and rewards authoritarian management and further undermines the ability of workers collectively to resist unlawful or unreasonable demands made of them. There is no definition of 'industrial action' in section 62, either as originally conceived or as amended, so that the matter is one of fact for the tribunals. As we shall see, it may well involve a concerted refusal to work in unsafe conditions or to comply with an instruction (such as agreeing to do overtime) which the employer has no right to give under the contract.[22] Yet anyone who refuses to comply may find himself liable to dismissal, with his isolation reinforced by the fact that the union has no immunity to take official industrial action on behalf of someone dismissed for taking unofficial action.[23] Related to this is the second cause for concern, namely the unlimited scope of the power to victimize. For offensive though it may be that the employer should be free to act without restraint or accountability against what Mr Howard referred to as 'a handful of trouble-makers',[24] the power to victimize is not confined to such people, and no guarantees were given in Committee that it would be. The employer can dismiss whomever he likes for whatever reason, which might well include a desire to avoid liabilities arising under what is left of the Employment Protection (Consolidation) Act 1978. So if the dismissal of Mr Howard's so-called 'trouble-makers' sits uneasily with the protection for trade union members and officials in EPCA, ss. 23 and 58, and ILO Convention 98,[25] what about dismissals of pregnant women in order to avoid maternity rights,[26]

---

[20] Mr Tony Lloyd, Official Report, Standing Committee D, 8 Mar. 1990, col. 314.

[21] Ibid.

[22] Note that the government refused to accept an Opposition amendment which would have restored the right of employees in unofficial action where the reason of the employee for taking part in the action was a reason connected with health and safety or physical or verbal intimidation by the employer. See Official Report, Standing Committee D, 15 Mar. 1990, col. 369 et seq.

[23] Employment Bill 1990, cl. 9(2), amending TULRA 1974, s. 13.

[24] 166 HC Debs. 47 (29 Jan. 1990).

[25] See here the concerns expressed by Dr K. Howells, 166 HC Debs. 96 (29 Jan. 1990): 'For most of this century legislation by Governments of all political shades has recognised the role of those in trade unions who are chosen by their fellows to act as spokespersons and local organisers—a task which is frequently difficult and thankless and requires more than a little personal courage as well as ability . . . Clauses 6 and [9] threaten to take away even the fragile protection of existing legislation from men and women who are local trade union officials. The clauses threaten to undermine one of the central pillars of responsible and valuable trade unionism. No one in his or her right mind will put himself forward for a trade union position if, as a result of unofficial industrial action which he may have opposed in the first place, he finds himself at the wrong end of the law. There may be those in the Government who rejoice at such a prospect, but I fear that theirs will prove an extremely limited prospective, for they will be undermining a central pillar of that often fragile platform on which industrial harmony is based.'

[26] Official Report, Standing Committee D, 13 Mar. 1990, col. 348 (Mr Jim Wallace).

or the dismissal of people with more than two years' service in order to evade imminent redundancy payments and unfair dismissal obligations?[27]

III.   THE JUDICIAL RESPONSE

The provisions of section 62 of the EPCA have been described from the Bench, rightly, as conferring a 'special privilege of immunity from unfair dismissal claims' on employers.[28] Waite J. continued by pointing out that this immunity:

is subject (as is now well known) to stringent sanctions, designed to deter employers from abusing the immunity by treating a strike as a pretext for dismissing the unwanted elements in their workforce and retaining the remainder. The stringency permits no exceptions. If the employer omits to dismiss every single one of those participating in the strike action and retains in his employment (or re-engages) so much as one such participant, his immunity becomes forfeited and the entire dismissed workforce will be entitled to make unfair dismissal claims. Motive is irrelevant. Inadvertence makes no difference. The rule is wholly rigid and inflexible.

The result, as the authorities show, has been to turn the process of dismissal of a striking workforce into something like a game of hazard in which the winner takes all, in which defeat or victory turns upon the fall of a single card, and in which the stakes increase dramatically according to the numbers involved. It is a game requiring intense concentration, each side closely watching the other. It is also, one suspects, a game in which no one does half so well as the lawyers who have become indispensable as its croupiers. The appeal and cross-appeal in the present case both give rise, in different factual contexts, to the question how far the rules of the game permit the cards to be played face down.[29]

Although it is highly questionable whether the employer is subject to 'stringent sanctions' (failure to comply with section 62 merely opens the door to the industrial tribunal without guaranteeing the employee a remedy), there is no doubt that the legislation does give rise to difficult questions of scope. For the most part, however, any problems have been resolved by the courts in the employer's favour, thereby adding significantly to the weight against employees. The pro-management response of the courts in an already remarkably pro-management framework of legislation is highlighted forcefully in several of the areas of contention to which we now turn.

A. *The Scope of the Employer's Immunity*

The first problem which has arisen for adjudication by the courts is to determine to which action the employer's immunity extends. The Act simply provides that the immunity applies where at the date of dismissal the employer was conducting or instituting a lock-out, or the employees were taking part in a

---

[27] Official Report, Standing Committee D, 13 Mar. 1990 col. 320 (Mr John Evans).
[28] Hindle Gears Ltd. v. *McGinty* [1985] ICR 112, at p. 113.
[29] At pp. 113–14.

strike or other industrial action. But none of the crucial terms (lock-out, strike, other industrial action) is defined anywhere. So it has been left to the courts to give them some content. And in performing this role the courts have made it clear that the immunity extends to a wide range of action and that it applies regardless of the cause of the strike or the circumstances surrounding it. First, it is immaterial to the existence of the immunity that the strike or industrial action has been provoked by the unreasonable conduct of the employer. This is highlighted by *Thompson* v. *Eaton Ltd.*,[30] where employers sought to introduce new machinery into a plant. They did this without consulting the work-force, some of whom gathered round the newly-installed machines with a view to preventing them being tested for use. When they refused to return to their normal places of work, the employees were dismissed, the employer claiming successfully before an industrial tribunal that the employees had been dismissed for taking part in industrial action. The appeal to the Employment Appeal Tribunal was rejected despite the fact that 'there were faults on the side of the management'; that 'had the management acted somewhat differently at an earlier stage in the trouble the dispute might well have been settled'; and that 'had a proper discussion taken place otherwise than under the imminent intention of the management to carry out the installation of the [machines], there would have been a happier outcome'. Nevertheless the appeal tribunal rejected the argument that the employer's immunity does 'not apply to a case where the employer is wholly or substantially to blame for the occurrence of the strike or other industrial action'. In the view of the appeal tribunal, such a proposition is unwarranted by the language of the statute and it would in any event be impossible to apply in practice, it being 'very rare for strikes, or other industrial action, to be wholly the fault of one side or the other'. It was suggested that immunity would not apply in the case of a strike which had been 'provoked, or even engineered, by the employer in some gross manner'. But this depended on the view that a repudiation by one party automatically terminated the contract without the need for acceptance by the other. This is probably not now the law,[31] with the result that workers who wish to preserve a remedy in such a case must accept the employer's repudiation by resigning. If they strike they may then be dismissed by the employer who will retain the immunity notwithstanding the fact that the strike was provoked by him in the first place.

But the immunity applies not only where the strike is provoked by the unreasonable conduct of the employer. It also applies where the strike is provoked by the unlawful conduct of the employer. This point is illustrated forcefully by *Wilkins* v. *Cantrell and Cochrane (GB) Ltd.*[32] where three applicants were employed as drivers by the respondent company. On a number of occasions lorries had been sent from their depot in an overloaded condition. Following a number of complaints from the staff, a strike was called when the

[30] [1976] ICR 336.
[31] *Rigby* v. *Ferodo Ltd.* [1987] IRLR 516.   [32] [1978] IRLR 483.

management practice continued. The employees were then dismissed following a warning from management. The employees argued, first, that in sending the lorries out on the road in an overloaded condition the employers were in breach of the Road Traffic Act and therefore in breach of the law. Secondly, it was contended that by sending the drivers out with the loads in question the employers were exposing the drivers to the risk that they, too, might be charged with an offence under the same Act. And, finally, it was argued that the employers were in breach of contract which entitled the employees to respond to the repudiatory conduct in the way they did. The industrial tribunal came to the conclusion that 'at the worst these instances were insufficient, and at the worst these instances indicated negligence not amounting to deliberate breaches of the law'. In the EAT, however, it was pointed out that the employees 'knew that there had been instances where vehicles had gone out overloaded' and had made proper and sensible representations to no avail. Nevertheless the EAT held for the employer, rejecting the justification put forward by the employees that their conduct was in response to a fundamental breach of contract. The EAT concluded that if an employer repudiates the contract 'the employee has to act upon the situation' by making it clear that he regards the contract as having been brought to an end. The taking of strike action does not terminate the contract in the face of the employer's repudiatory conduct but rather gives the employer new grounds for termination which under the Act cannot then be challenged unless the employer discriminates in his dismissal of the strikers.

So the immunity applies even where the employer acts unreasonably or unlawfully. The fact that the strike is purely defensive is of no avail. If this is not remarkable enough, the position was developed still further by the Court of Appeal in *Power Packing Casemakers Ltd.* v. *Faust*[33] where a group of employees were in dispute with their employer about wages. The company made 'packing cases for goods for despatch and they got a rush order for an export job, which they claimed, and the employees denied, required their workmen to work overtime' to meet a deadline. All the workmen, when threatened with dismissal, complied with the 'request' to work overtime, except three who were dismissed. The crucial point in the case is that the employees were not under a contractual obligation to work overtime. They were acting perfectly lawfully under the contract and were dismissed effectively for refusing to submit to the employer's demand to do something which the employer had no *right* to demand, and which was beyond the terms of the contract. The question before the Court of Appeal was whether there could be a strike or other industrial action under section 62 when the conduct of the employees did not amount to a breach of contract on their part. For the employees it was argued that the legislation could not possibly be construed in favour of the employer. For if the legislation was so construed, 'unscrupulous

[33] [1983] ICR 292.

employers will be allowed . . . to dismiss unfairly and unjustly those who take legitimate industrial action, without any fear of the circumstances being investigated by the statutory tribunals, or having to pay compensation or reinstate those unfairly dismissed employees'.[34] And, if the legislation was so construed, it 'would open the floodgates of abuse, and strike at the whole object of the legislation providing employment protection'.[35] Yet although confirming that the interpretation proposed by the company was 'a gift to employers',[36] the Court of Appeal nevertheless accepted it. The Court justified its decision on two grounds, the first being the intention of Parliament to remove 'from the areas of consideration of the industrial tribunal saving only the special aspects of discriminatory treatment, any question which arose out of a strike or other industrial action'.[37] Secondly, there was 'no justification, let alone a mandate, to import, by interpretation or implication, the words "breach of contract" to qualify the meaning of "other industrial action" and . . . the words must be given their plain and ordinary meaning'.[38]

B. *Lock-outs*

Staggeringly, perhaps, section 62 gives the employer immunity where the employer was conducting or instituting a lock-out at the date of the employees' dismissal. In such a case an industrial tribunal may not determine whether the dismissal is fair or unfair unless it is shown that one or more relevant employees of the same employer have not been dismissed. For this purpose 'relevant employees' means employees who were directly interested in the dispute in contemplation or furtherance of which the lock-out occurred.[39] Before 1982 the word 'dispute' read 'trade dispute', this being defined in terms similar to the definition of a trade dispute for the purpose of immunity from liability in tort. With the narrowing of that definition in that context in 1982, the employer's immunity in section 62 would be correspondingly yet unintention-ally narrowed as well. Presumably the amendment was made to avoid this problem with the result that the employer's immunity has been extended (by applying to all disputes and not just to trade disputes as statutorily defined) whereas the immunity of trade unions and their officials has been significantly reduced. Nevertheless other limbs of the definition of the term 'relevant employees' in this context makes this head of the immunity difficult for employers to use and perhaps for this reason it is apparently infrequently relied upon. So in *Fisher* v. *York Trailer Co. Ltd.*,[40] seven employees out of a work-force of thirty-four were suspended from duty when they refused to work normally following the introduction of new productivity proposals. They were eventually dismissed, but following proceedings by six for unfair dismissal, the tribunal declined jurisdiction on the basis that they had been dismissed while

---

[34] At pp. 299–300 (Stephenson L.J.).   [35] At p. 301 (Purchas L.J.).
[36] At p. 296 (Stephenson L.J.).   [37] At p. 304 (Purchas L.J.).
[38] Ibid.   [39] EPCA, s. 62(4)(b).   [40] [1979] IRLR 385.

the employer was conducting a lock-out. Although this last finding was upheld, the EAT also held that the industrial tribunal had wrongly declined jurisdiction on the ground that not all relevant employees had been dismissed. On the facts it was held that the dispute in this case (to accept an ultimatum from management) was such that all thirty-four employees were 'relevant employees' in the sense that they were all 'directly interested in the trade dispute at some time while the trade dispute was going on'. Consequently, as all the relevant employees had not been dismissed the industrial tribunal was held to have had jurisdiction to hear the complaints.

But although *Fisher* suggests that there may be difficulties in the way of using the lock-out as a basis of immunity, the reality is that the employer need rarely if ever rely on it as a means of securing immunity. If presented with the facts in *Fisher* today, a well-advised employer could simply argue that the tribunal has no jurisdiction, on the ground that at the time of dismissal the employees were engaged in industrial action. As all those engaged in the action at the time of the applicants' dismissal were also dismissed, the immunity would be retained without the need to dismiss the bulk of the work-force who had returned. It is indeed a feature of this area of law that the adjudicating authorities have read the term 'strike' or 'industrial action' so widely to preclude the employer ever having to rely upon the lock-out clause as a condition of immunity. And in this context it is important to emphasize the extent to which it is in the employer's interest to rely upon the strike or industrial action clause: to do so means dismissing only those still on strike at the date of dismissal in contrast to all those directly interested in the dispute. This was the 'crucial' issue highlighted forcefully by *Express and Star Ltd.* v. *Bunday*,[41] which concerned a dispute about 'single keying' in the newspaper industry. Again the trouble arose when a number of employees refused to submit to a management ultimatum regarding working practices. As a result access to the employer's premises was closed, the employees being suspended without pay and finally dismissed. An industrial tribunal held against the employees who argued that they had been dismissed while the employer was instituting a lock-out, favouring the view that the employees had been engaged in industrial action. The tribunal also held, however, that it had jurisdiction to hear the complaint on the ground that one relevant employee had been dismissed but subsequently re-engaged. Although the EAT[42] reversed this last finding of the industrial tribunal (a decision subsequently approved by the Court of Appeal), it also held that the industrial tribunal had erred in regarding the employees as having been engaged in industrial action rather than having been locked out.

The Court of Appeal was concerned only with the employer's appeal that he had not been engaged in a lock-out at the time of dismissal but that the employees had been engaged in industrial action. The matter was litigated this

---

[41] [1987] IRLR 422.   [42] [1986] IRLR 477.

far by the employer because it would be easier to show that he had dismissed all relevant employees if the facts supported the view that the employees had been engaged in industrial action rather than that he had been conducting a lock-out. In deciding for the employer, the Court of Appeal made two important contributions to this area of the law. First, it was held (by a majority) that the question whether or not employees are engaged in industrial action or have been locked out is a matter of fact for the tribunal of first instance to determine. In the view of May L.J., '[w]hat are the necessary elements of a lock-out, or for that matter of a bicycle or an elephant is not . . . a question of law'.[43] If it is not a question of law then there can be no appeal, with there being no right of appeal to the EAT on questions of fact. It was also argued, however, that the industrial tribunal had misdirected itself to the extent that it had allegedly held that there could not be a lock-out without a breach of contract on the part of the employer and, as in this case there was no breach of contract, there could be no lock-out. In a potentially remarkable passage, May L.J. replied:

Even if they had done so, I do not think this was necessarily a misdirection. It must depend on the facts of the particular case. In one case, whether or not the employers were in breach of contract may be a critical factor in deciding if there has been a lock-out. In at least a substantial number of cases in my opinion it will at least be a material consideration.[44]

By parity of reasoning with *Faust*,[45] it was accepted that employers could institute a lock-out without a breach of contract, though in this context, unlike in *Faust*, the breach of contract was not necessarily irrelevant. In the event, however, the tribunal was in the clear, principally because in the view of the Court of Appeal it had simply taken into account whether the employer had acted in breach of contract and had not laid this down as a condition of a lock-out. Nevertheless, *Bunday* stands in sharp contrast to *Faust*. In the latter the Court extended the definition of industrial action to breaking point, to include concerted action which was not a breach of contract, thereby increasing further the disadvantage of employees. In the former, by contrast, by emphasizing (if not yet formally requiring) the need for a breach of contract by the employer, the Court has significantly reduced the utility of s. 62 for employees by restrictively construing this more onerous route to immunity.

C. *Who is a Relevant Employee?*

The third point of concern relates to the concept of the relevant employee. Under the Act, if there is a strike, lock-out or other industrial action, the employer will have immunity if it is shown that 'one or more relevant employees of the same employer have not been dismissed'. The term 'relevant

---

[43] [1987] IRLR 422, at p. 425.
[44] At p. 426.
[45] [1983] ICR 292.

employees' was in turn defined to mean in part: 'in relation to a strike . . . employees who took part in it'. The phrase is now defined to mean:

(i) in relation to a lock-out, employees who were directly interested in the dispute in contemplation or furtherance of which the lock-out occurred, and

(ii) in relation to a strike or other industrial action, those employees at the establishment who were taking part in the action at the complainant's date of dismissal.[46]

The major problem here is to determine precisely who is taking part in the action, this key phrase again being undefined in the body of the Act.[47] Can an employee be dismissed for participating in a strike if on the date of his and his colleagues' dismissal he is absent from work on account of sickness or bad weather conditions?[48] If an employee refuses to cross a picket line because of fear and is not dismissed, can those who are dismissed for taking part in a strike bring a claim for unfair dismissal on the ground that one employee has participated and has not been dismissed?[49] And, is an employee who attends a meeting which decides to impose an overtime ban participating in industrial action with the result that his non-dismissal enables those dismissed to bring a claim for unfair dismissal?[50] These are only some of the problems which have arisen. Again, however, any difficulties have been resolved to the advantage of employers, with the longer-term interest of employers clearly in mind even in several decisions which were favourable to applicants; points made forcefully by two decisions of the Court of Appeal.

In the first, *McCormick* v. *Horsepower Ltd.*[51] a number of boilermakers in dispute with their employer were dismissed for going on strike. Another employee, a Mr Brazier, was a fitter's mate who was a member of a different union from the boilermakers, his union having no quarrel with the employer. Because of his trade union principles, however, Mr Brazier refused to cross the boilermakers' picket line, though he did so eventually and before the applicants were dismissed for their industrial action. In fact Mr Brazier was himself dismissed for redundancy shortly after some of the striking engineers were dismissed. The questions for consideration were first whether Mr Brazier had been taking part in the strike (as the applicants argued in order to establish jurisdiction) and, if so, whether he had been dismissed as a result, the applicants arguing that in order to retain the immunity the employer must dismiss relevant employees while they are on strike at the time of the applicants' dismissals. Restoring the industrial tribunal, the Court of Appeal held that Mr Brazier had not been taking part in the action and so was not a relevant employee. Thus, although Mr Brazier 'may be said to have gone on

---

[46] EPCA, s. 62(4)(b).

[47] The question whether someone is 'taking part in a strike or other industrial action' is one of fact for the tribunal to decide: *Coates* v. *Modern Methods and Materials Ltd.* [1982] IRLR 318.

[48] *Williams* v. *Western Mail and Echo Ltd.* [1980] IRLR 366; *McKenzie* v. *Crossville Motor Services Ltd.* [1989] IRLR 516.

[49] *Coates* v. *Modern Methods and Materials Ltd.* [1982] IRLR 318.

[50] *Naylor* v. *Orton & Smith Ltd.* [1983] ICR 665.   [51] [1981] IRLR 217.

strike, he did not take part in the same strike' as the boilermakers. His strike, it seems, was a one-man strike. But it was also held that even if he had taken part in the strike, it was not necessary to show that he had been dismissed while taking part in the strike. The employer would be covered provided the employee had been dismissed at any time up until the time of the tribunal hearing. The Court of Appeal reached this conclusion following 'the plain meaning' of the statute, there being 'no statutory words to indicate how long before or whether the dismissal should have been for any reason connected with or relevant to the strike'.[52] Such a position was adopted despite the 'undesirable results' that could follow. Lawton L.J. gave as an example 'an employer who had enticed back to work one or more strikers [and who] could defeat claims for unfair dismissal by the other strikers by dismissing those he had taken back a day or so before the hearing'.[53] Significantly, he pointed out that in such a case the employer 'might have to face damages for wrongful dismissal but in industry such damages would probably be small compared to what might be awarded by way of compensation for unfair dismissal'.

Following the 1982 amendments, on its facts *McCormick* would be decided on the more straightforward ground that even if Brazier had taken part in the strike, he was not doing so at the date of dismissal of the complainants. Nevertheless the decision is still relevant, for instance, in a case where the employer does not dismiss everyone on strike at the date of an applicant's dismissal. It also illustrates just how sanguine the courts are about reaching decisions which are 'certainly' anomalous and undesirable. Also important in this context is *P & O European Ferries (Dover) Ltd.* v. *Byrne*[54] where the respondent was one of 1,025 employees dismissed while on strike. They subsequently claimed that industrial tribunals had jurisdiction to deal with their complaints of unfair dismissal because one of their number (albeit inadvertently, it seems) had not also been dismissed. One of the questions before the Court of Appeal was whether the applicant was under a duty to identify the relevant employee who had not been dismissed. This he had refused to do because it would have led inevitably to the dismissal of the employee in question with damaging consequences for the application by Mr Byrne and subsequently by his 1,024 fellow strikers. Significantly, both the industrial tribunal and the EAT refused the employer's request. This they did in order to prevent Mr Byrne from being irrevocably prejudiced, with the EAT contending that the failure to disclose would not in contrast prejudice the employer for 'it would be possible after the identity was known for the employers to obtain an adjournment to enable them to prepare their case against the contention that there had been discrimination'. On this point the Court of Appeal reversed: an employee who has been dismissed for taking part in industrial action must provide the employer with the information which will enable the employer to defeat the application on jurisdictional grounds. As

[52] At p. 220 (Lawton L.J.).   [53] At p. 221.   [54] [1989] IRLR 254.

events unfolded, however, this proved to be inconsequential, for even if the information had been allowed to be withheld until the hearing was under way, the employer would still have been able to defeat the claim on jurisdictional grounds. This is because of the extension of *McCormick* by the Court of Appeal in *Byrne*, it being held now that the employer is free to exercise the power of dismissal over anyone who may give jurisdiction, not at the start of the hearing, but at any time up until its conclusion. So even if Byrne had been permitted to withhold his hand until the hearing, the unnamed employee could then have been dismissed and Byrne's claim defeated. Unlike in *McCormick* there was no concern that this might lead to undesirable results.

D. *Re-engagement*

As already pointed out, the employer's immunity is lost in the event of selective dismissal or re-engagement of those engaged in a strike, industrial action or a lock-out. In the words of Lord Denning, the employer 'must offer to re-engage all those who have been dismissed. He must not be selective. He must not re-engage the passive and indolent and refuse to re-engage the ringleaders and activists'.[55] Before 1982 re-engagement of a participant at any time would be enough to activate the jurisdiction of tribunals. Now employers may begin to re-engage striking workers after a period of three months has elapsed from the dismissal of the workforce. More specifically, the tribunal will have jurisdiction to determine whether a dismissal is fair or unfair if, before the expiry of the three-month period beginning with the applicant's date of dismissal, one or more relevant employees have been *offered* re-engagement which the complainant has not.[56] It is then provided that an offer of re-engagement means an offer to re-engage an employee, either in the job which he held immediately before the date of dismissal, or in a different job which would be reasonably suitable in the case of the complainant.[57] The word 'job' is in turn defined to mean 'the nature of the work which [the employee] is employed to do in accordance with his contract and the capacity and place in which he is so employed'.[58]

But although the employer must offer to re-engage everyone or no one involved in the strike, lock-out or other industrial action as a condition of retaining the immunity, it seems that he need not offer to take everyone back on the same terms, the Court of Appeal having been willing to tolerate the discriminatory and vindictive use of disciplinary sanctions in the re-engagement process. In *Williams* v. *National Theatre Board Ltd.*[59] a dispute at the National Theatre led to an unofficial strike by about thirty members of the stage staff, causing the cancellation of eight performances and a loss of £20,000. When the strike continued, the strikers were suspended and then

[55] *Williams* v. *National Theatre Board Ltd.* [1982] IRLR 377, at p. 378.
[56] EPCA, s. 62(2)(b).   [57] EPCA, s. 62(4)(c).
[58] EPCA, s. 153(1).   [59] [1982] IRLR 377.

dismissed. Subsequently, however, management wrote to all the strikers offering re-engagement on the condition that they would be treated as being on a second warning, which is a serious disciplinary step in the sense that a third warning entitled the employer to suspend an employee pending dismissal. In other words, they were offered re-engagement on the condition that if they stepped out of line on one more occasion they could be dismissed. That is to say, all but one of the relevant employees were offered re-engagement on these terms. The exception was a secretary who had participated in the strike for part of the time but who was offered re-engagement on the same terms and conditions as before her dismissal. The question for consideration was whether the employer had acted in a discriminatory manner, on the ground that while the secretary had been offered re-engagement the thirty or so other strikers had not been offered re-engagement 'in the job which they held before the date of dismissal'. Both the industrial tribunal and the EAT held that there was no jurisdiction because the offers of re-engagement satisfied the statutory requirements. The Court of Appeal agreed (unanimously), with the principal question being what is meant by re-engagement in the 'job' which the employee held before the dismissal? Did the fact that disciplinary penalties had been imposed and the fact that the employees would be returning under new conditions mean that they were not being offered re-engagement in the old jobs? The answer to this question depended upon the statutory definition of 'job' which we have already encountered.

The employees fell prey to drafting differences between the 1971 Act and its successors. The 1971 Act made the immunity conditional on the employer re-engaging the employees to the *position* each held, a term defined to mean 'the following matters taken as a whole, that is to say, his status as an employee, the nature of his work and his terms and conditions of employment'.[60] The definition of 'job' in the 1975 Act was drafted in much more flexible terms, and as Fox L.J. pointed out in *Williams*, the 'reference to his "terms and conditions of employment" ' is dropped altogether, a 'significant' change which 'indicates that an offer of re-engagement upon something less than the precise terms and conditions upon which the employee was employed at the time of his dismissal can now satisfy the requirements of the statute'.[61] But the crucial question, as Fox L.J. rightly pointed out, was 'how much less'? Yet although it was accepted that 'the statute was concerned with limiting the risk of discrimination and victimisation after a strike'[62] it will come as no surprise that the Court concluded in direct conflict with 'the general policy of the legislature',[63] holding on this occasion that the employees had been offered re-engagement in their old jobs, notwithstanding the disciplinary penalties. The underlying premiss of Lord Denning's reasoning was sadly predictable:

It seems to me that these men were offered re-engagement in the same 'capacity' as before. It was quite reasonable for the management to treat them as on second warning.

[60] Industrial Relations Act 1971, s. 107.
[61] [1981] IRLR 377, at p. 380.   [62] Ibid.   [63] Ibid.

It must be remembered that they had been guilty of most serious misconduct. They had been guilty of repudiatory breach of their contract. They had inflicted heavy losses on the National Theatre. They could not fairly claim to be re-engaged on precisely the same terms as the large number of loyal employees who had stayed at work throughout the strike. It was only fair all round that these 30 men should be told: 'Yes, we are ready to re-engage you in the same job in the same capacity as before, but, mark you, you must not do anything of this kind again. Otherwise you will be liable to be suspended, and may be dismissed'. That condition does not, to my mind, derogate from the fact that they were offered re-engagement in the same job as before.[64]

He did say, however, that the terms of re-engagement offered to employees would have to be reasonable in all the circumstances, though some difference in terms and conditions, such as 'some re-arrangement of hours or duties' would not make it unreasonable.[65] Nevertheless, the message is clear. Employees who are re-engaged after a strike may be disciplined, and indeed the employer may lawfully choose to discipline some but not all of those involved. And in concluding this section, it may be noted that although Lord Denning criticized the workers acting in breach of contract and causing loss to their employer, the opportunity was not taken to reflect on the cause or origins of the dispute. The fact is that this disciplinary power and this power to offer re-engagement on fresh terms applies as much to a defensive strike as it does to an offensive one. Indeed workers may be striking in order to resist a unilateral variation concerning 'some re-arrangement of hours or duties'. The employer may then dismiss the workers involved and offer lawfully to re-engage them on terms which are a material variation of the original contract and in fact the very subject of the dispute between the parties.

E. *The Question of Fairness*

An employee who can successfully show that he has been victimized for taking part in a strike or other industrial action has only negotiated one of the hurdles which have to be surmounted before a successful claim may be made. For the fact is that victimization only gives the industrial tribunals jurisdiction to deal with a complaint of unfair dismissal; it is not unfair dismissal on its own. This means first that the employee must meet the various qualifying conditions for bringing a claim, including the requirement that he has been employed by the respondent employer for a minimum of two years. In one case[66] it is to be noted that although seven employees were dismissed, an application for unfair dismissal was made by only six, with the seventh being unable to comply with the qualifying condition then in force. There is, however, an important exception to the requirement of two years' service, namely dismissals where the reason or principal reason is either that the employee was a member of an independent trade union, or that the employee had taken part in the activities of such a union at a time outside working hours, or at a time during working

---

[64] Ibid., at p. 379.   [65] Ibid.
[66] *Fisher* v. *York Trailer Co. Ltd.* [1979] IRLR 385.

hours with the consent of the employer.[67] In these cases the dismissal is automatically unfair without any need to show that the employer has acted unreasonably. Mere participation in a strike does not, however, constitute taking part in trade union activities for this purpose.[68] As a result it would be necessary to convince the tribunal that the employer was genuinely motivated by a desire to get rid of an employee simply because the person was a union member or a union official.

The general provisions on unfair dismissal are contained in section 57 of the EPCA. This provides that a dismissal shall be unfair unless it relates to one of five grounds laid down in the Act: capability and qualifications; conduct; redundancy; that continued employment would lead to a breach of a statutory duty; or some other substantial reason which would justify the dismissal of an employee. If the dismissal relates to one of these grounds, it will still be unfair unless the tribunal is satisfied that the employer acted reasonably in accordance with equity and the substantial merits of the case in treating the reason for dismissal as sufficient justification in the case in question.[69] This means, in effect, that the employer must normally act in accordance with the requirements of procedural justice (warnings and hearings) and that the penalty of dismissal should not be disproportionate in the circumstances. But perhaps because the jurisdictional barrier is so high, there is little direct authority on the application of these principles to the situation of discriminatory industrial action dismissals. One case, for example, is concerned with a highly technical question of interpretation following a selective re-engagement of strikers.[70] There are, however, cases which deal with more general questions, such as those concerned with redundancies allegedly caused by a strike. The issue which has arisen here is whether an employer may reasonably select for dismissal employees who took part in the strike at the expense of those who remained loyal to management. And indeed, there are now at least two cases where the courts have responded positively to such employer conduct.

The most significant of these is *Cruikshank* v. *Hobbs*[71] where, at the end of a stable lads' strike, a trainer made five employees redundant. In selecting the employees for redundancy the trainer selected five of the six lads who had been on strike, retaining all those who had worked during the strike. In an application for unfair dismissal the lads complained that they had been wrongly selected for redundancy. Their application failed, and in the Employment Appeal Tribunal it was accepted that 'a strike may be relevant to selection for redundancy in a number of ways'. In fact the EAT indicated that there were three circumstances in which the strike could be taken into account. First, if 'the strike has caused or aggravated the redundancy, it may be reasonable to take account of the conduct of the strikers as causing the redundancy, so that it

[67] EPCA, s. 58.
[68] *Drew* v. *St Edmundsbury DC* [1980] IRLR 459.
[69] EPCA, s. 57(3).
[70] *Edwards* v. *Cardiff City Council* [1979] IRLR 303.
[71] [1977] ICR 725.

is a factor that points to their selection rather than any of those who did not by their conduct reduce the number of jobs available'. Secondly, 'if the withdrawal of labour lasts long enough, the reintroduction into the reduced force of men who have been long absent may give rise to practical difficulties arising from technical or administrative changes which have occurred during their long absence'. And thirdly, they offered the situation where 'passions may be aroused during the strike, or incidents of abuse or violence between strikers and those remaining at work may have the effect that to sack men who stayed on and replace them with strikers may be expected to cause such friction between opposing groups on the shop floor that the morale and efficiency of the undertaking will be significantly impaired'. On the facts it was held by the EAT that Cruikshank's appeal fell into the last category and that the employer was 'reasonable in giving great or paramount weight to this factor'.

The apparent equity of such reasoning is, however, only very superficial. For the fact is that one of the members of the EAT, Mrs Lancaster, dissented:

Her reasons are that the fact that five stable lads had been on strike was only one of a number of factors to be taken into account in selection for redundancy. The trainer said in evidence that the strike did not cause the redundancy situation—it was there in any case. Furthermore, he said that had there been no strike the five eventually chosen would not necessarily have been the ones to go. In all these circumstances, therefore, it would not be unreasonable to expect that when the strike was over the trainer would review the total situation, taking all his employees into account, their length of service, their merit and whether or not they had been on strike, and come to a considered judgment on who should be made redundant. He did nothing of the kind.[72]

As regards the evidence of friction at the work-place:

Much was made during the hearing of the trouble there would be in the yard if any of the striking stable lads were re-employed in favour of those who had not struck. Yet the only evidence on this point is a single sentence from the trainer's evidence in cross-examination: 'Rather than upset the staff who were working for me, the fairest thing was to dismiss those on strike'. The trainer was not examined on this point to see what weight it bore. If, as his counsel argued at the appeal, the likelihood of trouble was a very important factor in the trainer coming to his decision, it is surprising that he did not probe his client before the industrial tribunal. It was open to the tribunal to question the witness in order to assess the weight of the statement, but they did not do so. The trainer's single answer in cross-examination has been made to carry a weight quite inconsistent with the explanation which he gave in chief and which he himself was too honest to suggest that it should carry.[73]

And, perhaps most tellingly, Mrs Lancaster concluded on this point by claiming:

The note of the trainer's evidence shows that he was completely blind to his obligation to be fair to the strikers as well as the non-strikers, even though he said in evidence that he was not anti-union. He simply chose between those who were loyal to him and those

---

[72] At p. 737.   [73] At pp. 737–8.

who were disloyal to him. It never occurred to him to try to explain to the non-strikers, most of whom were union men, that with the strike over and five redundancies on his hands he now had to consider how to be fair to everyone. He never sought to argue before the tribunal that he had even considered such a possibility and rejected it because to re-employ any of the striking stable lads would lead to real trouble, either immediately or in the future. The obvious risk of victimisation after a strike has ended is so grave to all union members, that an employer who selects for redundancy in a way which can be construed as having exactly that effect must clearly explain to an industrial tribunal all the factors he took into account when embarking on such an unattractive course. The trainer admitted that the only thing he took into account was the fact that the five men had been on strike.[74]

Nevertheless, the message from the majority is clear (and all the clearer for this lucid dissent). The selective dismissal or non-re-engagement of strikers may be fair on the basis of rather flimsy evidence.[75]

IV.   CONCLUSION

Section 62 of the EPCA, even without the 1982 and 1990 amendments, is a truly remarkable measure. As we have seen, even where the jurisdiction of the tribunal is opened up, it seems to be very difficult to secure a finding of unfair dismissal. Yet even then another major weakness is the fact that employers cannot be required to reinstate a worker unfairly dismissed for participating in industrial action, or indeed in any other situation. This is a general weakness of the legislation which badly needs to be corrected. But so far as the dismissal of strikers is concerned, there is enough evidence in the pages of this chapter alone to suggest that cosy assumptions about employers not dismissing were hopelessly misplaced. Even without Wapping, aggressive demands for reform would have been quite justified. As it is the Wapping dispute has led a number of trade unions to propose that section 62 be re-examined. We return to consider some of these proposals and to examine the question of reform in Chapter 8. In the mean time we have yet to complete our examination of the measures which may be taken against striking workers.

---

[74] At p. 738.
[75] See also *Laffin and Callaghan* v. *Fashion Industries (Hartlepool) Ltd.* [1978] IRLR 448.

[5]
Unemployment Benefit: The Trade Dispute Disqualification

I. INTRODUCTORY

We have concentrated so far on the powers of the employer over employees in a dispute. Both common law and statute confer a near absolute legal power, all the more remarkable for the fact that the strike may be a defensive one in response to the unreasonable, unlawful or illegal conduct of the employer. But the striker is subject not only to penalties imposed by the employer. Also important is the way in which the machinery of the state, in the form of unemployment benefit and social welfare benefits, is used, advertently or inadvertently, to reinforce the power of the employer, again regardless of the circumstances of the dispute. In this chapter we begin the examination of state sanctions (as opposed to permitted employer sanctions) by considering the trade dispute disqualification from unemployment benefit. It is perhaps worth pointing out at this stage that the effect of disqualification is to deny unemployment benefit to the claimant in respect of both himself and any dependants. This contrasts with the social welfare benefits discussed in the next chapter where the disqualification applies principally in respect of the claimant but not his family (subject to amendments introduced in 1980). But back to unemployment benefit. After first looking at the function of the trade dispute disqualification, attention is directed to the way in which the measure has evolved and has been basically liberalized since its introduction in 1911. This is followed by a discussion of the principal features of the present law, as it now operates under the Social Security Act 1975, s. 19, as amended by the Social Security Act 1986.

II. THE RATIONALE OF DISQUALIFICATION

As originally drafted in the National Insurance Act 1911, the trade dispute disqualification was written in wide terms, applying where the claimant 'lost employment by reason of a stoppage of work which was due to a trade dispute at the factory, workshop, or other premises at which he was employed', continuing for the duration of the stoppage unless the claimant had become bona fide employed elsewhere in an insured trade.[1] Yet despite the scope of the

---

[1] National Insurance Act 1911, s. 87(1). It was also provided that 'Where separate branches of work which are commonly carried on as separate businesses in separate premises are in any case

disqualification, the measure appears to have been relatively uncontroversial. Thus, during the Standing Committee stage of the Bill, Sir John Simon explained that the principle of the fund was that it should provide for the man who finds himself out of work owing to fluctuations of trade; it was not a fund which would support one side or the other in industrial warfare. This, he said, was a principle which everybody on the Standing Committee accepted, including those representing Labour.[2] Indeed, the Labour leader, Ramsay MacDonald, acknowledged that he did not 'want to subsidise those who are on strike or locked out from this fund; they must look after themselves. . . . There is no dispute on that point at all'.[3] Similarly, nine years later during the debate on the Unemployment Insurance Act 1920, J. R. Clynes acknowledged that 'men who are parties to a dispute, men whose interests are involved in the dispute, men who are part of the issue in respect of wage claims or conditions of employment, have no claim on the State for unemployment pay. They must provide their own benefit—as it were, their own ammunition—during the struggle in which they may be engaged'.[4]

But what is the justification for disqualifying claimants who are unemployed because of a trade dispute? Perhaps the most obvious starting point is to examine the views of Sir John Simon, one of the architects of the insurance scheme. Speaking in 1924, he defended the disqualification on the basis that it was consistent with the fact that the scheme was an insurance-based one, which was supported by contributions made by employers, employees and the state.[5] The suggestion here is that the fund should not be used to support voluntary unemployment (which would be inconsistent with insurance principles), and that being a fund to which premiums are paid by three parties, it should not be used in the interests of one (employees) at a time when that party is in conflict with the other two (employers and the state). The first point was reinforced by his reminder that by the scheme the government was not trying to provide a compassionate allowance out of a state fund for individuals who may be unfortunate in their industrial history or opportunities. The second point was reinforced by a Conservative backbencher, also in 1924, who said that 'It would be as outrageous to use [the] fund in any way to advance a strike in the interests of people who are interested in the strike as it would be to use that fund to finance employers in a lock-out. Both sides are contributing to the fund, and you would cut at the root of the whole principle of contributory insurance if you allowed it to be touched in the interests of employers or employed.'[6]

carried on in separate departments on the same premises, each of those departments shall, for the purposes of this provision, be deemed to be a separate factory or workshop or separate premises, as the case may be.'

[2]   31 HC Debs. 1729–30 (7 Nov. 1911).
[3]   31 HC Debs. 1731 (7 Nov. 1911).
[4]   131 HC Debs. 938–9 (2 July 1920).
[5]   176 HC Debs. 773–80 (18 July 1924).
[6]   176 HC Debs. 783 (18 July 1924) (Sir P. Lloyd-Greame).

The departmental view was expressed in written and oral evidence to the Royal Commission on Unemployment Insurance 1930–32. In a memorandum submitted on 17 April 1931, the Ministry of Labour claimed that 'It has always been regarded as of the first importance that the Umpire and the other statutory authorities for the determination of benefit claims should not be called upon to pronounce directly or indirectly on the merits of the issues arising between employers and workers in a trade dispute.'[7] These remarks were amplified by Mr J. F. G. Price CB, Principal Assistant Secretary at Ministry of Labour, who in the course of oral examination said that the trade dispute disqualification 'is an attempt to hold the balance between the two sides—not to give either side the benefit of the Unemployment Insurance Acts or to deprive them of its assistance if it is proper they should have it. Speaking generally it does rough justice between the parties.'[8] Both of these points relate to the same theme; namely that the insurance fund should be neutral in trade disputes in the sense that it should not be used generally to support one side or the other, and in the sense also that the adjudicating authorities should not become engaged in assessing the merits of a dispute in any particular case. This in fact was one of three principal justifications for the disqualification identified in the memorandum prepared by the Ministry of Social Security (1967a) for the Donovan Royal Commission of 1965–8 which to this day is still the fullest official account published to justify the existence of the disqualification.

The first justification offered by the Ministry was that the payment of benefit to those engaged in a dispute would conflict with the 'conditional basis of unemployment benefit', and in particular the insurance principles on which it is based. So, it was claimed that the 'object of unemployment benefit is to compensate people who are out of work provided that they have not only lost employment involuntarily and through no fault of their own but also are fit to work and ready to accept at once any offer of suitable employment'. The argument continued that 'It would be difficult to maintain that everyone who was unemployed as a result of a trade dispute had lost employment involuntarily and through no fault of his own. Nor could it generally be said that such people would in any real sense be available for alternative employment; the intention on both sides is usually to resume the relationship of employer and employee as soon as the dispute is settled.' The second justification was the neutrality point. Thus

It has always been regarded as an important objective that the National Insurance Fund, to which both employers and employees contribute, should not become involved in industrial disputes and that the scheme should not be open to the criticism that it is supporting one side or the other.

[7] Under the legislation operating before the National Insurance Act 1946, appeals by claimants were made in the first instance to the Court of Referees, and from there to the Umpire. The Umpire corresponds for practical purposes to the modern-day Social Security Commissioners, known previously as National Insurance Commissioners.

[8] Royal Commission on Unemployment Insurance 1930–32. Minutes of Evidence taken on 36th day, Friday, 10 July 1931. Q. 9779.

In the evidence submitted by the Ministry the opportunity was taken for the first time to explain why this was thought to be so important:

If the payment of benefit depended on a prior examination of the merits of the issues in dispute, this would be likely to harden the attitude of both sides. This could well prolong the dispute. It would certainly slow down the determination of benefit claims which is an important consideration with a benefit which is intended to meet current needs. It might often transpire that neither side in a dispute was entirely to blame but the adjudicating authorities would nevertheless have to come down firmly in favour of, or against, disqualification for benefit. The reputation of the adjudicating authorities for impartiality which has long been accepted and respected could be gravely impaired if such a task were to be imposed upon them, even if it were at all a practicable one.

The case in favour of disqualification was not, however, based only on grounds of principle. The third justification related to considerations of administrative convenience, it being pointed out that:

It is essential to the purpose of unemployment benefit that there should be speedy adjudication of claims and that any benefit due should be put into payment promptly. Practical considerations are particularly relevant in trade dispute cases where an employment exchange may suddenly be confronted with large numbers of claimants in circumstances where feelings run high and facts are not always easy to establish. Accordingly the statutory provisions must not only be sound in principle but must provide tests of eligibility for benefit which are workable in these extremely difficult conditions.

III. THE EVOLUTION OF THE MODERN LAW

Although there was a broad measure of political agreement about the principle of the trade dispute disqualification, from the inception of the unemployment insurance scheme there was some concern that the disqualification was too widely drawn. Thus, in Standing Committee on the 1911 Bill, Mr Ramsay MacDonald said:

I should like to suggest to the Committee one point upon which the draft is not quite clear. . . . Supposing a dispute arose say between the Amalgamated Society of Engineers and some employer. Suppose that the labourers who had nothing whatever to do with that dispute, although they are employed by the same employer and at the same factory or on the same premises, are, in consequence of it, locked out of employment. If the dispute is successful so far as the engineers are concerned, the labourers get nothing at all. In no way, and in no sense are they the gainers; yet . . . under the wording of the [clause] they will be unable to get any benefit.[9]

This issue was raised subsequently in Parliament on many occasions, and again in 1920 during the debates on the Unemployment Insurance Bill. J. R. Clynes complained that unions were being forced to finance a number of innocent victims who were disqualified from unemployment benefit. He continued by

[9] 31 HC Debs. 1731–2 (7 Nov. 1911).

claiming that '[t]here is a very serious sense of injustice in the mind of large bodies of workmen who in recent disputes have suffered very severe financial losses because of stoppages to which they were no parties at all'.[10] In one particularly notorious case, a strike by skilled moulders caused the lay-off of the moulders' labourers. The strike lasted for four months, and the labourers were disqualified for the whole of this period because they worked at the same establishment as the moulders. Indeed, the incident led directly to an unsuccessful attempt to restrict the application of the disqualification to people who had withdrawn their labour in order to participate in a trade dispute. But despite this concern, the 1920 disqualification remained almost identical to the original. In fact, the only significant difference was that the 'bona fide employed elsewhere' exemption was modified, with the extension of the scheme, so that a worker would cease to be disqualified if he became 'bona fide employed elsewhere in the occupation which he usually follows or has become regularly engaged in some other occupation'.[11]

A. *The 1924 Amendments*

It was not until 1924, with the election of the first Labour government, that two major changes were made, both being contained in section 4 of the Unemployment Insurance (No. 2) Act 1924. On the first of these changes, however, the terms of the 1924 Act did not go as far as the government had originally planned, although on the second the scheme was taken in an interesting and unprecedented direction. The first government Bill simply provided that the disqualification would not apply if the claimant could prove that he was neither participating in the dispute nor a member of a grade or class of workers any of whom were participating in the dispute. Sir John Simon— who had been one of the Liberal ministers responsible for carrying the legislation in 1911—was concerned that this proposal was over-generous, in the sense that the insurance fund could be open to misuse and manipulation by union officials. He was particularly concerned that 'key men' could be called out, thereby preserving the right to benefit by workers who were laid off but who might nevertheless have an immediate interest in the outcome of the dispute. Consequently he proposed successfully that in order to escape disqualification a claimant should be required to establish not only that he was neither participating in the dispute, nor a member of a participating grade or class, but also that he was neither financing nor directly interested in the dispute, nor a member of a grade or class of workers who were financing or directly interested in the dispute.

Although the criticism appeared to be made less frequently, trade unionists also objected to the original formula of the disqualification on the ground that participants in disputes were disqualified from benefit, regardless of the merits

---

[10] 131 HC Debs. 938 (2 July 1920).
[11] Unemployment Insurance Act 1920, s. 8.

of the dispute. Concern was expressed that workers were disqualified where the stoppage was caused by a lock-out. Similarly, at the annual conference of the Miners' Federation of Great Britain in 1922, delegates expressed concern and astonishment at decisions of the Umpire which held that the claimants would be disqualified from benefit even though the trade dispute was caused by an employer's breach of a collective agreement. In one case, *Case No. 6781*, it was simply held that 'A dispute in which one party seeks to induce the other party to abrogate or vary an existing agreement as to wages is a trade dispute'. Such decisions led one delegate at the 1922 MFGB Conference to argue that the disqualification was operating

unjustly and unfairly, and undoubtedly it has been used for the purpose of driving our men's wages below the level which is payable under [the] Agreement. An effective protest ought to be made from this Conference.

Another delegate agreed that the disqualification 'was used as an instrument for the reduction of wages' and suggested that Members of Parliament sponsored by the miners' unions could 'assist in getting this clause amended'. An earlier deputation to the Minister of Labour by miners' leaders about one of these decisions had met with the response that the Minister had no power to interfere because the decision had been made by an independent judicial authority.

The introduction of the Unemployment Insurance (No. 2) Bill in 1924 presented an opportunity to the unions to secure a satisfactory solution to this problem. No initiative was taken by the government, however, and it was left to a trade union sponsored Labour backbencher, Mr George Spencer, to introduce a suitable amendment in Committee. This provided that the trade dispute disqualification would not apply where

the stoppage is due to an employer acting in a manner so as to contravene the terms or provisions of any agreement existing between a group of employers where the stoppage takes place, or of a national agreement to either of which the employers and employees are contracting parties.[12]

The amendment was heavily defeated by eighteen votes to five, with Labour ministers voting against the measure. But Mr Spencer persisted, and a similar amendment was successfully introduced on Report.[13] Introducing his amendment, Mr Spencer explained that it was designed to make collective agreements 'more sacred'. He complained that under the law as it then stood

If an employer . . . puts up a notice stating that he is going to close down his works, and that he cannot continue working, his men get unemployment benefit; but if he throws the works open and offers terms other than those included in the agreement, no matter what these terms are, whether or not they are sufficient for maintenance, it is a trade dispute if the men refuse to accept, and they cannot get unemployment pay.

[12] Report of Standing Committee D on the Unemployment Insurance (No. 2) Bill, pp. 20–1.
[13] 176 HC Debs. 803–11 (18 July 1924).

Other Labour backbenchers spoke in favour of this proposal. One referred to the amendment as the outcome of the experiences through which the unions had passed, while another argued: 'If an agreement is made it ought to be honoured. That is the claim that is made on this side of the House. Agreements are made that are dishonoured by employers.' On a free vote, the Commons approved the amendment, despite doubts expressed by the Minister of Labour as to whether the proposal would work.

The House of Lords, by contrast, was not so sympathetic to Mr Spencer's amendment. Opposition was evident in the Second Reading Debate,[14] and an amendment to exclude the provision was successfully moved in Committee.[15] Complaints were made that the measure had been 'hurried', that it was not 'model drafting', and that it was 'incomprehensible'. A more fundamental objection was raised by Lord Askwith. He said:

This question of a breach of agreement is one of the most difficult things in industrial disputes that it is possible to imagine. . . . [I]t was one of the most difficult things in the labour world to determine, and it seems extraordinary that the question as to whether there is a breach of an agreement or not should be handed over to an official of an Employment Exchange to decide, with a possibility of its going to a referee or umpire after the strike or lock-out has begun.

Similarly, Viscount Cave thought that it was very dangerous for the Insurance Fund to take sides in trade disputes. He continued by saying:

It is very difficult for even the most experienced person at times to say, first, whether an agreement is binding upon everybody whose name is in it; secondly, whether there has been any breach of that agreement; and, thirdly, whether the trade dispute is *bona fide* due to a breach of the agreement.

But despite this criticism, some support for the principle expressed in Mr Spencer's amendment came from Lord Parmoor, the Lord President of the Council. He argued that it was necessary to examine who was at 'fault' in breaching an agreement, and that 'innocent' workmen should not be disqualified. He also suggested that the difficulty in determining where 'fault' lay was no greater than other issues with which the insurance authorities had to deal. These arguments were not enough, however, to prevent the Lords from supporting a motion to leave out the Spencer amendment and from rejecting Lord Parmoor's own amendment which accepted the principle of the employer's breach exemption but which sought to improve its drafting. The Spencer amendment was saved only when the Commons refused to accept its deletion.[16]

---

[14] 58 HC Debs. 1006–24 (24 July 1924).
[15] Ibid., cols. 1063–8 (28 July 1924).
[16] For an account of the operation of this provision, see Ewing (1981).

B. *Blanesburgh and the 1927 Act*

The reforms of 1924 survived only a few years longer than the ill-fated Labour administration which had introduced them. In 1925 a Departmental Committee chaired by Lord Blanesburgh was appointed to 'consider in the light of experience gained in the working of the Unemployment Insurance Scheme, what changes in the Scheme, if any, ought to be made'. The Committee received evidence from both sides of industry concerning the 1924 amendments. The National Confederation of Employers' Organizations did not wish to commit itself to any position on the Simon amendments without fuller experience of their operation. One of their representatives did say, however, in the course of examination, that he preferred the 1920 drafting 'in the interests of the relationship between employers and workers and industry generally'. The principal concern of the employers' organization was in fact with the employer's breach exemption to which several objections were raised. The first was that the Court of Referees and the Umpire were called upon to interpret collective agreements without giving employers, who were parties to the agreements, the right to be heard. A second objection raised by the Confederation was that

the interpretation of collective agreements—which may involve a full knowledge of technical conditions in the industry and the negotiations, which may have far-reaching effects, and the interpretation of which may, under the Industrial Courts Act of 1919, be a matter for consideration under that Act—cannot appropriately be left for incidental decision by tribunals set up for a totally different purpose.

A third objection to the exemption was evident in the following exchange which took place when representatives of the Confederation were examined by the Committee:

More often than not, you mean, a dispute arises on a clause of that kind, a clause which is uncertain?—Clearly. Really the action of the Umpire in these particular cases was, in fact, the interpretation of an agreement, as there is an alleged breach of it.[17]

Not surprisingly, such criticisms were not forthcoming from the unions. So rather than question the propriety of the employer's breach exemption, the TUC argued that it did not go far enough. The TUC thought the provision defective because it applied only to agreements involving a group of employers, arguing that since the violation of an agreement between a single employer and his employees was just as serious, the exemption should be amended to cover the contravention of such agreements. For its part the Iron and Steel Trades' Confederation argued that the Simon amendment also did not go far enough. Thus, while it agreed that the unemployment insurance fund 'should not be used to finance either employers or employees who are direct participants in a trade dispute', it submitted that the dispute clause even as amended by section

[17] Unemployment Insurance Committee, Minutes of Evidence, Q. 759.

4(1) of the 1924 Act 'involves the refusal of benefit to innocent victims of trade disputes and those who are in no sense associated with the cause of the stoppage of work'. Thus it pointed out that as the disqualification presently stood it was possible 'for a trade union having a few members in each department of a large works to be engaged in a dispute with an employer which results in a stoppage of the whole of the plant. The membership of this union may be a minority of the employees of the firm; the remaining workpeople and their trade unions may actually disapprove of the claims of their fellow workmen who are parties to the dispute, but they are nevertheless refused . . . benefit because they are of the same "grade or class" as those who are participating in the dispute.' Similar concerns were expressed by the National Federation of Colliery Enginemen, Boilermen, and Mechanics which argued that an employee should be disqualified only if he belonged to a grade or class of workers, the majority of whose members were participating in or financing the dispute. In the view of the Federation, it was opposed to justice that a grade or class of workmen should be penalized because of the acts of some men or associations over which it has no control.

The unions in fact raised a number of other issues of concern about the scheme. Nevertheless, the Committee confined its remarks to the grade or class provision and to the employer's breach exemption. The purpose of the first, it said, was 'to place on one and the same footing all workers who may be presumed to be bound together by community of interest, and to limit exemption from disqualification to classes of workers none of whom have any part or lot in the dispute' (Blanesburgh 1927: 65). In fact the Committee referred to other justifications for the drafting: it made for ease of administration 'at a time when there is likely to be considerable pressure on the benefit machinery'; while the wider the disqualification the less tendency there would be for 'a stoppage of work to be embarked on by the withdrawal of a small number of pivotal men in the knowledge that the majority of those who lose employment as a result of the stoppage will get benefit and so augment the workers' fighting funds'. The Committee did, however, appear to acknowledge that 'innocent victims are disqualified in the type of case where, for example, the union covering the occupational grade or class primarily concerned in the dispute also covers a relatively small proportion of another grade or class, the majority of which have no direct part in the dispute and are not members of that union'. Nevertheless it did not recommend any change to the principle of the grade or class provision, but proposed only a minor revision to deal with a problem which had arisen during the general strike relating to 'the refusal of benefit claims of colliery deputy men and safety men'. Apparently, '[m]en of these grades and classes who were unemployed as a result of the dispute were held disentitled to benefit everywhere by reason of the fact that in some districts members of the grade or class belonged to the Miners' Union affiliated to the Miners' Federation and, as such, were participating in or financing the dispute. The remainder of the men—it was contended, the great majority—

were not participating in the dispute at all, and . . . were thrown out of work and could not draw benefit' (Blanesburgh 1927: 64).[18] The Committee suggested that this particular difficulty could be met by amending legislation, a suggestion acted upon in the Unemployment Insurance Act 1927.[19]

So far as the employer's breach exemption is concerned (the so-called Spencer amendment), the Committee concluded 'after careful consideration' that the provision should be repealed. In making this recommendation, the Committee was convinced that 'collective bargaining and the authority and usefulness of associations both of employers and workers will be strengthened thereby'. The reasons for this were explained in the following terms:

in a trade dispute of this kind any discrimination by the unemployment insurance scheme would have to be based on the merits of the dispute—a question too remote or, at any rate, too difficult for unemployment insurance to concern itself with. Further, it is better, it is suggested, that industrial agreements should carry their own sanction, and the tendency of the clause is to discourage employers from making long-term agreements, an unfortunate result, inasmuch as such agreements are frequently of great value, especially to employers who have long contracts, while the Trade Unions themselves often have much to gain from them. Again, from the point of view of the State, it is urged that anything which tends to disturb industrial stability is to be avoided. Moreover Courts of Referees and the Umpire are not set up to interpret industrial agreements of this kind. The provision, too, as it stands, appears to discriminate against the employer with no corresponding discrimination against the worker. Although, when an employer breaks an agreement, his workers can obtain benefit, on the other hand, when the workers break an agreement, though they themselves are disqualified, the employer may be unable to fill their places, since the vacancies are 'due to a trade dispute' and may under the law be refused by other workers with impunity. (Blanesburgh 1927: 66–7).

Despite opposition expressed by both TUC (1927) and the STUC (1927), the Conservative government endorsed these views,[20] and by the Unemployment

---

[18] The problem is perhaps best illustrated by the following example. Suppose that the deputies' union in Durham had participated in the dispute. There was a stoppage of work in Nottingham, for instance, because the (imaginary) miners' union came out laying off the deputies who wished to work. Under the Simon amendments the deputies in Nottingham would be disqualified: they were unemployed because of a stoppage due to a trade dispute at their place of employment; and although they were not participating etc. in the dispute themselves, there were members of their grade or class (in Durham) who were. Blanesburgh thought it 'irrational that a colliery deputy, say, in Nottingham should be disqualified simply because some deputies in Durham, with whom he has nothing to do, are participating in the dispute'.

[19] As amended in 1927, the proviso to the disqualification in the principal Act provided that the disqualification 'shall not apply in any case in which the insured contributor proves that he is not participating in or financing or directly interested in the trade dispute which caused the stoppage of work, and that he does not belong to a grade or class of workers *of which immediately before the commencement of the stoppage there were members employed at the premises at which the stoppage is taking place any of whom* are participating in or financing or directly interested in the dispute . . .' The 1927 amendments are in italics. The words they replaced were 'members of which'. The effect of the 1927 reform on the example in n. 18 would be that the deputies in Nottingham would not now be disqualified because, in our imaginary example, there would be no one in their grade or class at the place where they were employed who was participating etc. in the dispute.

[20] See especially 211 HC Debs. 868–70; 880–4 (2 Dec. 1927).

Insurance Act 1927, the employer's breach provision was repealed. In taking this step, the government successfully resisted Labour amendments at the Committee and Report stages in the Commons which were designed to ensure the retention of the exemption. Labour speakers alleged that the government action would encourage employers to break collective agreements and would facilitate attacks on workers, since employers would now have the right to bludgeon workers into any position they liked.

C. *The Donovan Commission*

The 1927 amendments were hardly a satisfactory solution to the problems of the disqualification. As a result the TUC lobbied hard both before and after the war for further reform. Representations to the Royal Commission on Unemployment Insurance 1930–2 fell on deaf ears, and regular meetings with ministers were no more fruitful (Ewing 1981). In view of this lack of success spanning a period of almost forty years, the TUC used the Donovan Commission as yet another platform in its campaign for further reforms to the trade dispute disqualification. Shortly after their appointment in 1965 the Commissioners were asked by the Minister of Social Security, Margaret Herbison, if they would examine the trade dispute disqualification. They agreed, and the TUC took the opportunity to submit a wide-ranging memorandum. In contrast to its earlier memoranda on the subject this proposed a number of reforms, and for the first time did not concentrate attention on the restoration of the employer's breach exemption (though this was also proposed). According to the TUC the basic issues calling for examination were first 'the extent to which disqualification can be more closely limited to those with a real community of interest in a dispute', and secondly, 'the extent to which account should be taken of the merits of a dispute'.

As to the first, a major concern was the wide sweep of the grade or class limb of the proviso (despite the 1927 amendment), which led to the wholesale disqualification of workers with no real community of interest in a dispute. As an example of this, reference was made to a dispute at the British Motor Corporation, Longbridge, where 300 fitters in the maintenance department stopped work in a pay claim. The action was officially supported by the AEU, ETU and the Heating and Domestic Engineers' Union. The dispute led to some 18,000 workers being laid off, many of those being in the other unions in the plant. In some departments almost everyone was a member of the NUVB, while in another all but one employee were members of TGWU. Nevertheless, although neither of these unions was participating in the dispute, their members were disqualified because they could not show that their grade did not include any members of the unions financing the dispute. Indeed, '[a]fter numerous test cases between 16,000 and 17,000 workers were disqualified in this way'. But despite setbacks of this kind the TUC fell far short of proposing the removal of the grade or class limb of the proviso, taking the remarkable view that 'the disadvantages—not least the resulting discrimination against collective action and consequent undermining of fundamental trade union principles—would outweigh advantages which might well prove illusory'. Illusory because simply to abolish the grade or class proviso, and 'leave all claims to be decided under the very wide terms' of the participating, directly interested or financing limbs, 'might well result in the emergence of new and equally unsatisfactory case-law'. The extent of the TUC's recommendation was that the financing limb should be removed, 'thus limiting the collective disqualification . . . to grades or classes which include members who are "participating" or are "directly interested"'. In the view of the TUC, this would limit the disqualification more closely to those with 'a real community of interest in a dispute without . . . affording unreasonable relief to those with such interest'.

As to the second general area of concern, the TUC again noted that no account was taken of the merits of a dispute and that consequently, where a stoppage was due to unreasonable conditions being imposed by an employer, the disqualification applied. In this light, the TUC recommended that the disqualification should not apply when there had been a breach by the employer of an established agreement. It was suggested that the question whether or not the employer was in breach should be determined by the Industrial Court, access to which would be conditional upon the consent of the unions concerned. But the proposal was once again rejected, this time for two reasons. First, the Commission endorsed the Blanesburgh Committee's view that the insurance authorities should not enter into the merits of industrial disputes, nor into disputed questions of interpretation of collective bargaining. Secondly, the Commission took the view that if insurance officers or the Industrial Court had to decide whether an agreement had been breached, much delay would result, 'and delay in the matter of paying unemployment benefit should be avoided as far as possible'. This latter view was thought to be persuasive despite the TUC's recommendation that the Industrial Court should be required to give priority to matters of this kind; despite the point made by TUC representatives in oral examination that trade dispute questions already had to be resolved under the present law, and that they took some time to resolve; and despite an earlier remark by the Commission in a discussion on another point (but also related to the disqualification) that 'Administrative convenience . . . is not much of a commendation for a provision which is also capable of considerable injustice.' Yet, however persuasive the Commission's views may or may not be the matter now seems to be conclusively resolved by the Donovan recommendations. For despite the persistence of the campaign for reform ever since the Spencer amendment was repealed in 1927, there is no evidence of the matter having been raised since 1968.

The Commission did, however, make other important recommendations significantly to limit the scope of the disqualification. First, contrary to TUC submissions, it recommended the total abolition of the grade or class provision.

The Ministry of Social Security had justified the disqualification on this ground in the following terms:

The grade or class provision . . . assumes that a group of workers doing much the same kind of work in the same place and under the same conditions and circumstances have a corporate identity and a special relationship one with another—a 'community of interest'—quite apart from their position in relation to any particular trade dispute. The argument runs that just as members of a particular grade or class are treated alike in so many other aspects of their working life in the factory so they should be treated alike for purposes of the trade dispute disqualification (Ministry of Social Security 1967*b*).

The Commission, in contrast, concluded that the reasoning underlying the provision was 'fallacious', noting that 'no investigation is required to disqualify [an entire grade or class] from receiving unemployment benefit beyond discovering whether there is at least one of the class participating in the trade dispute, or financing it, or directly interested in it. This seems to us not so much the recognition of [a common] interest [with those in dispute] as the invention of it' (Donovan 1968: 251). They then gave examples of the 'capricious results which the provision can and does produce':

1. If . . . the process workers at a particular works go on strike on an issue which concerns them alone and one member out of a total of 100 maintenance workers strikes in sympathy, the remaining 99 if laid off will all be disqualified from receiving unemployment benefit, though they have no interest in the strike and indeed are hostile to it.
2. . . . if 'A' were a storeman in a works comprising different departments and a dispute occurred in the foundry shop which led to a stoppage of work, during which the union concerned paid strike benefit, 'A' would be disqualified for receiving unemployment benefit if he happened to belong to the same union. So also would all the other storemen, although they might belong to a different union or unions (Donovan 1968: 251–2).

Because of these and other considerations, the Donovan Commission recommended abolition, pointing out in the process that this would not lead to benefit being paid to large numbers of undeserving claimants. For any employee 'who became unemployed by reason of a stoppage of work due to a trade dispute at his place of employment would still have to prove that he was not participating in the dispute, not financing it, and not directly interested in it'. But Donovan also recommended that the financing limb of the disqualification should be removed. The effect of this measure was to disqualify from benefit anyone who was unemployed as a result of a trade dispute at his place of employment if he was a member of a trade union paying strike pay to other members who were participating in the dispute. In the view of Donovan, the effect of this measure was to disqualify people thrown out of work by a dispute, 'who may have no interest in the dispute whatsoever'. It was also pointed out that a claimant could evade disqualification 'simply by resigning from his trade union at any time during the trade dispute', for by so doing the claimant would no longer be 'financing' the dispute. Finally it was suggested that this limb of the proviso gave an advantage to those engaged in unofficial action—which was a feature of contemporary industrial relations the Commission was anxious to end. This arose because the disqualification would apply where the dispute was supported by the union paying strike pay, but not where strike pay was not being made. There were of course many unions which did not pay strike pay in official disputes, but they were much less likely to make such payments when the dispute was unofficial. This recommendation was acted upon by the Labour government in its Employment Protection Act 1975. And to complete the first significant amendment to the disqualification since 1927, the 1975 Act also implemented Donovan's other recommendation in this area by abolishing the grade or class limb of the disqualification.[21]

IV. THE MODERN LEGAL FRAMEWORK

As a result of the 1975 amendments, a worker would be disqualified for receiving unemployment benefit if he was unemployed by reason of a stoppage of work caused by a trade dispute at his place of employment. This disqualification would not arise, however, if the employee could show that he was neither participating nor directly interested in the dispute which caused the stoppage, even though it did take place at the claimant's place of work. And the disqualification would cease if, during the stoppage, the employee became bona fide employed elsewhere. This represented a major advance on the form of drafting originally employed in 1911. Whereas at that time all those affected by a dispute at their workplace—whether or not they had an interest in the issue—were disqualified, now the disqualification was confined largely to those with a community of interest with those engaged in the dispute. Yet although the 1975 reforms are genuinely important modifications of the 1924 and 1927 revisions, they were not the last word on the matter. In the Social Security Act 1986, section 44, further revisions were made, although these were much less dramatic than the reforms of 1924 and 1975. The 1986 Act substitutes the following for section 19(1) of the Social Security Act 1975 (which is now the principal statute dealing with social security benefits):

(1) Subject to the following provisions of this section—
    (a) an employed earner who has lost employment as an employed earner by reason of a stoppage of work due to a trade dispute at his place of employment is disqualified for receiving unemployment benefit for any day during the stoppage unless he proves that he is not directly interested in the dispute; and
    (b) an employed earner who has withdrawn his labour in furtherance of a trade dispute but does not fall within paragraph (a) above is disqualified for receiving unemployment benefit for any day on which his labour remains withdrawn.
(1A) A person disqualified under subsection (1)(a) above for receiving unemployment benefit shall cease to be so disqualified if he proves that during the stoppage—

---

[21] Employment Protection Act 1975, s. 111.

(a) he has become bona fide employed elsewhere; or

(b) his employment has been terminated by reason of redundancy within the meaning of section 81(2) of the Employment Protection (Consolidation) Act 1978; or

(c) he has bona fide resumed employment with his employer but has subsequently left for a reason other than the trade dispute.

The definitions of 'place of employment' and 'trade dispute' remain unchanged, and are to be found in the 1975 Act, section 19(2).

So far as the 1986 amendments are concerned, three differences may be noted. First, section 19(1)(a) provides now only one of the original 1924 provisos to the disqualification, namely that the claimant is not directly interested in the dispute. It hardly follows, however, that anyone who is 'participating' in the dispute will now qualify for benefit. Quite apart from the new provisions of paragraph (b), an employee on strike or lock-out will presumably be directly interested in the dispute causing the stoppage. Secondly, the terms of section 19(1)(b) are entirely new, though it is unlikely to have any major practical impact. According to the government, it is designed to cover a loophole whereby 'a person participates in a dispute by withdrawing his labour although there is no stoppage of work. That sometimes happens when some people go on strike while others keep working'.[22] It was surely not the case, however, that people in that situation would qualify for benefit. For under section 20 of the 1975 Act a person is disqualified for receiving unemployment benefit on several grounds but including the loss of employment through misconduct or the voluntary leaving of employment without just cause. Although the maximum period of disqualification has been six weeks ever since 1911, this was extended in 1986 to 13 weeks[23] (an extension condemned by the Opposition as being harsh and nasty[24]) and more recently to 26 weeks. But whatever the merits of the extension, it seems almost inconceivable that a worker on strike (albeit not causing a stoppage) would escape disqualification on one or other of the grounds already referred to. It would, however, always have been possible for the authorities to conclude that there had been no misconduct and that there was good cause for leaving in a situation where the dispute was engineered by the employer. And it would always have been possible in the case of other strikes for those engaged in a long dispute to qualify for benefit after the 13-week period expired. But while the amendment extends the disqualification slightly (thereby reversing the trend of liberalization albeit marginally), the third difference in the new clause restricts the disqualification in one important respect. Under the 1975 drafting, the disqualification once attached would be lost before the end of the dispute only if the claimant became bona fide employed elsewhere during the stoppage. If he lost work in this new occupation, benefit would be payable even though the

---

[22] Official Report, Standing Committee B, 17 Apr. 1986, col. 1505.

[23] Social Security Act 1986, s. 43.

[24] Official Report, Standing Committee B, 30 Apr. 1986, cols. 1835–6.

strike at the former establishment remained on foot. The new subsection (1A) allows for the disqualification to lapse where the employee is dismissed during the stoppage for redundancy. It also allows for the disqualification to lapse where the employee returns to work with the employer during the strike, but has left for a reason other than the dispute.[25] We may now turn to consider some of the problems which have arisen in seeking to determine the limits of the statutory provisions.

A. *The Meaning of a Trade Dispute*

The disqualification applies where the claimant is unemployed because of a stoppage of work caused by a trade dispute at his place of employment. A trade dispute is defined in section 19(2)(b) of the Social Security Act 1975 to mean:

any dispute between employers and employees, or between employees and employees, which is connected with the employment or non-employment or the terms of employment or the conditions of employment of any persons, whether employees in the employment of the employer with whom the dispute arises, or not.

This is almost identical to the original definition in the 1911 and 1920 Acts. It is also almost identical to the definition of trade dispute employed in the Trade Disputes Act 1906. Together these two measures produced a nice symmetry: where a trade dispute was in operation an employer could not obtain an injunction or damages against the union or the union officials involved; and where a trade dispute was in operation those involved would not be eligible for unemployment benefit from the state. That symmetry was shattered, however, with the repeal of the Trade Disputes Act in 1971. Although the Labour government in the 1970s restored the tortious immunity of trade unions and their officers, it did so by extending the definition of a trade dispute to make it more watertight. The definition in the Social Security Act was not similarly extended. Since 1980 the definition of a trade dispute in the context of tortious immunity has of course been significantly narrowed, without any corresponding narrowing of the definition in the context of the disqualification. As a result, industrial action may not now constitute a trade dispute for the purposes of the tortious immunity, but it may be a trade dispute for the purposes of the disqualification, with the definition of the latter being wider in some key respects than the definition in the former. One obvious example of this is that a dispute need only be connected with one of the specified matters for the purpose of the disqualification, but must relate wholly or mainly to (an admittedly longer list of) specified items for the purpose of the immunity.[26]

---

[25] These amendments effectively reverse the Court of Appeal's decision in *Cartlidge* v. *Chief Adjudication Officer* [1986] 2 All ER 1.

[26] So while the facts in *Mercury Communications Ltd.* v. *Scott-Garner* [1984] 1 All ER 179 did not constitute a trade dispute for the purposes of tortious immunity, they would almost certainly have constituted a trade dispute for the purposes of the disqualification.

But although the trade dispute concept is applied in rather different contexts, different policy considerations nevertheless suggest that it would be narrowly construed in both. Thus it is to be expected that the judges would interpret very narrowly an immunity from tortious liability, and it is to be expected that a disqualification (a penalty) on claimants would also be narrowly construed and confined in its application. But this is not how matters have transpired. The immunity from tortious liability was eventually interpreted very widely by the House of Lords,[27] and the Social Security Commissioners and their predecessors have similarly taken a wide approach to its meaning, despite the punitive consequences. Perhaps the most remarkable feature of the cases is the fact that the merits of the dispute are irrelevant, with a tribunal of Commissioners expressing the view in *R(U)17/52* that

The manifest object of the subsection is to prevent the insurance fund from being used for financing employees during strikes or lock-outs. For this reason . . . the disqualification is made absolute and the merits of the dispute are irrelevant. Provisions in earlier Acts which would have involved the consideration of the merits of the dispute by the Statutory Authorities in certain circumstances had been repealed before the passing of the Unemployment Insurance Act, 1935.[28]

In the same vein, the Commissioner in *R(U)3/71* observed that 'The definition is wide and in deciding whether or not there is a "trade dispute" the merits of the dispute do not enter into the matter'. As a result workers are disqualified even where the dispute is a response to the unreasonable, unlawful or illegal conduct of the employer. The insurance fund is thus placed behind the employer who has provoked a dispute by conduct which could not possibly be defended and which may be contrary to public policy. The point is in fact nicely illustrated by *R(U)4/65* where the Commissioner said that the definition of trade dispute was 'very wide', and continued by observing that he could 'visualise a trade dispute about . . . the provision of safety clothing or equipment, or about safety precautions. Or there might be a trade dispute turning on, say, racial discrimination in employment.' A trade dispute, it seems, 'may relate to conditions of employment in respect of safety, or convenience, or health, or comfort'.

Cases *R(U)4/65* and *R(U)3/71* both illustrate the fact that workers may be disqualified when defending themselves from the unlawful or illegal conduct of the employer. *R(U)4/65* related to a walk-out by platers who complained that heating provision was inadequate, while *R(U)3/71* concerned the safety of a machine. Both were held to be 'trade disputes' despite the facts in the latter case that the machine was allegedly improperly fenced, that a worker had cut his finger, and that there were allegations that the employer was in breach of the Factories Act 1961, section 14 (a criminal offence). The point is also

---

[27] See especially *N.W.L. Ltd.* v. *Woods* [1979] ICR 867.
[28] This was a consolidating measure giving way in turn to the National Insurance Act 1946, and subsequently the National Insurance Act 1965.

illustrated most recently by *R(U)5/77* where the dispute was related to the provision of protective clothing for workers exposed to dust from lagging operations. While the employer was willing to provide the clothing, the employees insisted that it should not be at their expense as the employer proposed. This led to a long stoppage, and to a claim for unemployment benefit by the workers involved. They appealed successfully against their disqualification to the local tribunal, but were ultimately unsuccessful following an appeal by the insurance officer to the Commissioner. The argument for the claimant related to the Health and Safety at Work etc. Act 1974, it being submitted that 'there would have been a breach by the employers of section 2 (to ensure, so far as is reasonably practicable, the health, safety and welfare at work of all their employees) and a breach by the employees of section 7 (to take reasonable care for the health and safety of themselves) had the men worked in certain areas without protective clothing'. From this it was argued that a stoppage of work because of the illegal conduct of the employer could not be the result of a trade dispute, a position supported by some of the pre-war decisions of the Umpire —a point to which we return in Chapter 8. But after reviewing the legislative history of the disqualification, referring to the Donovan Report, and having regard to leading decisions such as *R(U)17/52*, the Commissioner concluded that he should not follow and apply the approach of the Umpire, and involve himself in consideration of the legal merits of the dispute, a point which, needless to say, was subsequently endorsed by the Lord Chief Justice in an unsuccessful application for *certiorari*.[29] The significance of the case is barely affected by the Commissioner's decision that even if he had considered the legal merits, the claimant would still have been disqualified on the ground that the employer's conduct did not amount to a breach of the 1974 Act. The employer was willing to comply with the statute by providing the clothing and was under no obligation to pay for it.[30]

B. *Place of Employment*

The second rock on which the disqualification continues to rest is that the stoppage due to the trade dispute takes place at the claimant's place of employment. Under the Act the term is defined by section 19(2)(a) to mean 'the factory, workshop, farm or other premises or place' at which the claimant was employed.[31] The definition is thus not very helpful, though it is subject to a proviso which restricts the meaning of the term by providing that 'where

---

[29]   *R. v. National Insurance Commissioner, ex parte Thompson*, Appendix to *R(U)5/77*.

[30]   These cases put into proper perspective *R(U)2/53* which has attracted considerable academic criticism. In that case the claimants were turned away from work by the illegal acts of pickets. This was held to constitute a trade dispute between the pickets and the claimants. It is to be borne in mind that a strike caused by an employer's illegal conduct is also a trade dispute. Cf. *R(U)3/69*, and *Valois* v. *Attorney General of Canada* (1987) 32 DLR (4th) 381.

[31]   The inclusion of farms was made in 1936 when the legislation was extended to agriculture: Unemployment Insurance (Agriculture) Act 1936.

separate branches of work which are commonly carried on as separate businesses in separate premises or at separate places are in any case carried on in
separate departments on the same premises or at the same place, each of those
departments shall . . . be deemed to be a separate factory or workshop or farm
or separate premises or a separate place, as the case may be'. There are thus two
issues to be considered if there is any question about the location of a stoppage:
first, a claimant may escape disqualification if he can show that the dispute did
not take place at his place of employment; and secondly, if it did, that the
proviso was applicable, the purpose of the proviso being 'to secure that where
businesses which are commonly run as separate businesses are run in separate
departments on the same premises, each of those departments is to be treated
as a separate place of employment for the purpose of [the trade dispute
disqualification], and a trade dispute affecting one department will not be held
to affect another department merely because they are on the same premises'
(Ministry of Social Security 1967).

It has been pointed out by the Commissioner that 'the definition of "place of
employment" is a very wide one. The inclusion in it of a farm, which may well
be intersected by a road or a railway, supports this view. The presence of, and
necessity for, the exception in the second part does not suggest that the first
part should be narrowly construed. It has always been widely construed by the
Commissioner'.[32] There is, however, clearly no need for the disqualification to
be widely construed. Indeed, to recognize that it has been so construed is to
recognize also that it is capable of being narrowly construed. A narrow
approach would arguably be more appropriate in the construction of what is in
effect a penal provision. The implications of this wide approach to construction
are highlighted by the decision in the leading case, *R(U)1/70*, which arose as a
result of a dispute in the trim shop at the Ford estate at Dagenham, Essex. The
dispute caused the lay-off of workers in other parts of the estate, including
those in the assembly and body plants. The question for decision was whether
those laid off as a result of the dispute at the trim shop were unemployed
because of a stoppage at their place of work. The insurance officer argued that
the dispute was at the claimants' place of employment (even though they were
not engaged in the trim shop) on the ground that 'the whole estate constitutes
one factory, workshop, farm or other premises or place'. After referring to the
definition of a 'factory' in the *Oxford English Dictionary* ('A building, or
buildings, with plant for the manufacture of goods; a manufactory; works') the
Commissioner agreed, reaching the remarkable conclusion that the entire
Dagenham estate 'was for national insurance purposes a factory for the
production of motor vehicles and not merely a number of factories for
the manufacture of component parts of them'. This then brought into play the
proviso which, as the Commissioner pointed out, would apply only if the trim
shop and the other sites at Dagenham 'were separate places or premises, where

[32] *R(U)1/70*.

separate branches of work were carried on, which are commonly carried on as separate businesses in separate premises or at separate places'. In this case, however, the persuasive and convincing evidence of the insurance officer established that 'trim manufacture is certainly not commonly carried on as a separate business and indeed is probably not carried on at all except by the one supplier whom the company prevailed on to do the work when they were in difficulties'. It was not argued that separate branches of work were carried on in either the assembly plant or the body shop.

In view of the wide interpretation given to the 'place of employment' test, it is surprising that the CBI should have proposed in its evidence to the Donovan Commission that the definition should be widened still further to disqualify those laid off by a trade dispute occurring elsewhere than at the claimants' own place of employment, provided it occurs within one company. According to Donovan, the implication of the proposal was that an employee at one factory of a company may easily be directly interested in the outcome of a trade dispute at another factory belonging to the same company, and accordingly ought not to be paid benefit if the dispute involves him in unemployment. An alternative response was that of the TUC which had argued that 'a new formula, relating disqualification much more closely to different departments within the same place of employment, can and should be found' (TUC 1967). The TUC continued by pointing out that the 'existing provisions have not been altered since 1911. Since then large scale production has greatly increased. Increasingly branches of production previously carried out in separate workplaces are now carried out under the same roof as part of an integrated process'. The TUC rightly pointed out that in 'a large factory employing perhaps many thousands a dispute affecting a handful of workers may lead to wholesale denial of benefit to men who have no concern with, or indeed knowledge of, the dispute' (TUC 1967). But as with the proposals of the CBI, the submission of the TUC was rejected by the Commission which raised the 'serious objection' that it would 'open the door to selectivity in the matter of strikes', a common concern of policy makers in this area. In particular, it was suggested by the Commission that a union, which organized the workers in a factory where an integrated process is carried out under one roof, would need to call out only the workers in one department. As Donovan (1968: 250) concluded:

Production being integrated, the probability is that work would have to stop in the other departments too. But the employees there would qualify for unemployment benefit, and the union need pay strike benefit to its members in one department only. Yet all the employees might have a direct interest in the outcome of the dispute.

This led a majority to conclude that the present law should remain unchanged, the minority dissenting on the ground that the risk of selectivity 'ought to be accepted in order to avoid the greater injustice of penalising men who are not concerned in a trade dispute simply because it is the common practice of an industry to locate people doing their work in a particular way' (Donovan 1968: 250).

C. *Directly Interested*

The definitions of both 'trade dispute' and 'place of employment' are thus very wide. Consequently, a lot of weight is placed on the meaning of 'direct interest', the claimant having to show that he has no such interest in order to escape disqualification. As with the place of employment test, there are two issues which arise for consideration. These are the nature and the extent of the interest in another person's dispute which will lead to the disqualification of the claimant. As to the former, this too has been very widely construed. Thus, the interest leading to disqualification may be insubstantial, a point highlighted by two cases in 1962. In the first, *R(U)3/62*, a loader in an export dispatch department of a firm which made heating appliances was laid off following a trade dispute in another section. The dispute arose as a result of management proposals to impose minor alterations to working practices, of which only the abolition of the afternoon tea-break would affect the claimant. It was thus argued that the nature of the claimant's interest was 'too insubstantial to be worthy of consideration'. This, however, was rejected by the Commissioner who held that the disqualification applied, observing that 'the claimant stood to be affected by the outcome of the trade dispute in question, in respect that, if the employers prevailed, he would lose his afternoon tea-break. This may well be regarded as a small matter: but it was in my view a matter of direct interest to the claimant'. The Commissioner also made it clear in the following case, *R(U)4/62* arising from the same dispute that he was not concerned with the magnitude of the claimant's interest. On that occasion workers in the enamelling department were disqualified even though their interest in the dispute was an alteration in their lateness allowance. According to the report '[t]he alteration was only a small one, constituting a reduction from 7 minutes to 5 minutes, cumulative over the 5-day week'. In so holding in these cases, the Commissioner rejected a submission that in order to disqualify from benefit, the interest must be 'substantial and material'. The matter was raised by the TUC in its evidence to the Donovan Commission, submitting that workers with merely a minor interest in a dispute should not be disqualified. This, however, was rejected by the Commission on the ground that 'the line between major and minor interests could . . . not be drawn with precision'.

On the extent of the interest in another person's dispute, the TUC has complained in the past that the authorities had blurred the distinction between direct and indirect interest. It is indeed difficult to find more than one Commissioner's decision before 1971 in which a claimant has unsuccessfully claimed that he was not directly interested in the trade dispute in question.[33]

---

[33] See also *Punton* v. *Ministry of Pensions and National Insurance (No. 2)* [1964] 1 All ER 448.

Since 1971, however, a number of important decisions on this point have been made by the Commissioner, the Court of Session, and the House of Lords. In all of them the term has been narrowly construed, though as we shall see there is scope for an even narrower approach. The starting point is *R(U)13/71* where the Commissioner wrote as follows:

The statute does not require proof of *no* interest. It requires proof of no *direct* interest: and it is essential that proper value be given to the qualifying word *direct*. Unfortunately the adjective 'direct' has a variety of meanings, depending on the substantive which it qualifies; and the statute provides no specific definition.

Without attempting to define precisely what is meant by 'direct interest', I think that a claimant should not be regarded as having a direct interest in another person's dispute ... unless there is a close association between the two occupations concerned, and the outcome of the dispute is likely to affect the claimant, not at a number of removes, but virtually automatically, without further intervening contingencies.

This approach was subsequently endorsed in *R(U)8/72*, though in that case the Commissioner disapproved the requirement that there must be a close connection between the two occupations concerned:

In my opinion, whatever formulation is used the concept which must be expressed is that of a break in a chain of causation. Supposing that the outcome of a trade dispute might lead to a change in the terms of employment of a person, then that person will have a direct interest in the dispute if the change would occur without any act or event breaking the chain of causation between such outcome and the change. On the other hand, his interest will not be direct if some act or event must be interposed between the outcome of the dispute and the occurrence of the change. I believe that this is what the learned Commissioner who decided *R(U)13/71* meant by 'further intervening contingencies'.

R(U)13/71 was also endorsed by the Court of Session in *Watt* v. *Lord Advocate*,[34] though the Commissioner's remarks were interpreted more widely by the Court than they had been in *R(U)8/72* where a claimant would be disqualified only if the outcome of the dispute causing the lay-off would automatically affect his employment. In *Watt*, by contrast, the Lord President read *R(U)13/71*:

as having in mind ... the particular outcome of the particular dispute and what seems to me to be necessary is that the terms of settlement of that dispute should themselves affect the claimant's wages or conditions of work virtually automatically and as a necessary consequence thereof. What seems to be required is that the issues in the dispute should embrace not only the interests of those taking part in it but the interests of others including the claimant as well with the result that its outcome is likely to have consequences, virtually immediate and automatic, for workers other than those engaged in it.

Although the differences between *R(U)8/72* and *Watt* are not great, the latter, unlike the former, does allow for the possibility of a worker being

---

[34] 1979 SLT 137.

disqualified on the ground of direct interest even though the claimant's terms and conditions will be affected only by some intervening event. It is precisely this point which was at issue in *Presho* v. *Department of Health and Social Security*[35] where the claimant was employed as an instructor/machine operator at a Brooke Bond Oxo food factory in Lancashire. As such she was a member of USDAW. Also employed at the factory were fifty-seven maintenance engineers who were members of the AUEW which made a pay claim to the management on behalf of its members. The claim was rejected, a work-to-rule was imposed by the union, and eventually work came to a standstill. This in turn led to the lay-off of the production workers (including the claimant) as machines were not being repaired. Although the claim was made only by the AUEW, and not also by the claimant's union USDAW, the Commissioner found that it was 'incontrovertible on the evidence that . . . if the demand by AUEW were conceded it would automatically be applied to the USDAW workers as well'. Unsurprisingly, perhaps, the Commissioner held that the claimant was disqualified, having failed to show that she did not have a direct interest in the dispute, given that its outcome would be applied across the board to all the other workers including in particular production workers such as the claimant. Remarkably, the Court of Appeal reversed, with Kerr L.J. holding:

In this context, as it seems to me, the word 'directly' should be construed strictly and narrowly. To construe it as 'automatically' would clearly satisfy this construction. However, to extend the meaning to 'virtually automatically', and then to apply it to facts such as those in the present case, in my view goes further than the meaning which should properly be given to 'directly' in this context. The proper meaning of 'directly', I think, given the remainder of the extensive gloss which has already been placed upon the words 'directly interested in the dispute', is that the circumstances are such that the probable outcome of the dispute will automatically affect the claimant by virtue of some pre-existing agreement, whether legally binding or not.[36]

In this case, it was merely the policy of management that any changes would be applied across the board. But this would not happen automatically because it would require negotiation. So although the Court accepted that the claimant would be disqualified if directly was equated with 'virtually automatically', it was held, equating directly with 'automatically', that the disqualification did not apply. In so holding Slade L.J. expressly endorsed the decision in *R(U)8/72*.

This was a remarkably broad-minded decision. Not only does it effectively clarify the distinction between direct and indirect interests, but it goes a long way to meeting the TUC's proposal that a claimant 'should not be disqualified

---

[35] [1983] IRLR 295 (CA); [1984] IRLR 74 (HL).

[36] These remarks were preceded by the long overdue observation that 'The context in which this issue arises is that of a disqualification from the receipt of unemployment benefit when a claimant has lost her job without being in any dispute with her employers, and without in any way having participated in a dispute involving other members of the workforce [which] has led to their stopping work and her being laid off in consequence.'

unless his terms or conditions of employment are the subject of, *or are immediately in issue in*, the trade dispute' [emphasis added]. Predictably, perhaps, this was not allowed to stand for long, with the House of Lords reversing. But in delivering the only judgment of their Lordships, Lord Brandon served further to confuse an already complicated situation. He held that where different groups of workers, belonging to different unions, were employed by the same employer at the same place of work, and there was a dispute between the employer and one of these unions, those workers in the other groups represented by different unions were directly interested in the dispute provided that two conditions were fufilled. The first was that the outcome of the dispute would be applied by the employer not only to those participating in it, but also to the other groups of workers who belonged to the other unions concerned. The second condition was that this application of the dispute across the board 'should come about automatically as a result of one or other of three things: first, a collective agreement which is legally binding; or, secondly, a collective agreement which is not legally binding; or, thirdly, established industrial custom and practice at the place (or possibly places) of work concerned'. Lord Brandon continued by pointing out that it was a pure question of fact whether in any particular case these two conditions were satisfied. The decision of the Commissioner was thus restored after his Lordship noted that the Commissioner had found 'as a fact that these two conditions were satisfied, in that the employers would, by reason of the factual situation at the factory, by which he clearly meant the established industrial custom and practice there, apply automatically the outcome of their dispute with AUEW to other groups of workers belonging to other unions at the same factory, including the group of workers belonging to USDAW'. It appears, then, that the difference between the Court of Appeal and the House of Lords lay not on a point of law (both concluded that a direct interest would arise only if someone else's dispute would apply automatically to the claimant), but in the power of the Court of Appeal to challenge a finding of fact. And despite Lord Brandon's claim that his approach accorded substantially with the ratio of the majority in *Watt*, his approach on the question of construction goes beyond both *Watt* and *R(U)13/71* on which it was based. *Presho* in the Court of Appeal (expressly) and in the House of Lords (impliedly) is in effect a strong endorsement of the more restrictive yet liberal approach to interpretation adopted by the Commissioner in *R(U)8/72*.

But although *Presho* is the culmination of a gradual narrowing of the direct interest ground of disqualification, it need not lead to uncontrolled rejoicing. For the fact is that despite that decision the disqualification still operates to disqualify claimants who are not in fact participating in a trade dispute. In *Presho* an attempt was made to take their Lordships one step further when it was argued that 'a worker can only be directly interested in a trade dispute if it is his own pay or conditions of work which form the subject-matter of such dispute'. Without giving very convincing reasons, the House of Lords found such an interpretation 'impossible', though one factor which may have been important was the concern that if 'a narrower and more legalistic interpretation' of this kind was adopted 'the way would be wide open for deliberate and calculated evasions' of the disqualification 'with the result that the effectiveness of the [measure] to achieve its manifest object would be much reduced'. The concern here appears to be similar to the concern which moved the Donovan Commission not to recommend any legislative narrowing of the direct interest limbs of the disqualification. Thus, the Commission was concerned that 'a claim recognised as potentially of general application in a place of employment might be advanced and made the subject of a dispute by one section alone'. But this concern to prevent abuse may not necessarily justify the non-payment of benefit to workers who are not in fact participating in a dispute. It is arguable, admittedly, that the desire to promote state neutrality would be undermined if the disqualification was to apply to only a small and selective number of strikers who formed part of a much larger group in dispute with their employer. The state would be supporting workers in dispute to the extent that the disqualification was applied only to those physically on strike. It is arguable also that in such a situation it is not only the workers on strike who were voluntarily unemployed, so that disqualification on the ground of direct interest could be sustained on both of the principal grounds for the disqualification discussed in Section II above. On the other hand, however, it is difficult to see how either justification dictates the disqualification of workers in a dispute where the nature of the interest is either minor or prejudicial, or both. It would be hard to argue seriously, for example, that the claimants in *R(U)3/62* or *R(U)4/62* were voluntarily unemployed or that the non-payment of benefit was necessary in the interests of state neutrality. The same is true of the many cases in the bound volumes of Commissioners' decisions which deal with the disputes between an employer and one union, the outcome of which could lead to the reduction of the work available to the members of another. Even if it is proper to disqualify on the ground of direct interest in some cases, it is difficult to see the rational basis for disqualifying the members of other unions who stand only to lose if the strike is settled to the satisfaction of the union in the dispute.

V.   CONCLUSION

The trade dispute disqualification has undergone a number of important modifications since the remarkably sweeping measure first introduced in 1911 whereby everyone participating in and everyone laid off by a dispute at his place of work was disqualified. These modifications have gradually narrowed the range of people affected by the disqualification to exclude innocent victims caught up in the dispute. To that extent the statutory initiatives generally are to be welcomed, as are the judicial decisions such as *Presho* tending in the same direction, if only because they may tend to reduce the pressure for a settlement from those other workers. But for all that the central feature of the disqualification remains uncompromising and untouched. That is to say, claimants participating in a dispute are disqualified, regardless of whether the stoppage of work is caused by a strike or a lock-out, or whether the trade dispute is a consequence of unreasonable or unlawful conduct on the part of the employer. Despite persistent pressure from the TUC, successive governments have been extraordinarily impervious to the need to reform this feature of the legislation, with the employer's breach exemption crumbling to employer political power in the absence of any clear evidence one way or another as to its effect in practice. Equally, just as in the law relating to unfair dismissal, with only a few notable exceptions those exercising judicial authority have been unwilling to moderate the harsh and inequitable consequences of the legislation, though, as we shall see in Chapter 8, precedents of the Umpires before World War II provided ample scope for imagination and initiative. As a result, the disqualification serves to reinforce the common law powers of the employer, and is an even greater 'instrument of coercion'[37] than it need be. The point is poignantly illustrated by the disqualifications upheld by Commissioners' decisions in the 1950s where workers were dismissed and offered re-employment on less favourable terms,[38] or dismissed because of union membership and activities following a union claim for recognition.[39] In such circumstances neither the common law nor even employment protection legislation offers any effective remedy to the workers involved. The trade dispute disqualification helps to undermine self-help remedies, and may tend towards inducing employees 'to accept terms of employment which are unsatisfactory, and which they would not otherwise accept'.[40] We return in Chapter 8 to consider whether these coercive qualities can be justified on grounds of state neutrality or indeed on any of the other grounds presented in justification. But first we must deal with the treatment of strikers in social welfare law.

---

[37] *In Re Application of William N. McKay* (1946) 53 Man. Reps. 364.
[38] *R(U)19/53.*
[39] *R(U)27/56.*
[40] *In Re Application of William N. McKay* (1946) 53 Man. Reps. 364.

[6]
Industrial Action and Social Welfare

I. INTRODUCTORY

With those engaged in industrial action denied unemployment benefit, we have now to consider rights of access to social welfare benefits provided by the state to those who have no other sources of income or those whose supply of income is inadequate. Since the origins of trade unionism and consequently the use of the strike weapon in its modern form, five different schemes have been in operation to provide (in different degrees) for the unemployed without the means of personal support, or for the support of dependants. The schemes in question have been the poor law; unemployment assistance; national assistance; supplementary benefit; and now income support. Yet this diversity in the nomenclature of the different schemes masks what has been a considerable degree of continuity in state policy regarding the poor which has evolved very gradually. So far as the relief of those engaged in industrial disputes is concerned, the degree of continuity is even more profound. It would be no exaggeration to claim that the policy pursued to this day is one laid down in principle by the Court of Appeal in 1900. Paradoxically indeed, the reviled poor law which operated until the late 1930s was in many respects more favourable for many strikers and their families than the law which is in force at the time of writing.

II. THE POOR LAW

A. *General Principles*

Twentieth-century poor law had its origins in the Act of 1601. This imposed a duty on parish authorities to relieve discrete categories of poor citizens. Although the Act of 1601[1] was largely replaced by the great reforming Act of 1834,[2] the categories of poor citizens to be relieved by the poor law remained largely unchanged until its formal abolition in 1948. Thus, in section 15 of the

---

[1] Poor Relief Act 1601.
[2] Poor Law Amendment Act 1834.

consolidating Poor Law Act 1930, those responsible for the relief of the poor were under a duty

(a) to set to work all such persons, whether married or unmarried, as have no means to maintain themselves, and use no ordinary and daily trade of life to get their living by;
(b) to provide such relief as may be necessary for the lame, impotent, old, blind and such other persons as are poor and not able to work;
(c) to set to work or put out as apprentices all children whose parents are not . . . able to keep and maintain their children.

Under the 1601 Act, the first category of citizens was to be relieved only by being set to work, with only the second category being entitled to relief without work. 'If a poor person able to work, and for whom work was found by the parish authorities, would not work, he became liable to imprisonment under s. 2 of the statute of Elizabeth and the subsequent Vagrancy Acts.'[3]

According to Jennings (1936: 3), however, there had 'been no attempt to put into force the principle of 1601, that the men were to be set to work. Relief had been given without the exaction of a task of work, with the result that there were plenty prepared to take the meagre allowance from the parish and supplement it with begging or crime, without worrying about obtaining work'. An additional source of difficulty was the so-called Speenhamland system first introduced by Berkshire magistrates in 1795 whereby some parishes supplemented low wages from the poor rate in response to 'desperate need because of food shortages and increased prices' (Fraser 1973: 33). For these and other reasons, poor relief was becoming an increasingly heavy burden on those who had to pay for it, and in response to political pressure from landowners in particular, a Royal Commission was appointed in 1832, its report of 1834 'to be a classic document in the history of English social policy' (Fraser 1973: 38–9). For present purposes, three important principles were at the heart of the Report. The first was the abolition of outdoor relief for able-bodied persons, while the second was the principle of 'less eligibility' whereby the able-bodied poor 'who applied for relief would be offered maintenance in a workhouse in which their lives would be regulated and made less comfortable than those of their fellows who chose to stay outside and fend for themselves' (Rose 1972: 8). The third underlying theme of the Report was for the 'appointment of a Central Board to control the administration of the Poor Laws' (Jennings 1936: 4), with powers to frame regulations and control local practices. In the words of one social historian, 'Poor relief was to become for the first time in its history uniform and centrally directed' (Fraser 1973: 45).

But although there was thus a central authority regulating the poor laws

---

[3] *Attorney-General* v. *Guardians of the Poor of the Merthyr Tydfil Union* [1900] 1 Ch. 516, at p. 541. By the Vagrancy Act 1824, s. 3, 'Every person being able wholly or in part to maintain himself or herself, or his or her family, by work or by other means, and wilfully refusing or neglecting so to do, by which refusal or neglect he or she, or any of his or her family whom he or she may be legally bound to maintain, shall have become chargeable to any parish . . . shall be deemed an idle and disorderly person,' and be liable to prosecution by the guardians.

(initially the Poor Law Commissioners[4]), this was not wholly effective and did not provide the degree of control which the Commission of 1834 had anticipated.[5] In consequence a considerable degree of autonomy and discretion remained vested in the Poor Law Unions under the direction of Boards of Guardians. One notable feature of this was that outdoor relief was never completely abolished in England and Wales as had been recommended by the Royal Commission and proposed by the 1834 Act:

Sometimes the new regimes refused point blank to implement the workhouse test, and in the case of Liverpool special Parliamentary dispensation was given to . . . return to the former system of administration under a local Act. Popular opposition gradually subsided when it was realised that outdoor relief could not be dropped. Indeed the Poor Law Commission devised the 'labour test' (i.e. outdoor relief was given provided some work was done) in order to reconcile the continuation of outdoor relief with the principles of 1834, and by 1854 84 per cent of paupers were on outdoor relief (Fraser 1973: 48).[6]

Pressure was particularly acute during periods of high unemployment, such as the 1860s (Bruce 1968: 124) and the 1920s (Ryan 1976: 359–60). In the latter period Boards of Guardians are said to have had little alternative to granting outdoor relief on a large scale. Although the 'Poor Law Department of the Ministry of Health . . . deplored these new developments', they could do little about them, partly because of the wide discretion of the local Boards and partly because of the endemic fear of social and political disorder (Ryan 1976: 360).[7]

B. *The Relief of Strikers*

So far as the relief of strikers by the poor law is concerned, the author of one leading study has written that 'Little seems to be known about the treatment of strikers under the Poor Law in the nineteenth century, but it would perhaps not be unfair to assume that Boards dominated by small tradesmen, businessmen and rate-payers would not be sympathetic to strikers' (Ryan 1976: 361). It may be, of course, that many workers who did strike had other concerns about the law, with criminal conspiracy and prosecution under the Master and

[4] For constitutional reasons the powers of the Commissioners were transferred to a Poor Law Board, with a political head who was responsible to Parliament. In 1871 the powers of the Board fell under the authority of the new Local Government Board and in 1919 responsibility for Poor Law became that of the Ministry of Health.

[5] According to one historian, 'the central Poor Law Commission had very limited powers when faced with a union which failed to co-operate' (Fraser 1973: 48). At the end of the day the Commission performed a purely supervisory role: 'it could cajole, encourage, reprimand, inspect, but could not compel' Ibid.: 49).

[6] It has also been pointed out that there were administrative barriers to the effective implementation of the 1834 reforms: 'there were not yet sufficient workhouses, wages were too low, and the sudden change would cause undue hardship' (Jennings 1936: 4).

[7] In 1921 the practice of outdoor relief was officially sanctioned, with a circular from the Ministry accepting that relief could be given albeit on a lower level than wages currently payable (Ryan 1976: 359).

Servant Acts being very real dangers until well into the second half of the century. But to the extent that it ultimately became an issue, the little evidence which is available reveals some differences in the practices of different Poor Law Unions. During the Hull dock strike of 1893, 'the Poor Law Guardians openly acted as recruiting sergeants for "free labour" when able-bodied labourers applied for relief' (Saville 1967: 330). In contrast, during a coal strike in South Wales in 1898 the Merthyr Tydfil Union 'established labour yards and relief works, and, partly by these yards and works, and partly by gifts of food or money, the necessitous workmen and their families were relieved'. It was this episode which led to the landmark decision of the Court of Appeal which was to form the bench-mark for state policy in this area to the present day.[8] The action to challenge the payments was brought by a coal company, a rate-payer of the Merthyr Tydfil Union. The company sought a declaration that the provision of outdoor relief to able-bodied persons who were able to maintain themselves and their families constituted a breach of statutory duty. Evidence produced at the trial revealed that the striking colliers who had been relieved at the labour yards 'were offered work upon terms which they did not think proper to accept, and that notices containing the offer of such terms were posted at the . . . collieries'.

The action failed before Romer J. who noted that under regulations of 1870 the guardians were empowered to provide outdoor relief in cases of sudden and urgent necessity. In so holding, he rejected the contention that 'the guardians in no case could relieve able-bodied men who could but would not work'. It is important to note, however, that strikers were not entitled to relief as of right but only to relieve 'temporary urgent necessity'. Here, 'each case relieved by the guardians during the strike seems to have been investigated by their officers and to have been one of actual destitution'. This, however, was not the only ground for the decision, with the Court holding additionally that judicial review was not an appropriate remedy given the availability of other means of redress. Here Romer J. referred in particular to the rate-payers' right to make representations to the auditor which was 'clearly the ordinary and proper course'. But in a seminal judgment the Court of Appeal reversed, though it did hold that it was proper to give relief to the wives and children who had been reduced to destitution because of the strike. The Court also held that the guardians could lawfully provide relief to able-bodied men who were laid off because of the strike, and were unable to obtain work and maintain themselves while it lasted. This is clearly an important concession which contrasted sharply with the trade dispute disqualification in the National Insurance Act 1911. It seems that even those with an interest in the outcome of a dispute would be eligible for poor relief. There was no suggestion in the judgment of the Court of Appeal that such people could be required to maintain themselves by performing the work of those on strike for the duration of the dispute.

---

[8] *Attorney General* v. *Guardians of the Poor of the Merthyr Tydfil Union* [1900] 1 Ch. 516.

Rather different considerations applied to the strikers themselves, with rather uncompromising policy factors being paramount. Thus, the poor laws imposed on the comparatively well-to-do the duty of supporting those who by reason of their poverty could not support themselves. That being the case, a person was not justified in refusing to support himself 'on the ground that he cannot obtain work which, as between him and his employer, he considers reasonable. What is a reasonable agreement for a man to enter into is one thing; what is a reasonable justification for a man compelling others to support him is quite another thing.' This is not to say that strikers would never be entitled to poor relief. Lord Lindley appeared to leave open a window to deal with exceptional circumstances where 'as between him and the rate-payers', the striker was justified in refusing to support himself on the employer's terms. What would constitute exceptional circumstances was not specified.[9] In one later case, however, it was suggested by inference that the guardians would be entitled to grant relief where the employer was seeking to impose wages at a level insufficient to support the striker, his wife and family.[10] But returning to the *Merthyr* case, the general policy position was one of hostility to the idea of relief being provided to strikers. With such considerations being prominent, the Court then turned to an examination of the legislation from which it was unable to find any section 'which entitles able-bodied persons to support out of the rates, if they can obtain work and can support themselves and their families, if they choose to do so'. In this case the strikers were able-bodied men who could have obtained work, and who could have maintained themselves and their families had they chosen to do so.

Different considerations would have applied if the men had been physically too weak and ill to work, or if they had been prevented by fear of violence from accepting work. But although it was accepted that strikers were 'destitute' in the sense that 'they had neither food nor money', it seems that they were not destitute enough, not being physically unable to work by starvation: '[t]hey were not so weak as to be unable to work'. If they had been, then relief might have been given, the Court accepting that 'poor persons able to work and able to procure it might, by refusing to work, become so weak as to be no longer able to work, in which case they become entitled to relief out of the rates'. But they also became liable to imprisonment as idle and disorderly persons under the Vagrancy Act 1824, section 3. The right to relief in this type of case was referred to by Lord Lindley as 'an anomaly, for it enabled a person to obtain a legal advantage by his own wrong-doing'. The anomaly was, however, 'justified

[9] But it seems that the conduct of employers during the General Strike did not amount to an exceptional circumstance. It appears that a number of Boards insisted that 'the miners were going to be helped in their struggle against the mine-owners' campaign' (H. H. Elvin, TUC (1926: 463)). This led in turn to the Guardians (Default) Act 1926, passed on 15 July 1926 and authorizing the Minister of Health to reconstitute a Board of Guardians where it appeared to him that the existing guardians were not properly performing their duties. This conflict forms part of a wider conflict between central and local government in the 1920s, on which see the article by Fennell (1986).

[10] *Attorney-General* v. *Poplar Guardians* (1924) 40 TLR 752.

on grounds of humanity', in the sense that the penalty for refusing to work was 'imprisonment, not death by starvation'. But the fact is that the restriction on poor relief to strikers was underwritten ultimately by the criminal law. It should be pointed out, however, that prosecutions under the Vagrancy Act were instituted by the guardians who were unlikely to use their powers in many cases. And in one important instance where a prosecution was brought, a worker was held entitled to refuse to accept an offer of employment, and thereby maintain himself, where to do so could have led to disciplinary sanctions being imposed by his trade union.[11]

C. *The Position in Scotland*

In England and Wales there was thus some scope for use of the poor law to relieve poverty during an industrial dispute. Relief could be provided for the wives and children of those on strike; it could be provided for those laid off as a result of the strike, even though they may have an interest in its outcome; and in exceptional circumstances it could be provided to the strikers themselves—where the strikers had reasonable cause as between themselves and the rate-payers, or where the strikers had themselves become destitute to the extent described by Lord Lindley in the *Merthyr* case. So far as the relief of the strikers themselves was concerned, the *Merthyr* case thus left some scope for judgment on the part of local guardians, even though the underlying policy favoured a less than generous approach.[12] In Scotland, in contrast, the position was rather different. An important feature of Scots poor law was that no express provision was made in the Poor Law Act (Scotland) 1845 (the governing statute) for the relief of the able-bodied, or for providing work for those who were unemployed. The absence of any such right was established in a long line of cases,[13] with one judge in 1925 referring to 'the broad general principle that no able-bodied man . . . however burdensome his family obligations, and whatever his difficulties in getting remunerative employment, is legally entitled to parochial relief either *per se* or *per* the wife and children whom he is bound to maintain'.[14] It was not until 1921 that large-scale unemployment led to a modification of the position with the Poor Law Emergency Provisions (Scotland) Act authorizing relief to be granted to

---

[11] *Lewisham Union Guardians* v. *Nice* [1924] 1 KB 618.

[12] One leading authority has commented that 'As a clear-cut statement of policy laying down guidelines for Boards of Guardians the judgment was entirely unsatisfactory. In effect, the decision as to whether to give relief or not involved a judgment on the merits of the dispute by the Guardians, and clearly in the majority of cases, the political complexion of the Board would be the determining factor' (Ryan 1976: 362). The same author writes of how many Boards were 'confused' by the judgment during the General Strike (1976: 370). But note that the Ministry of Health (1926) Circular 703 states (wrongly) that 'The function of the Guardians is the relief of destitution within the limits prescribed by law and they are in no way concerned in the merits of an industrial dispute'. See further Appendix 2.

[13] *Adams* v. *McWilliam* (1849) 11 D. 719; *Petrie* v. *Meek* (1859) 21 D. 614.

[14] *Glasgow Parish Council* v. *Rutherglen Parish Council*, 1925 SC 79, at p. 95.

'destitute able-bodied persons out of employment' if such persons could satisfy the parish council that they were unable to obtain employment.

The leading case on the provision of poor relief to strikers and their families in Scotland is *David Colville & Sons Ltd.* v. *The Parish Council of the Parish Dalziel*[15] which arose out of the General Strike of 1926. On 8 May 1926 the Scottish Board of Health had issued a circular accepting that strikers could be relieved under the 1845 Act if they were no longer physically able to work. The circular also acknowledged that relief could be provided for the dependants of striking miners, with the Lord Advocate (William Watson) subsequently explaining that this step had been taken to introduce a measure of parity between Scotland and England.[16] But although this seemed fair, so far as Scots law was concerned it was nevertheless unlawful. In so holding, Lord Constable examined the position under both the 1845 Act and the 1921 Act. So far as the former is concerned, the position seemed clear and the authorities conclusive: the absence of any power to relieve the able-bodied unemployed or their families meant that the payments could not be authorized under 'the ordinary rules of the poor law'. So far as the 1921 Act is concerned, the position was rather more tricky, and in order fully to understand the legal arguments it is necessary to reproduce section 1 of that Act in full. It provided:

Notwithstanding anything in . . . the Poor Law (Scotland) Act, 1845 . . . assessments imposed and levied for the relief of the poor shall extend and be applicable to the relief of destitute able-bodied persons out of employment, so, however that *nothing in this Act contained shall require the parish council of any parish to provide relief to any such person unless he satisfies the parish council . . . that he is destitute and unable to obtain employment* (emphasis added).

The council argued that the payments were authorized under section 1 on two grounds. The first was that the section must be read in two parts. The first part conferred a discretion on the authorities to grant relief to any destitute able-bodied person, and the second conferred a duty to provide relief to any such person who was unable to find employment. But this argument was rejected, with the Court preferring the view that the section was to be read as a whole and that the words in italics qualified the first part of the section. In other

---

[15] 1927 SLT 118.

[16] 202 HC Debs. 1610 (22 Feb. 1927). The government had decided that relief must be given 'whether it was strictly within the law or not'. Mr Watson explained that 'the Government decided in the beginning of May that, whether it was actually legal or illegal, it was right such relief should be given, and for this reason—there are many other reasons—that it seemed quite impossible, administratively or with any fairness, to have the dependants of those engaged in the dispute in England receiving relief out of the rates while the dependants of those in Scotland were not receiving such relief at all.' There was also concern that to treat dependants differently in Scotland 'would of itself tend to promote ill-feeling and possibly disturbance'. It appears, however, that neither equitable arguments nor the fear of disorder were widely accepted throughout Scotland as reasons for paying relief. One author has written that in 'some areas the "city fathers" were indignant at having to give any relief at all' and that it took 'vigorous efforts' from trades councils and others to enforce payment even on the meagre scale rates laid down in the Circular. (Arnot 1955: 175–6).

words, no able-bodied person could be lawfully provided with relief unless he was unable to find employment. The second argument for the council then was simply that this condition had been fulfilled—the men were unable to find employment and so the parish council was entitled to relieve their families. But this argument was also rejected, although if it had succeeded it would have authorized payment not only to the families of the strikers, but to the strikers themselves. In the view of Lord Constable:

having regard to the admitted facts in the case, I think that on its merits the contention clearly fails. So far from satisfying themselves that the applicants for relief were unable to find employment, the respondents put no questions to applicants on the subject. They assumed that all applicants were unable to obtain employment. But that assumption was quite unwarranted, because there were notices at the pitheads that employment was open. It was argued that ability to find employment necessarily involves a consideration of the terms upon which employment is open. But the respondents never considered the terms which were open to the applicants. It was further argued that employment at a pit necessitated the attendance of a number of miners, and that no employment was open to an individual miner. This might have been a good answer by any applicant who proved that he attended at the pits and was debarred from work because no other miners presented themselves. But it is admitted that no miner attended at the pits and asked employment.

The Court consequently decided in favour of the pursuers, who were local rate-payers, possibly connected with the mining industry.

The *Colville* case thus created the anomaly that relief could be lawfully granted in England and Wales, but not in Scotland. The anomaly was all the greater in the context of the General Strike, 'the dispute being common to both countries and in many cases the employers being common to both countries'.[17] In an interesting development, however, the government legislated to bring the Scottish position closer into line with that prevailing in England and Wales. The Poor Law Emergency Provisions (Scotland) Act 1927 provided by section 1:

Notwithstanding anything in the Poor Law (Scotland) Act, 1845, the assessments imposed and levied for the relief of the poor shall extend and be applicable to relief to the destitute dependants of any destitute able-bodied person who is out of employment owing to his being directly involved in a trade dispute.

What is more, the provision was made retrospective to 30 April 1926, thereby reversing *Colville* and validating the Health Department's circular of 8 May 1926. It will be noted, however, that the position was not quite the same as in England and Wales, with no provision being made in the statute for the relief of the striker himself. It is possible, however, that creative use of the 1921 Act together with benevolent reading of the passage from the Constable judgment quoted above could have produced an outcome similar to the position under English law whereby strikers themselves could be relieved under exceptional

[17] 202 HC Debs. 1610 (22 Feb. 1927) (Lord Advocate).

circumstances, and the same ones at that. Yet whatever the limitations of the 1927 Act, it was nevertheless quite a remarkable piece of legislation from a government which was more concerned with reparations from rather than relief for those engaged in the strike.

III. NATIONAL ASSISTANCE AND SUPPLEMENTARY BENEFIT

A. *General Principles*

The Poor Law was abolished in 1948 and replaced by national assistance which was modelled to a large extent on the non-contributory unemployment assistance scheme which had been introduced in 1934 to relieve unemployment under the central direction of the Unemployment Assistance Board.[18] The National Assistance Act 1948 imposed a duty on the newly-created National Assistance Board 'to assist persons in Great Britain who are without resources to meet their requirements',[19] the duty to be met by the payment of means-tested assistance grants. As originally conceived by Beveridge (1944), national assistance would fulfil a quite secondary role in the social security system, operating mainly as a safety net for those who were not eligible for one of the comprehensive insurance-based benefits. But as is well known, this is not how events unfolded, so that by the time national assistance was replaced with supplementary benefit in 1966, the number of people in receipt had risen from 800,000 in 1948 to over 2,000,000 in 1966, partly as a result of the low rate of insurance benefit but in part also because of the increasing number of claimants such as single mothers for whom there was no appropriate insurance benefit. The 1966 changes were designed to improve the public image of means-tested benefit (Rowell and Wilton 1982), mainly by insisting that claimants had a right to benefit when their requirements exceeded their resources.[20] Benefit was now to be administered by the Supplementary Benefits Commission which, unlike the National Assistance Board before it, was not a government department.

B. *The Treatment of Strikers*

Both national assistance and supplementary benefit were available to unemployed claimants who either did not qualify for or were disqualified from unemployment benefit. This was with the exception of those unemployed because of a trade dispute who have been disqualified since the National Assistance Act 1948.[21] A remarkable feature of the disqualification is not just

---

[18] Unemployment Act 1934, Part II.   [19] National Assistance Act 1948, s. 4.
[20] Ministry of Social Security Act 1966, s. 4.
[21] National Assistance Act 1948, s. 9(3).

the fact that it was introduced into the national assistance scheme and retained in its progeny by Labour governments, thereby providing further evidence, perhaps, that Labour can be relied upon to be responsible. Also remarkable is the fact that no attempt was made to defend either the principle of the disqualification, or indeed its scope. Historians will look long and hard in a vain search for ministerial statements in either 1948 or 1966, with the fullest account appearing to be brief remarks by the Ministry of Social Security in its evidence to the Donovan Commission, where it submitted that 'The general considerations which argue against the payment of unemployment benefit to a person who has lost employment because of a trade dispute in which he is involved also argue against the payment to him of national assistance in the sense that it is not in the public interest to allow those involved in industrial action to receive financial assistance from public funds.' We return to these arguments in Chapter 8, but at this point it needs to be said that such assumptions (no doubt sincerely held) are simply unsustainable. The Ministry justified the disqualification from unemployment benefit on insurance principles, arguments from state neutrality, and administrative convenience. Clearly the first has no bearing on the present context, while the second and third could be met by treating the striker like anyone else who is voluntarily unemployed, allowing benefit to be paid (at a reduced rate) without any need on the part of the authorities to enquire into the merits of the dispute.

Like many of the other features of the national assistance scheme, the trade dispute disqualification appears to be a legacy inherited from the poor law, though the influence of unemployment assistance and national insurance law is also readily apparent. Indeed, the heavy hand of the poor law was so obvious to one Labour back-bencher (Mr William Blyton, a Durham miner for thirty years before his election in 1945) that in Standing Committee he claimed that the terms of the new legislation were 'exactly the same . . . as the Merthyr Tydfil decision'.[22] Thus, under both the 1948 and 1966 Acts the striker himself was not entitled to benefit. But, as under the poor law rules determined by the Court of Appeal, the disqualification of the striker did not extend to his family for whose requirements both national assistance and supplementary benefit were payable. And as was also the case under the poor law, the striker could in exceptional cases be relieved, with the urgent needs payments of national assistance being an equivalent to the payment for destitution under the poor law. This is not to deny that there were important differences between the poor law and national assistance. As Mr James Griffiths, the responsible Minister, pointed out in Committee, payments to strikers' families would be paid in cash, by a 'money grant', and not partly in kind as was the practice under the previous regime.[23] Similarly, so far as the strikers themselves were concerned, any urgent needs payments would not be dependent upon a 'full report' from a medical officer certifying that the claimant 'though ordinarily

---

[22] Official Report, Standing Committee C, 17 Dec. 1947, col. 2417.
[23] Ibid., cols. 2417–18. See Appendix 2.

able-bodied is, as a result of continued unemployment or otherwise, no longer physically able to perform work' (Ministry of Health 1926).[24] But ultimately these are matters of practice and administration rather than principle, particularly as in some areas medical certificates stating that strikers were unable to work were freely signed by District Medical Officers (Ryan 1976: 371).

If the poor law determined the principle of disqualification, the rules inherited from the unemployment assistance scheme determined its scope. The trade dispute disqualification under the 1934 Act was tied in closely with the disqualification under the unemployment insurance law, it being provided that 'during any period during which a person is disqualified for receiving unemployment benefit under the Unemployment Insurance Acts owing to his having lost employment by reason of a stoppage of work which was due to a trade dispute, or during which he would have been so disqualified as aforesaid if he had been an insured contributor under those Acts, he shall . . . be deemed not to be a person to whom this Part of this Act applies'.[25] Yet although there is no compelling reason why a scheme for the relief of need should carry a disqualification as wide as that contained in the insurance scheme, the 1948 Act retained this link to the disqualification from unemployment benefit, providing that

An assistance grant shall not be made to meet the requirements of a person, other than requirements to provide for any other person, for any period during which he is without employment by reason of a stoppage of work which was due to a trade dispute at his place of employment and during which the stoppage of work continues, unless during the stoppage of work he has become bona fide employed elsewhere in the occupation which he usually follows or has become regularly engaged in some other occupation: Provided that this subsection shall not apply in the case of a person who proves—
(a) that he is not participating in or financing or directly interested in the trade dispute which caused the stoppage of work; and
(b) that he does not belong to a grade or class of workers of which, immediately before the commencement of the stoppage, there were members employed at his place of employment any of whom are participating in or financing or directly interested in the dispute.[26]

This was similar but not quite identical to the trade dispute disqualification from unemployment benefit (Mesher 1985a), as was the corresponding provision in the 1966 Act.[27] So simply for reasons of administrative

---

[24] The Minister also said that the value of school meals would not be taken into account in assessing the requirements of the family, as they had been under the poor law.

[25] Unemployment Act 1934, s. 36(1).   [26] National Assistance Act 1948, s. 9(3).

[27] Ministry of Social Security Act 1966, s. 10. In both the 1948 and the 1966 Acts a 'trade dispute' was defined by reference to the National Insurance Act 1946 (in the case of the 1948 Act) and the National Insurance Act 1965 (in the case of the 1966 Act). And having thus extended the same body of law to the national assistance and supplementary benefits schemes, Parliament also intervened to remove the danger that the adjudicating authorities under one regime might hold benefit to be payable in a particular dispute while those under the other reached a different conclusion. This danger was averted by a provision in both the 1948 and 1966 Acts to the effect that a person disqualified from national assistance or supplementary benefit would appeal not to the

convenience,[28] claimants were disqualified from both national assistance and supplementary benefit because they happened to work beside someone who was a member of a trade union engaged in a trade dispute in which neither was participating or even directly interested, or because they happened to work beside someone who had a direct interest in someone else's dispute.

C. *The 1971 Act*

In the twenty years following the introduction of the National Assistance Act 1948, it seems that only a relatively small amount of money was used for the relief of strikers and their families. The amounts paid out annually to dependants ranged from £9,327 in 1950 to £375,330 in 1967, with the annual sum between 1950 and 1968 exceeding five figures on only five occasions. The amount paid to strikers themselves ranged from a total of £85 in 1956 to £2,114 in 1955.[29] There were in fact several factors which helped to keep down the number of claimants. One was the disqualification of single strikers (subject to the availability of urgent needs payments), it being estimated on one occasion that probably about 20 per cent of all strikers are single.[30] A second and perhaps more significant consideration was that 'in general supplementary benefit is not payable for the first two weeks of a strike'.[31] This arose because 'Wages or salary earned by a claimant in the period immediately prior to a dispute, and paid at the beginning of or during the dispute, are treated as a current resource' (TUC 1978: 6). This meant in practice that 'if a person is paid a week's wages for previous work at the beginning of the dispute he or she is regarded as having resources for the week after ceasing employment'(ibid.).[32] And apart from the fact that wages in arrears were treated as a current resource, since 1959 a two-times rule was used in the treatment of a striker's prior income. The effect of this rule was to assume that higher income earners could make the last pay packet last up to two weeks.

Yet despite the punitive way in which an already punitive disqualification was applied, the payment of benefits to strikers and their families began to cause serious concern in the late 1960s. In 1969 the £747,141 paid out to

national assistance appeal tribunals or subsequently to the supplementary benefit appeal tribunals, but to the national insurance local tribunal created by the National Insurance Act 1946. The disqualification in both jurisdictions would thus be applied consistently by the same people.

[28] In Official Report, Standing Committee C, 17 Dec. 1947, col. 2418, the Minister, James Griffiths, explained that 'it was thought wise to incorporate the definition already known, and well understood, of what is or is not a person engaged in a trade dispute'.

[29] These figures are drawn from information provided by Gennard and Lasko (1974).

[30] 816 HC Debs. 53 (26 Apr. 1971) (Sir Keith Joseph, Secretary of State for Social Services).

[31] Ibid.

[32] This is a rule which seems to have its origins in the poor law. The Ministry of Health Circular 703 observed that 'there have been instances of applications for relief being made by persons immediately on cessation of work, when they would normally have just received at least the wages for the previous week's work'. The Circular suggested that in such cases 'destitution is [not] present'. See Appendix 2.

strikers' dependants almost doubled the record levels of 1967, and this in turn was to double in 1970 to £1,445,912, which in turn almost quadrupled in 1971 to stand at £4,309,149. The figure for 1971 was mainly the result of two long national disputes, one in the Post Office which led to £3,024,199 being paid out to strikers' dependants, and the other at Ford which cost £626,466. In other words, these two disputes in the first few months of 1971 had led to more than £3,650,000 being paid out to dependants, with still more being paid out to strikers themselves. This exceeded the total of all national assistance grants and supplementary benefits paid out in connection with strikes from the end of World War II until 1970. But despite the increasing amounts paid in benefit, fewer than 30 per cent of all strikers were eligible for supplementary benefit in 1971 (because of the length of their strike), and of these only slightly more than one in three received benefit (Gennard and Lasko 1974). Yet the government claimed to be 'startled'[33] by the evidence and responded with a number of initiatives contained in its Social Security Act 1971, which was given the Royal Assent on the same day as the Industrial Relations Act 1971 which it immediately follows in the statute book. Both might well be seen as designed to deal with the same problem, with the Industrial Relations Act 1971 seeking to regulate and constrain the circumstances in which industrial action might lawfully be taken, and the Social Security Act 1971 designed to discourage both lawful and unlawful industrial action indirectly by the use of financial sanctions.[34]

The purpose of the Social Security Act 1971 was to force unions and workers to bear a greater part of the cost of strikes themselves. This was done by changing a long-standing administrative practice of the National Assistance Board, a practice which the Supplementary Benefits Commission had inherited. Workers engaged in a long dispute might have been able to sustain themselves in a variety of ways apart from supplementary benefits. Such alternatives included income tax rebates[35] which would be payable on account of unemployment resulting from the dispute, and strike pay from the appropriate trade union. The practice which had developed was for these sources of income to be disregarded up to the full amount of the claimant's personal requirements which in 1971 was £4.35. In other words, although claimants in dispute could not obtain benefit for their own needs, any income which they received up to the supplementary benefit scale rate was not taken into account in determining the resources available to the family unit. The union could pay strike pay without this being knocked off the benefit payable to the striker in

---

[33] 816 HC Debs. 54 (26 Apr. 1971) (Sir Keith Joseph).

[34] During the Second Reading debate, Sir Keith Joseph observed that 'A large number of people whose views are entitled to respect believe that the right to strike is often exercised irresponsibly and it is unreasonable that the taxpayer should be expected to help finance strikes by men whose normal earnings are often quite sufficient to enable them to finance the strikes themselves' (ibid., col. 53).

[35] For an account of the background to law and practice relating to PAYE refunds, see Tiley 1981: 167–8.

respect of his family. But 'although this was a discretionary but long-standing rule with no statutory basis, it was felt that an Act of Parliament was necessary to reduce the disregard'[36] (Gennard and Lasko 1974: 4–5). This was done by section 1 of the 1971 Act providing that such income was now to be taken into account in assessing the resources of a striker who was claiming for the requirements of his family. This was subject to a disregard of only £1, which was what other claimants were allowed. The result would be 'a cut of £3.35 a week in household income of a person connected with a trade dispute wherever such a household has tax refunds or strike pay of £4.35 or more'.[37]

But the 1971 Act did not penalize people only while they were participating in a strike or other industrial action; a second change penalized workers who returned to work after the strike. The general prohibition against paying benefit to people in full-time employment was subject to an exception in both the 1948 and 1966 Acts permitting the Minister to make regulations allowing 'persons becoming engaged in remunerative full-time work'[38] to be paid benefit for a short period after the commencement of their employment. This is presumably because, although in full-time employment, need will continue until wages are paid, wages normally being paid in arrears. In 1970, the position as explained in the Supplementary Benefits Commission's handbook was that 'When a trade dispute ends, the disqualification provisions no longer apply, and persons who have been involved in the dispute may receive supplementary benefit for up to 15 days to supplement part payments (or advances) of wages payable by their employers or any other income they may have' (Supplementary Benefits Commission 1970: 37).[39] Again the government was concerned about the 'dramatic' increase in the number of claims during this period,[40] as '[m]ore and more people have realised that, whereas the sub from the employer is repayable—that is to say, it is merely on account of future earnings and comes out of taxed income—supplementary benefit is neither repayable nor taxable'.[41] So in order to encourage employees 'to revert to the traditional practice of accepting subs [from the employer] to tide them over the period after a trade dispute',[42] the 1971 Act introduced the general rule that benefit paid during this fifteen-day period would be recovered by deductions

[36] An unsuccessful attempt was made by the Labour government to place the practice on a statutory base: National Superannuation and Social Insurance Bill 1970, cl. 110(3), and Sch. 6(2).

[37] 816 HC Debs. 56 (26 Apr. 1971) (Sir Keith Joseph).

[38] Ministry of Social Security Act 1966, s. 8(2).

[39] The limit of 15 days was provided for in the Supplementary Benefit (General) Regulations 1966, SI 1966/1065, reg. 2.

[40] It may be noted that the previous Labour administration's National Superannuation and Social Insurance Bill 1970, cl. 110(1) would have enabled 'the Secretary of State to provide by Regulations that the entitlement on return to work of people involved in the trade dispute is to be the same as before they returned to work' (Supplementary Benefits Commission 1970: 37).

[41] 816 HC Debs. 58 (26 Apr. 1971). According to Sir Keith Joseph the total paid out in 1964 after trade disputes ended was some £4,000, whereas in 1970 the equivalent figure was 'very nearly £900,000'. This was 'an abuse which no Government could contentedly accept'.

[42] 816 HC Debs. 59 (26 Apr. 1971).

from future wages at source.[43] This would be normally at the rate of 10 per cent per week subject to the protected earnings level which was a sum equal to the full supplementary benefit requirements including housing costs, plus £3, but minus any family allowances which were payable.

The 1971 reforms were strongly opposed by the Labour opposition and by the TUC, principally on two grounds. The first was that the supplementary benefits scheme was being used in a punitive way against those engaged in a dispute, and the second that non-participants with only a remote interest in the dispute were being penalized even more.[44] Yet, surprisingly, on its return to power in 1974 the new Labour government failed to remove the provisions of the 1971 Act which had been so strongly condemned. The government could hardly claim that it had no opportunity to do so. The Employment Protection Act 1975 contained provisions removing the financing and the grade or class limbs of the trade dispute disqualification from unemployment benefit, a modification which was extended to supplementary benefit.[45] A second opportunity to deal with the 1971 Act was presented with the enactment of the Supplementary Benefits Act 1976 which replaced its predecessor of 1966, but which in doing so retained both the 1971 innovations in section 8 where the trade dispute disqualification was now to be found. Difficulties in the administration of benefit during the national dispute in the fire service in 1977/8 led, however, to a meeting between TUC General Council representatives and the Minister for Social Security who undertook to set up a special review of the rules governing social security entitlement during disputes. In 1978 the TUC submitted a lengthy and detailed document which not only renewed the attack on the 1971 reforms, but also attacked the disqualification on a number of other grounds. Thus, it was submitted that the disqualification had no place at all and that strikers should have the same rights of access as everyone else 'to the minimum subsistence level income'. It was also argued that the 'disqualification is particularly unjust because it operates even in cases where the stoppage of work is entirely due to the actions of the employer' (TUC 1978a: 3). But nothing came of the review before the fall of the government in 1979.

---

[43] Social Security Act 1971, s. 2, and Sch. 1.

[44] In a meeting with the Secretary of State, TUC General Council representatives pointed out that 'because of the arbitrary operation of the trade dispute disqualification from unemployment benefit, the cuts would not only penalise the families of men actually taking part in industrial action without regard to the merits of the dispute, but would also affect families of non-participants whose connection with a strike was extremely remote' (TUC 1971: 114).

[45] This proposal, which was based on the Donovan recommendations, had been contained earlier in Labour's National Superannuation and Social Insurance Bill 1970. In 1971 the Conservatives decided not to carry out these recommendations which 'could facilitate manipulation of the National Insurance Fund by the withdrawal of a few key workers'.

IV.   THE 1980 REFORMS

A. *General Principles*

In 1980 two important statutes affected the law relating to supplementary benefits—the Social Security Act 1980 and the Social Security (No. 2) Act 1980. The first was the consequence of a departmental review which had concluded that the existing scheme had become too difficult to understand and too dependant for its operation on the discretionary exceptional needs payments which were used for a variety of purposes such as clothing, shoes and furniture. The purpose of the Social Security Act 1980 was purportedly to simplify the law and to eliminate much of the discretion by laying down in detailed rules contained in statutory instruments the precise entitlement of claimants. A number of other important changes introduced in 1980 included the abolition of the Supplementary Benefits Commission, with responsibility transferred to the DHSS with direct accountability of the Minister to Parliament. Also significant was the introduction of a right of appeal from the supplementary benefit appeal tribunals to the Social Security Commissioner (formerly the National Insurance Commissioner), a step which was perhaps necessary because of the growing legalism of the system, a process which it may well have helped to reinforce. The new law indeed became highly legalistic, betraying the intention of its authors to simplify the process. The law was now contained in regulations made under the authority of the 1976 Act (as amended in 1980) which were lengthy, complex and incomprehensible even without the frequent amendments to which they were subject.

B. *The Treatment of Strikers*

So far as strikers were concerned, the general position was largely unchanged. Section 8 of the Supplementary Benefits Act 1976 remained in force. This meant that the single striker was disqualified, and was eligible for urgent needs payments only, while the requirements of the wife and children of a married striker would continue to be met. This is not to deny, however, that the new arrangements discriminated against this class of claimant, retaining existing discriminatory provisions and introducing new ones. It is to be recalled that the right to benefit would arise only where the requirements of the claimant exceeded his resources. So far as the treatment of the claimant's resources are concerned, the Resources Regulations[46] gave legal authority to the practice of the Board and the Commission requiring 'the last wage payments received to be spread over a longer period than normal' (Mesher 1985: 228). Thus, 'If the last week's earnings are more than twice the family's normal and housing

---

[46] Supplementary Benefit (Resources) Regulations 1981, SI 1981/1527.

requirements, the excess is regarded as available income and set against the benefit requirements for the next week' (Department of Health and Social Security 1982: 105–6). So far as requirements are concerned, the new law provided a scale rate which was intended to meet all normal daily living expenses. Provision was also made, however, for what were known as additional requirements with claimants being entitled to extra payments to deal with problems of age, blindness, special diets, laundry costs, domestic help, extra baths, fares to visit relatives in hospital, attendance expenses for someone who is severely disabled, furniture storage, heavy wear and tear of clothing and heating.[47] A notable feature of the Requirements Regulations was that a family could be penalized by being denied some of these payments because one of their number was engaged in dispute.

The Requirements Regulations were in fact remarkable. Thus, so far as additional heating requirements were concerned, no payment would be made in the following circumstances where '*any* member of the assessment unit is a person affected by a trade dispute':

1 where extra warmth needed to be provided because of chronic ill-health (such as bronchitis);

2 where the home is difficult to heat adequately because of draught or damp;

3 where the home is part of an estate built with a heating system which the Secretary of State has in his discretion recognized the running costs as being disproportionately high to run.

An additional requirement for heating would be paid where a member of the unit is affected by a dispute only

1 where extra warmth needed to be provided because of physical illness or physical disability to the extent that the individual in question is confined to the home or unable to leave it alone;

2 where the person in respect of whom the payment is made suffers from a serious physical illness' such that a constant temperature must be maintained;

3 where the person in respect of whom the payment is made is entitled to specified benefits for disability (such as attendance allowance or mobility allowance).

But even in the last three cases the additional requirements would not be met if the person in need is the person affected by the dispute.

So far as other additional requirements are concerned, again no payment would be made in the following circumstances where '*any* member of the assessment unit is a person affected by a trade dispute':

1 where a member of the unit has special attendance needs in connection with bodily functions or to avoid substantial danger to himself;

2 where a member of the unit on medical grounds needs more than one bath a week;

[47] Supplementary Benefit (Requirements) Regulations 1980, SI 1980/1299.

3 where a person has special dietary needs which involves extra cost but is not included within the categories referred to in 2 below, even though in some cases the extra cost may be 'substantial'.

Again an additional requirements payment would be made where a member of the unit is affected by a dispute only in very limited circumstances:

1 where a member of the assessment unit is blind;

2 where a person has special dietary needs because of diabetes, tuberculosis, peptic ulcers, ulcerative colitis, throat conditions making swallowing difficult, or renal failure for which he or she is treated by dialysis;

3 where a member of the unit needs assistance with fares to visit a close relative in hospital.

Once again, in the last three cases the additional requirements would not be met if the person in need is the person affected by the dispute.

Any one of a number of epithets can be employed to evaluate and condemn these rules. All the more so when it is recalled (as is often forgotten) that the people with medical needs penalized in this are not themselves on strike, but are the innocent victims of a husband's or father's dispute. Indeed the husband or father may himself be an innocent victim of someone else's dispute in the sense that he is not a participant but only directly interested in a dispute which he does not support. Yet the discrimination against the striker and his family did not begin with the Resources Regulations and end with the Requirements Regulations. For although the scale rate and the additional requirements (together with housing requirements) were intended to cover regular day-to-day living expenses, it was recognized that there were 'other needs which arise from time to time' (Department of Health and Social Security 1982: 80) which in certain circumstances could be met by an exceptional needs payment under the Single Payments Regulations.[48] True to form, however, these provided that 'no single payment shall be made where any member of the assessment unit is a person whose requirements fall to be disregarded to any extent by virtue of section 8 of the [1976] Act (persons affected by trade disputes)'. Although it is true that some of the items provided for in the Single Payments Regulations could be met as Urgent Needs Payments under the Trade Disputes Regulations,[49] these, as we shall see, were available only in very restrictive circumstances. But even if the requirements for an urgent needs payment under the Trade Disputes Regulations were met, the provision of these needs was generally less favourable than the already meagre provision made by the Single Payments Regulations. And in some cases—such as funeral expenses—there was no equivalent to the Single Payment in the Trade Disputes Regulations. Mesher (1985a: 195) reminds us of the chilling episode

---

[48] Supplementary Benefit (Single Payments) Regulations 1981, SI 1981/1528.

[49] Supplementary Benefit (Trade Disputes and Recovery from Earnings) Regulations 1980, SI 1980/1641.

during the miners' strike when a family was denied a single payment to meet the funeral costs of a dead child.[50]

C. *The 1980 (No. 2) Act*

The 1971 reforms had failed to satisfy many in the Conservative Party who were becoming increasingly outspoken about the extent to which the state was subsidizing strikers. Indeed, the extent of the failure of the 1971 Act to encourage unions to bear a greater part of the cost of strikes is perhaps best reflected by the fact that in 1972 supplementary benefit to strikers and their families exceeded £8,500,000 which was almost double the record-breaking 1971 and more than the total paid out in all the preceding post-war years.[51] The continuing concern led to the publication in 1974 of *Financing Strikes*, by a sub-committee of the Society of Conservative Lawyers. This argued for further major reforms to the law then in force, partly because of the failure of the 1971 Act to induce unions to provide for members on strike, partly as a result of which the state was still heavily subsidizing strikers, some of whom '. . . may have as their purpose the frustration of policies approved by Parliament . . .'[52] Conservative Party interest in this subject assumed a new dimension in 1978 with the publication of details of the so-called Ridley Report which contained recommendations to prepare the next Conservative government for confrontation with a trade union in a vulnerable industry, predicted as being the coal industry. In order to deal with this threat the Report concluded that the 'eventual battle should be on ground chosen by the [government]'; that social security benefits for strikers should be cut; and that a large mobile police squad should be equipped and prepared to deal with violent picketing.[53] Here we have for the first time express recognition of the fact that the function of reform in this area is the coercive one of starving workers out of the right to strike.

The opportunity for amending legislation was quickly seized with the enactment of the Social Security (No. 2) Act 1980. Section 6 made three major changes to the Supplementary Benefits Act 1976, the governing statute which had replaced the 1966 Act. In the first place, it abolished completely the disregard of small sums received by the striker during the course of the dispute. All other claimants were entitled to receive what was by now up to £4 per week without this affecting total entitlement to benefit. So whereas before

[50] The regulations were subsequently amended in 1985 to allow for the payment of funeral expenses under the Trade Disputes Regulations: Supplementary Benefit (Trade Disputes and Claims and Payments) Amendment Regulations 1985, SI 1985/1016.

[51] But it was still the case that only 44.5 per cent of all strikers were eligible to apply for benefit (in the sense that the dispute dragged on for long enough), of whom only 32.5 per cent actually received benefit.

[52] For a critique of the pamphlet, see Lasko (1975) from which information about its contents is drawn.

[53] *The Economist*, 27 May 1978. It was believed that the greatest deterrent to any strike would be 'to cut off the money supply to the strikers, and make the union finance them'.

1971 strikers were in a privileged position over other claimants to the extent that they could receive up to the level of their own requirements without this affecting benefit,[54] now they were discriminated as against other claimants. But even this was of marginal importance when set against the second major change introduced in 1980. An index-linked sum, set then at £12 per week, was to be deducted from any benefit which would be payable to a striker in respect of his family. This much publicized measure was the principal method whereby the government gave effect to its election pledge 'to ensure that unions bear their fair share of the cost of supporting those of their members who are on strike'. In this respect the 1971 Act had been a lamentable failure. Quite simply, it was a disincentive rather than an incentive to unions supporting strikers. This is because whatever they paid over the disregard of £1 would immediately be deducted from the benefit which would otherwise be paid to the striker's family. From the government's point of view the 1980 reforms (which appear to have been proposed first by the backbencher John Page in 1973[55]) were a much more efficient way of ensuring that unions made a contribution to relieve the distress of members on strike, particularly as they were followed by an amendment to the Taxes Act 1970 in the following year which provided that tax rebates were not to be paid at any time to anyone disqualified from unemployment benefit because of section 19 of the Social Security Act 1975, or to anyone who would have been disqualified if he otherwise satisfied the conditions for entitlement.[56]

The third change introduced in 1980 was to tighten still further the already strangling law relating to urgent needs payments. Although strikers were disqualified from receiving benefits to meet their own requirements, this was subject to an overriding discretion on the part of the Supplementary Benefits Commission (and the National Assistance Board before it) to pay benefit if it was urgently needed. In making such payments under the Act, the Commission was not bound by the normal rules of assessment, whether in the Act or in the regulations made thereunder, if these appeared to be inappropriate in the

---

[54] But note the observation that 'The claim of apparent inequity between the disregards available to strikers and to other claimants prior to the 1971 Act ignores the fact that strikers were, and remain, disqualified from benefit in their own right. The pre-1971 Act disregard had the effect of partially redressing the legally enforced denial of the basic entitlement to strikers of S.B. at the prescribed scale rates' (TUC 1978a: 7).

[55] 852 HC Debs. 1699–1701 (16 Mar. 1973). Mr Page questioned whether taxpayers should be asked to subsidize 'those who very often, as in the case of gas or electricity or rail strikes, are closing their businesses and making their home and travelling life a misery'. Apart from proposing that trade unions would be assumed to provide £5 to strikers and their families every week, he also suggested that any benefit paid should be paid only as a loan and be recoverable in the same way as post-strike payments; benefit should be paid to the wife, not the striker; PAYE refunds should be postponed until the end of the strike; and no benefit at all should be paid during a state of emergency. By taking these steps, he urged, 'the community would have the satisfaction of seeing that the first charge of maintaining the striker's family rests on the individual himself and his union'.

[56] Finance Act 1981, s. 29(c), authorizing regulations to be made in these terms under the Income and Corporation Taxes Act 1970, s. 204. See now Income and Corporation Taxes Act 1988, s. 204.

circumstances.[57] In trade dispute cases, the Commission explained that these powers were exercised in accordance with the following criteria:

In deciding whether a striker is in urgent need the Commission take account both of personal circumstances at the time and of all income received since the beginning of the dispute. They expect the single striker to make the total amount he gets from final wages before the dispute, any subsequent wages in hand and any other income or available resource last at the rate of not more than £16.50 a week. Then, providing he has no parents or relatives to whom he could reasonably look for temporary help, payment may be made to bring any other income and resources up to a minimum of £12.50 a week (Supplementary Benefits Commission 1980: 82).[58]

The rate of £12.50 per week compared with a rate of £18.30 for a single householder at that time.

Section 6 of the 1980 Act provided that no urgent needs payments were to be made to strikers or their dependants, save in accordance with regulations, which would cover the rare compassionate case without opening the door to wholesale abuse.[59] The regulations[60] then provided that urgent needs payments could only be made if the need could not be met:

1 from capital (including that which was normally disregarded such as proceeds from the sale of a home) or from income which was normally disregarded in assessing resources;

2 by other persons (including working members of the same household), a public authority, a trade union, emergency relief or comparable service 'to whom or to which it is reasonable to expect the assessment unit to look for assistance';

3 from available credit facilities.

Only if the need could not be met in this way could a payment be made for a limited purpose specified in the regulations. These provided that help could be given only for:

1. immediate relief of distress in the case of fire, flood or similar disaster[61];

[57] Supplementary Benefits Act 1976, s. 4.

[58] During the 1972 miners' strike, the Commission is said to have issued a statement explaining how its officers were instructed to interpret what was then s. 13 of the 1966 Act in relation to single strikers: 'no payment is made to a single person in lodgings unless he can satisfy the officer that he will be evicted straight away if he cannot pay his landlady; and no payments are to be made where a single person lives with his parents unless the parents themselves are in poor circumstances, for example if they are living on supplementary benefit. If a single person lives alone, it will be accepted more readily that he may need money to buy food. If the officer decides to make a payment of supplementary benefit he will bring the person's other resources (including any available capital) up to the level which he considers necessary in the circumstances. In no case, however, is this level to exceed £4 and it may well be less than this' (Lynes 1972: 126–7).

[59] Baroness Young, 409 HL Debs. 1119 (2 June 1980).

[60] Supplementary Benefit (Trade Disputes and Recovery from Earnings) Regulations 1980, SI 1980/1641.

[61] The regulations actually applied 'where any member of the assessment unit is affected by a disaster (for example, a fire or a flood)'. In R(SB)24/85 a Tribunal of Commissioners refused to hold that a complete devastation of the household's ordinary financial arrangements caused by a

2. the extra cost of an exceptionally expensive diet medically prescribed for the striker;
3. fares to visit a partner ill in hospital or a close relative critically ill or dying;
4. essential fares for special transport for a disabled child to and from school;
5. immediate necessities for a baby born during the strike (provided the birth occurs 11 weeks or more after the beginning of the strike);
6. repair, replacement or provision of a substitute (whichever is the cheapest) of household equipment for heating and cooking essential to health or safety.

Payments made under category 1 above may be subject to recovery, as in other urgent need cases, on return to work
(Supplementary Benefits Commission 1981: 72).

V.   REFORM OF SOCIAL SECURITY

A. *General Principles*

In April 1988 the social security system underwent another radical reform. Supplementary benefit was abolished and replaced with what are now called income-related benefits.[62] The 1980 reforms had clearly failed, with the government contending in its Green Paper of 1985 that the supplementary benefit system was still too complex, swamped by the extra additions, and unable to target resources to the most needy as effectively as possible (Department of Health and Social Security 1985: 31). For present purposes the principal benefit of the new regime is income support. The claimant must first normally be of or over the age of 18. Second, the claimant must have no income, or if he does have income, this must not exceed the benefit rate. Thirdly, the claimant must not be engaged in remunerative work, nor must his partner if he is a member of a married or unmarried couple. Finally, except in prescribed circumstances, the claimant must be available for work and actively seeking employment, and must not be receiving relevant education. The Income Support (General) Regulations[63] provide that a number of claimants will not be treated as being available for work. These are the so-called work-incentive rules which effectively exclude from benefit a claimant who, for example, fails without good cause to apply for a vacancy of suitable employment which has been notified to him; or who places unreasonable restrictions on the nature, hours, rate of remuneration or locality or other conditions of employment which he is prepared to accept.

The amount of income support to which a claimant is entitled is set out in the Income Support (General) Regulations. These prescribe a set amount for single claimants, and for a couple. From April 1990 (the time of writing) the weekly amount for a couple where at least one is over the age of 18 is £57.60. An

strike is a disaster. As a result the regulation could not be used to replace shoes which a child had outgrown.
   [62] Social Security Act 1986, Part II, amended by the Social Security Act 1988, and the Social Security Act 1989.
   [63] SI 1987/1967.

additional amount is paid in respect of each child who is a member of the family, the amount varying according to the age of the child. So, for example, for each child aged under 11 years the applicable amount is £12.35, while for each child who is 16 or 17 years old the amount is £21.90 per week at the time of writing. In addition to these basic rates, additional payments may be made. The first is a family premium of £7.35 payable where the claimant is a member of a family of which at least one member is a child or young person. The second is one or more of the additional premiums laid down in the regulations, these being respectively the lone parent premium, the pensioner premium, the higher pensioner premium, the disability premium, the severe disability premium, and the disabled child premium. The third additional payment may be for housing costs, payable mainly for mortgage interest payments in respect of a home occupied by the claimant or his family. No payment is made here for rent costs. This is dealt with separately in the form of housing benefit, eligibility for which is similar to that for income support.

An important departure from supplementary benefit law is that no account is now taken of earnings paid on the termination of employment.[64] As a result, albeit inadvertently as a consequence of the drive for simplicity, the new rules operate less harshly in some respects than did the old. So payment of benefit is not postponed because of the last pay cheque, or because of the payment of wages in hand, or because of the operation of the two-times rule. On the other hand, however, income support is paid in arrears rather than in advance of the benefit period, while the regulations also provide that a claimant affected by a trade dispute is to be treated as engaged in remunerative work (and so ineligible for benefit) 'for the period of seven days following the date on which the stoppage of work due to a trade dispute at his . . . place of work commenced'.[65] So in practice no benefit will be paid under the new rules until the end of the second week of the dispute. Nevertheless, this seems (relatively) more civilized than the position operating before April 1988. The weekly paid worker with no wages in hand will continue to be entitled to benefit for the second week, as will the family of the weekly paid worker who does have a week in hand, even though the wages in hand are actually paid at the end of the first week of the strike. Even more beneficial is the position of the monthly paid worker who will also be entitled to income support at the end of the second week of the strike rather than in the second month of the strike. Any money saved from the salary would be treated as capital. It is thus possible now that benefit will be payable in some circumstances where it would not have been before 1988. Potentially those most likely to benefit would be the family of a salaried earner where the other partner is unemployed or is working for less than twenty-four hours per week.

---

[64] Income Support (General) Regulations 1987, SI 1987/1967, Sch. 8, para. 1, as amended by Income Support (General) Amendment No. 4 Regulations 1988, SI 1988/1445, reg. 24.

[65] Income Support (General Regulations) 1987, reg. 5(4).

B. *The Treatment of Strikers*

The position of strikers under the new arrangements is similar in principle to that which has pertained since 1948, with the 1971 and 1980 amendments having been built into the scheme from birth. Thus, the claimant for income support is disqualified in respect of his own needs.[66] This means that the single striker continues to be disqualified from the receipt of income support, though, as we shall discuss, there may be the possibility of a social fund payment being made.[67] So far as couples are concerned, a reduction is made for each member involved in the dispute. So, for example, if a striker claimed in respect of a couple, only half a couple's applicable amount would be paid. Where there are children, only half the couple's applicable amount would be paid, but the additions for children would continue to be paid, as would any relevant premiums payable in respect of a member of the household other than the person disqualified. So if we take a family of two adults and two children, both aged under 11, then provided that they are eligible, the weekly amount of income support would be £28.80 for the dependant adult (being one half of £57.60), plus £12.35 in respect of each child aged under 11, plus a family premium of £7.35. This would produce a total of £60.85 per week for a family of four with two children aged under 11 (though housing needs are met separately).

This, however, is not the end of the story. For although benefit may be payable, the various discounts must be added into the equation. The first is the notional strike pay introduced in 1980.[68] In 1990 the appropriate amount to be deducted weekly was £19.50, and it remains the case that the discount will be made regardless of whether or not the difference is made up by the union. This would thus reduce the family's entitlement to £41.35, despite the fact that a single adult is deemed to need £36.70 per week and a married couple without children £57.60 per week. Yet further deductions may be made in respect of other income actually received during the dispute. Thus any income tax rebates are to be treated as income and are not to be disregarded.[69] Where the amount exceeds one week's income support, the rebate is spread out by dividing it 'by the amount of income support which would be payable had the payment not been made'.[70] Because the amount of income support, after the claimant's disqualification and the assumed strike pay is knocked off, which would normally be payable will be very small, with the result that an income tax rebate may have to be spread out over a fairly extensive period. It

[66] Social Security Act 1986, s. 23.   [67] See *infra*, pp. 114–16.
[68] Social Security Act 1986, s. 23(5)(b).
[69] Social Security Act 1986, s. 23(5)(a). It would in fact be very unusual for an income tax rebate to be paid during a dispute, because of the operation of the Income and Corporation Taxes Act 1988, s. 204. It may, however, arise where an employer makes a payment despite the dispute; if workers have been dismissed during the dispute; or if a refund has been received during the dispute in respect of a period of earlier unemployment.
[70] Income Support (General) Regulations 1987, reg. 29.

may be noted that in circumstances other than trade disputes, tax refunds are treated as capital rather than income with the result that entitlement to benefit will not be affected.

But it is not only tax refunds which will be taken into account to prejudice benefit entitlement. The Act also provides that any other payment which the claimant or a member of his family receives or is entitled to obtain shall be treated as the claimant's income and shall not be disregarded.[71] So, for example, if a trade union were to pay strike pay at a higher rate than the assumed strike pay, the difference would be taken into account and would go to reduce income support otherwise payable. The same is now true of any emergency relief payments made under the Child Care Act 1980 or the Social Work (Scotland) Act 1968. By section 12 the latter impose a duty on every local authority to promote social welfare by giving advice, guidance and assistance on such a scale as may be appropriate for their area. The assistance may be given in cash or in kind, though before cash is provided to any person, the 'local authority shall have regard to his eligibility for receiving assistance from any other statutory body and, if he is so eligible, to the availability to him of that assistance in his time of need'. Financial assistance may be given unconditionally or may be repayable 'whether in whole or in part, as the local authority may consider reasonable having regard to the means of the person receiving the assistance'.

During the miners' strike in 1984–5, Fife Regional Council's Social Work Department provided financial assistance to a striking miner in order to enable him to meet payments on hire purchase instalments, representing four overdue weekly payments for a child's pushchair (about £7) and one monthly payment for a washing machine. The total payment of £15 was made by way of a loan, to be repaid following the return to work. This payment was treated in turn as income with the result that the recipient was disqualified from receipt of supplementary benefit for the week in question on the basis that his resources exceeded his requirements. The decision of the benefit officer was upheld by a social security appeal tribunal but was eventually overturned by the Social Security Commissioner who substituted a decision that benefit was payable, taking the view that the relevant payment was in the nature of a capital payment rather than income.[72] Although the payment was thus to be taken into account in assessing the claimant's capital resources, it did not affect the claimant's entitlement to benefit in view of the absence of any reckonable capital resources. The draftsman of the new legal framework has responded to this decision by providing in the regulations that in the context of trade disputes any such payment is to be treated as income, and to be fully taken into account, thereby reversing the Commissioner's decision.[73] Apart from trade

[71] Social Security Act 1986, s. 23(5)(a).   [72] *R(SB)29/85.*
[73] Income Support (General) Regulations 1987, reg. 41(3) (and Sch. 9, para. 28), extended by the Family Credit and Income Support (General) Amendment Regulations 1989, SI 1989/1034, reg. 7.

union strike pay and emergency payments from local authorities, other sources of income for those engaged in a long dispute will be charitable donations, whether in cash or in kind. During the miners' strike this was provided by street collections, donations by the trade unions, and from other sources. In its aggressive determination to ensure that all family income is to be set off against benefit, any charitable payments are to be taken into account,[74] as is any income in kind.[75] Again both are normally disregarded, the disregard in the former case being up to £10 weekly.[76]

C. *The Social Fund*

An important part of the government's thinking in remodelling the social welfare system was to reduce the role of the single payments. The government was concerned that these had got out of hand, with expenditure here having doubled at a time when the claimant population had increased by no more than 10 per cent. But although the government's intention was to increase the level of benefit generally so that there would be no need to rely on single payments, it was also accepted that however effective the main structure of income support, there would always be some people who run into particular difficulties or who have special needs which cannot sensibly be met by normal weekly payments (Department of Social Security 1985: 36). The government's answer was to provide a fund, to be known as the Social Fund, with regulations to be made prescribing the payment of maternity expenses and funeral expenses, and to meet other needs in accordance with directives given or guidance issued by the Secretary of State.[77] The question of whether a payment is to be made, and how much, is to be determined by Social Fund officers, specially trained departmental officers, vested with a wide discretion in deciding not only whether to make the payment, but whether it should be made in instalments, and whether it should be repayable. In determining whether or not to make a payment and if so, how much, the Social Fund officer is to have regard to a number of statutory criteria, including 'the nature, extent and urgency of the need' and 'the possibility that some other person or body may wholly or partly meet it'.[78] A particularly controversial feature of the fund is that social security offices are given an annual budget, which they are not permitted to overspend, for some of the purposes to be met from the Social Fund. Officials are required to meet the needs of local people in difficulty and to allocate priority between them.[79]

---

[74] Income Support (General) Regulations 1987, Sch. 9, para. 15, as amended.
[75] Income Support (General) Regulations 1987, Sch. 9, para. 21, as amended.
[76] Income Support (General) Regulations 1987, Sch. 9, para. 15, as amended.
[77] Social Security Act 1986, Part III, as amended by the Social Security Act 1988.
[78] 1986 Act, s. 33(9)(a) and (c).
[79] Cf. *R.* v. *Social Security Fund Inspector, ex parte Sherwin, the Independent*, 23 Feb. 1990. See now Social Security Bill 1990, cl. 15.

So far as the Social Fund is concerned, there are two principal pieces of subordinate legislation, both of which impact to some extent on trade disputes. The first is the Social Fund Maternity and Funeral Expenses (General) Regulations[80] which, as the title suggests, makes provision for Social Fund payments to deal with maternity expenses and funeral expenses. As to the former, a maternity payment is payable to a claimant awarded income support if the claimant or a member of the claimant's family is pregnant, has given birth to a child, or has adopted a child not more than one year old. The claim should normally be made any time from eleven weeks before the expected week of confinement until three months after the actual date of confinement (or adoption). In the case of trade disputes, however, the regulations continue the rule operating under the supplementary benefits regime. Thus where a claimant or the claimant's partner is affected by a trade dispute, a maternity payment shall be made only if the trade dispute has, at the date of the claim for payment, continued for not less than six weeks. This is less punitive than the old rules which provided that the dispute had to have been running for at least eleven weeks before a maternity payment would be made. In contrast to the maternity payment, a payment for funeral expenses will be made to a family where one of the members is engaged in a trade dispute as the need falls, in the same way as it will be made to any other family. It may be noted that in both cases if the claimant has capital of more than £500 this will reduce, and may indeed deny, an entitlement to a Social Fund payment. And in assessing capital, industrial disputants are again penalized to the extent that income tax rebates are treated as a capital resource rather than income.

The other major source of regulation of the Social Fund is the Social Fund Directions issued by the Secretary of State. These provide that Social Fund payments can be used in three cases other than maternity and funeral expenses, these being in the form of budgeting loans, crisis loans, and community care grants. Budgeting loans are to meet intermittent expenses for which it may be difficult to budget, though a large number of items are excluded. In order to qualify for a budgeting loan the claimant or his partner must have been in receipt of income support for the preceding twenty-six weeks. But even if this condition is satisfied, another condition of eligibility is that neither the claimant nor his partner must have been disqualified under section 19 of the Social Security Act 1975 for receiving unemployment benefit. So no budgeting loan from the Social Fund for those out of work because of a dispute. Crisis loans, in contrast, may be available, but only in very limited circumstances. These are generally available only to assist eligible persons (who need not be in receipt of income support but who are without sufficient resources to meet immediate short-term needs) to meet expenses in an emergency or as a consequence of a disaster, but only if such assistance 'is the only means by which serious damage or serious risk to the health or safety of that person, or

---

[80] SI 1987/481, as subsequently amended.

to a member of his family, may be prevented'. But for those subject to the trade dispute disqualification, a crisis loan is not available to meet all serious damage or obvious risk to health or safety. In such a case, 'the expenses for which a crisis loan might otherwise be awarded are limited to (a) expenses which are a consequence of a disaster; and (b) expenses, outside (a), in respect of items required for the purpose only of cooking or space heating (including fire-guards)'.

Community care grants exist to help people to remain in or return to the community rather than an institution. They may also be made to an eligible person or a member of his family to help with expenses of travel within the UK to visit someone who is ill, attend a relative's funeral, ease a domestic crisis, visit a child who is with the other parent pending a custody decision, or move to suitable accommodation. The only condition of eligibility generally is that the applicant should be in receipt of income support at the date of the application. In the case of trade disputes, however, the position is rather different. Thus, if the visit is made by a partner or dependant who is not affected by the trade dispute, an award may be made in respect of travelling expenses for:

(i) a visit to a patient who is a close relative or who was prior to his admission to hospital or similar institution a member of the same household; or

(ii) a visit to a person who is a close relative or who was prior to his illness a member of the same household as the visitor, and is critically ill but not in hospital or similar institution.

Where the visit is made by the striker or the person laid off or locked out by the trade dispute, an award may be made in respect of travelling expenses for:

(i)   a visit to a partner in hospital or similar institution; or

(ii)   a visit to a dependant in hospital or similar institution, if the person affected by the trade dispute has no partner living with him who would be eligible for an award within paragraph (a) of this direction, or the partner is also in hospital or similar institution; or

(iii)   a visit to a critically ill close relative or member of the household of the person affected by the trade dispute, whether or not he is in hospital or similar institution.

So a striker whose family is on income support may be eligible for a community care grant to visit a partner in hospital, but not a parent (unless critically ill), nor, significantly, a child (unless also critically ill). Before leaving the issue it may be noted again that if the claimant has capital of more than a prescribed amount of £500 this will reduce and may indeed deny the entitlement to a community care grant.

VI. CONCLUSION

Policy on the payment of social welfare to strikers has been inspired throughout the twentieth century by the *Merthyr Tydfil* decision of 1900. This was based on the premiss that neither the rate-payer nor the taxpayer should be required to subsidize those voluntarily unemployed and able to support themselves. But of course in the post-war period not everyone penalized was in this position for the scope of the disqualification (following the trade dispute disqualification from unemployment benefit) was so wide that it operated against those with a presumed rather than an actual community of interest with those in dispute. Since 1975 the scope of the disqualification here has admittedly been narrowed in line with the unemployment benefit reforms, so that perhaps some of the more outrageous aspects of the scope of the disqualification have been qualified. But this has been met by the more punitive treatment of those still afflicted by the disqualification, treatment which the Labour administrations of the 1970s did not see fit to modify. For it is to be kept in mind that these new punitive features of the scheme operate to deny the minimum level of subsistence to people in dispute and their families despite the fact that the individual affected may be the victim of unlawful or unreasonable conduct on the part of the employer, or may be the innocent victim of someone else's dispute. This seems hard to justify, particularly when it is recalled that the so-called voluntarily unemployed not engaged in a dispute (those dismissed for industrial misconduct), while penalized, are not denied benefit altogether, nor are their families punished. And it is even harder to justify when it is recalled that even the Court of Appeal in the *Merthyr Tydfil* case accepted that in some circumstances a 'workman' was justified 'as between him and the rate-payers' to refuse to work under the terms imposed by the employer. But if the blanket disqualification of those interested in a dispute may be unjustifiable, the current treatment of strikers' families seems downright wicked, and can be explained only as designed to reduce the number and length of disputes by a policy of starvation or the fear thereof.

[7]
The Social Welfare Tribunal in Ireland

I. INTRODUCTORY

Britain is not alone in imposing unemployment benefit and social welfare penalties on people who participate in a trade dispute, or who are affected by it. Indeed, in some jurisdictions the penalties are even wider. This would be true, for example, of the disqualification which operates in Australia, Canada, and some parts of the United States. In other jurisdictions, on the other hand, the disqualification is not as extensive, with the process of reform having been taken even further than the 1975 reforms in Britain. This is particularly true of the Republic of Ireland, all the more fascinating for the fact that the Irish inherited and adopted the British framework for unemployment benefit.[1] The purpose of this chapter is to describe this Irish initiative which was introduced by the Social Welfare (No. 2) Act 1982, and to consider how it has operated in practice. Section II sets out the trade disqualification rules operating before 1982 and examines the pressure for reform. Section III consists of an examination of the detailed provisions of the Act and the procedural regulations relating thereto. Section IV deals with aspects of how the law has operated in practice, looking in particular at the work of the Social Welfare Tribunal, the body set up to deal with applications for adjudication.

II. BACKGROUND TO THE LEGISLATION

The Irish law on the trade dispute disqualification has been very similar to the British. Indeed, the practice to date has been to adopt British statutory liberalizing measures, though usually several years after they have been implemented here.[2] The law is currently to be found in the Social Welfare (Consolidation) Act 1981 which as originally enacted provided by section 35(1):

---

[1] One major difference relates to the multiplicity of schemes for the relief of unemployment in Ireland, similar in many ways to the position in Britain in the 1930s. Thus apart from the insurance-based unemployment benefit scheme, there also operates an unemployment assistance scheme for people with an inadequate insurance record, or for people who have exhausted entitlement to unemployment benefit (Clark 1985).

[2] For a full account, see Kerr and Whyte (1985); Clark (1985a).

A person who has lost employment by reason of a stoppage of work which was due to a trade dispute at the factory, workshop, farm or other premises or place at which he was employed shall be disqualified for receiving unemployment benefit so long as the stoppage of work continues, except in a case where he has, during the stoppage of work, become *bona fide* employed elsewhere in the occupation which he usually follows or has become regularly engaged in some other occupation.

This was subject to the following proviso which had been introduced in 1952:

Provided that the foregoing provisions of this subsection shall not apply to a person who—
(a) is not participating in or financing or directly interested in the trade dispute which caused the stoppage of work, and
(b) does not belong to a grade or class of workers, of which, immediately before the commencement of the stoppage, there were members employed at his place of employment any of whom are participating in or financing or directly interested in the dispute.[3]

The term 'trade dispute' was defined in turn to mean 'any dispute between employers and employees, or between employees and employees, which is connected with the employment or non-employment or the terms of employment or the conditions of employment of any persons, whether employees in the employment of the employer with whom the dispute arises or not.'[4]

This formula—which it will be noted was similar to the British legislation before the 1975 amendments—was to contribute to the controversy surrounding two trade disputes in 1982.[5] The first and most significant was the Clover Meats dispute where the company had two factories in Waterford, one processing beef, and the other pigmeat. The dispute arose when the company announced an intention to close the beef factory and to lay off the workers employed there. The union (ITGWU) objected to this, arguing that the lay-off should apply to workers at both plants on the basis of seniority, a proposal to which the company objected because it would be inefficient if they were to lay off pigmeat workers to replace them with beef workers who would need to be retrained. When the parties were unable to agree, and when the employees refused to 'submit to [the] rationalisation programme',[6] the employer responded by dismissing the 356 workers employed at both plants. The workers then claimed unemployment benefit, but were held by the adjudicating authorities to be disqualified. In the view of the deciding officer, 'there was a trade dispute that had led to the stoppage of work even though no industrial action was taken or threatened' (Kerr and Whyte 1985: 364–5). In the High Court, McMahon J. refused to grant an order of mandamus directing the

---

[3] The 'financing' and 'grade or class' limbs of the disqualification were removed by the Social Welfare (No. 2) Act 1987, s. 13.
[4] A similar disqualification operates in respect of unemployment assistance (Kerr and Whyte 1985: 363).
[5] This paragraph draws heavily on Clark (1985a) to which I am greatly indebted.
[6] P. Gallacher, 334 *Dáil Debates* 574 (6 May 1982).

Minister to pay unemployment benefit. The Court took the view that the dismissal of the employees was the result of a failure by the union to agree on a formula to decide who would be retained in the pigmeat factory. This failure to agree constituted a trade dispute, and it was this dispute which had led to the stoppage of work (Clark 1985a: 662–3). But although the workers were thus without a legal remedy, the matter was not left unresolved. According to Clark, the dispute was 'controversial', located in a marginal constituency, and at a time of 'great political uncertainty'. This, it seems, led the Fianna Fáil government to agree to pay the workforce 'their respective social welfare "entitlements" from the date of dismissal until the resumption of work ten weeks later' (Clark 1985a: 663), a cost to the government of £186,000. The payments were made by the Department of Agriculture and not from the social welfare budget, as part of a rescue package for the company.[7]

Apart from making this financial contribution to the workers affected, the government also gave an undertaking to amend the legislation. Apparently both the Prime Minister and the Minister for Finance had given 'a very clear commitment' to amend the trade dispute disqualification 'to ensure that workers who were deprived of their employment in similar circumstances would get their unemployment benefit'. The Minister for Social Welfare, Dr Michael Woods, was reminded of this on 6 May 1982, and also of the fact that the promise was that the law would be altered 'forthwith'. The case for reform was now more urgent in view of the dispute at Comer International where ninety-seven workers employed by a large multinational had been disqualified. Here the circumstances were rather different from Clover Meats. On 26 February the work-force had participated in an unofficial strike, but following the intervention of the union the workers agreed to return to work on 15 March and to process their grievance through the normal procedures. When they reported for work on that day, they were forbidden access to the plant until an agreement had been reached on various matters 'to ensure the effective operation of the Company'. These various matters consisted of no less than fifteen changes to employment conditions, including a reduction in manning levels, increased productivity (without increased pay), reduced bonuses, smaller than average annual pay rises, and reduced holidays. Not surprisingly these demands were resisted and the dispute was not settled until 30 June 1982, with work resuming on a phased basis from 15 July. There was some concern that these workers were also being unfairly treated, and one Deputy took the liberty to remind Dr Woods in the Dáil on 6 May that 'Just because there is no election campaign at present they should not be left without payment', referring by implication to the suggestion that the Clover Meats case had been settled for reasons of political expediency during an election.

[7]   334 *Dáil Debates* 577 (6 May 1982).

III.   THE SOCIAL WELFARE (NO. 2) ACT 1982

A. *Proceedings in Parliament*

The Bill to amend the law was introduced in the Dáil, with the Second Stage and all remaining stages taking place on 15 July 1982, and with the proceedings in the Seanad taking place on 22 July 1982, following which the Bill was passed.[8] In introducing the measure the responsible Minister, Dr Woods, acknowledged the principle that unemployment resulting directly from a trade dispute in which the claimant is involved should not give him a title to unemployment benefit. This principle, which had been a feature of Irish law since 1911 and was a feature of unemployment insurance systems generally, was based on a belief that the social insurance fund should be neutral in relation to disputes. The Minister was satisfied that this general principle of disqualification was 'a sound one', but was not convinced that it should apply automatically in the case of all disputes, for 'all trade disputes are not the same'. The existing blanket disqualification of workers engaged in a trade dispute was 'unduly harsh and inequitable', a judgment reinforced by the Clover Meats and the Comer International disputes. But for all its harshness, the Minister was nevertheless concerned to emphasize the rather limited goals of his proposed reforms. Thus, the Bill would not 'involve any change in the existing situation whereby unemployment benefit or assistance is not payable where industrial action in the traditional sense is taken by employees'.

What, then, was the government's intention as to when benefit would be paid? In essence, it seems that eligibility would be reinstated only where workers were locked out by an employer who refused to comply with good industrial relations practice, or who was seeking to impose new terms on his work-force. Thus, according to Dr Woods, the Bill was 'designed only to redress the situation where workers are available for work, capable of work and willing to work but are deprived of their employment in what might be regarded as an unfair manner'. This question would be determined by a specially created tribunal which would be independent of the normal social welfare machinery, and would be tripartite in nature, representing the interests of employers and employees. The tribunal would be vested with wide discretionary powers to determine whether the workers involved had been 'unreasonably deprived of their employment', and while it would be charged with the duty of 'investigating the manner in which workers had been deprived of their employment and all the circumstances surrounding this', there was no intention that the tribunal should adjudicate 'on the merits or demerits of the fundamental industrial relations problems at issue'. This fine and perhaps

---

[8]   The debates of the Dáil are at 337 *Dáil Debates* 2611–42; 2883–929 (15 July 1982) (all stages). The debates of the Seanad are at 98 *Seanad Debates* (1390–1411) (all stages). The discussion in this section draws freely on the reports of these proceedings.

invisible line between examining the manner of depriving workers of their employment, and the merits of the dispute, not surprisingly attracted some scepticism from other members of the Dáil. The distinction was hardly clarified by an amendment to the Bill in Committee which directed the tribunal to have regard to the question 'whether the conduct of the applicant or of a trade union acting on his behalf was reasonable'.

Yet despite the ostensibly modest proposals of the government, the Bill was vigorously criticized by the Fine Gael opposition. First, a number of objections were taken to the political circumstances leading up to the introduction of the Bill, it being alleged that the measure was the result of a commitment to the Workers' Party, on whose support the government relied, without any regard to the overall consequences for the country. Secondly, from this, concern was expressed about the potentially damaging economic consequences of the measure, with one leading spokesman pointing out that the measure might serve only to encourage and prolong strikes. While it was accepted that there were hard cases under the existing law, concern was also expressed that the Bill might be used and abused for purposes other than those intended. In reply a supporter of the Bill said that 'If it is fair to say that the social welfare laws should not prolong strikes or assist strikers, then it is equally fair comment that the law should not be used to help an employer to impose detrimental working conditions on his employees'. The third concern, though important and significant, was as speculative and as uncertain as the second. This was the fear that the Bill would undermine the work of the existing agencies set up to provide a voluntary system for the conciliation and settlement of disputes (in Ireland the Labour Court, Rights' Commissioners, and conciliation services)[9] and that as a result 'tried and tested industrial relations procedures' would be 'thrown out the door'. Thus, it was pointed out that the tribunal created by the Bill would decide on the reasonableness of an employer's behaviour in a trade dispute. Having secured a determination that the employer acted unreasonably, why would a trade union bother discussing the matter any further at the Labour Court? The danger was that a tribunal determination would simply serve to harden attitudes and create rigidity on both sides, making the dispute more difficult to settle.

B. *The Substance of the Legislation*

The 1982 Act amends the Social Welfare (Consolidation) Act 1981, Ireland's principal social security statute.[10] The amendment provides that where a person is adjudged by the responsible authorities to be disqualified from unemployment benefit or unemployment assistance,[11] he may apply to the

---

[9] For an account of the work of these agencies, see Kerr and Whyte (1985: ch. 13).

[10] The 1982 Act adds new ss. 301A and 301B to the 1981 Act. The substantive provisions, referred to in the section, are all contained in s. 301A.

[11] See nn. 1 and 4 above. Although the trade dispute disqualification applies also to supplement-

newly created Social Welfare Tribunal for an adjudication. In making its adjudication, the tribunal has a wide discretion in determining whether or not benefit should be paid, the Minister explaining that it was necessary 'not to tie the tribunal's hands with regard to the matters which they should consider in arriving at their adjudication'. This flexibility was, however, a cause of criticism in the Dáil, with what was seen as a strength by the Minister being seen by others as a great weakness: thus the complaint was made that there are 'no substantive provisions telling the tribunal when they should or should not adjudicate in favour of an employee', and that 'Legislation establishing a tribunal should contain strict and definitive provisions that determine the manner in which the tribunal should make decisions'. Indeed the same speaker went so far as to claim that the measures were 'Kafkaesque in the extreme', to the extent that an employer 'might find himself trying to justify his actions before the tribunal without knowing what criteria at the end of the day the tribunal would apply in determining his case one way or the other'. It may be noted at this stage that the employer is not only entitled to be present, but may in fact be compelled to make submissions even though the legal question essentially is one between the claimant and the Minister of Social Welfare.

But what was the reason for the rather extraordinary parliamentary language, which does not sit very comfortably with the Minister's claim that this was a 'limited', 'specific', and 'exceptional' measure which 'applies only to people who want to go back, but who are locked out and cannot get unemployment benefit'? In fact the legislation is very much wider than the Minister suggested, without necessarily deserving the exaggerated epithets of the deputies. Under the Act the tribunal is required first to 'take into account all the circumstances of the stoppage of work concerned and of the trade dispute which caused the stoppage of work'. Without limiting the generality of this provision, the tribunal is directed to have regard to four matters in particular, the first three of which are concerned with the conduct of the employer. These are as follows:

(i) the question whether the applicant is or was available for work and willing to work, but is or was deprived of his employment through some act or omission on the part of the employer concerned which amounted to unfair or unjust treatment of the applicant,

(ii) the question whether the applicant is or was prevented by the employer from attending for work at his place of employment or was temporarily laid off by the employer, without (in either such case) any reasonable or adequate consultation by the employer with the applicant or with a trade union acting on his behalf, or without (in either case) the use by the employer or by any body acting on his behalf of the services normally availed of by employers in the interests of good industrial relations,

(iii) the question whether any action or decision by the employer, amounting to a worsening of the terms or conditions of employment of the applicant

ary welfare allowance and family income supplement, the Social Welfare Tribunal has no jurisdiction to entertain claims from strikers in respect of these payments.

and taken without any or any adequate consultation with, or any or any adequate notice to, the applicant, was a cause of the stoppage of work or of the trade dispute which caused the stoppage of work and was material grounds for such stoppage or such trade dispute.

These are the three factors to be taken into account by the tribunal contained in the Bill submitted by the Department to the Dáil. Although this looks very much like an attempt to legislate with particular disputes in mind, nevertheless the drafting is clumsy, with the result that a number of questions remain to be considered. First, it is not at all clear why the second of the three matters is included. For the most part the questions under (ii) are almost certainly covered by (i). So if an employer locks out or lays off an employee without any adequate consultation or without notice, surely this would be a deprivation of employment which amounted to unfair or unjust treatment of the applicant. Admittedly the employer's action may be defensive, so that in principle the tribunal could award the payment of benefit even though the employer was neither unjust nor unfair; the fact that he has locked out without notice or consultation in principle would seem to be enough to allow benefit to be paid. Yet although this would appear to have been possible under the Bill as originally drafted, it must now be remote following an Opposition-inspired amendment which requires the tribunal to have regard to 'the question whether the conduct of the applicant or of a trade union acting on his behalf was reasonable'. But even without this amendment, the tribunal already had the power to refuse benefit in a defensive lock-out where the employer has failed to give notice or consult. The itemized matters are presented as questions which the tribunal must take into account in exercising its wider discretionary powers; the tribunal is in no sense bound by them.

Also interesting is the third of the issues to which the attention of the tribunal is directed. The fact that this body is empowered to make an adjudication where a stoppage of work (whether a strike or a lock-out) was caused by the action of an employer intending to 'worsen' terms and conditions of employment indicates clearly that the Bill was not designed to deal only with lock-outs in exceptional cases as the Minister had suggested. At the very least the Act applies in order to allow benefit to be paid in the case of defensive strikes, provoked by the conduct of the employer. Indeed it is possible that the jurisdiction of the tribunal would extend to allow an adjudication to be made in favour of workers if they were struggling to improve their terms and conditions of employment. As one deputy argued:

We all know that a worsening of the terms or conditions of employment could mean for instance, an increase in wages, less than an increase in wages in a comparable employment, or an increase in wages less than the increase in the consumer price index over the period.

This point was made by way of criticism of the Bill because it could lead to benefit being paid in circumstances where wage rises are being held down in a particular industry in the interest of competitiveness. The point was also made that 'the State will end up subsidising strikes in pursuit of claims for increases in wages which are in excess of the Government's guidelines on what the country can afford'. But whether or not the specific duty to have regard to the employer's attempt to worsen terms and conditions would permit benefit to be paid in the case of a dispute designed to increase wages, it is clear that the general powers of the tribunal are wide enough to allow an adjudication in favour of workers in the case of a regular strike for the improvement of terms and conditions, where it would be reasonable to do so. This is despite the firm commitment by the Minister that his Bill did 'not involve any change in the existing situation whereby unemployment benefit or assistance is not payable where industrial action in the traditional sense is taken by employees'.

C. *Procedural Questions*

The members of the Social Welfare Tribunal are appointed by the Minister of Social Welfare, for 'such period as is specified by the Minister' when appointing each member.[12] There is no restriction in the legislation about the reappointment of members on the expiry of their terms, though members have no right to be reappointed and may indeed be removed from office by the Minister before their term expires. The tribunal consists of a chairman and four ordinary members, two of whom are nominated by the Irish Congress of Trade Unions, and the other two by employers' organizations. There is no requirement that the chairman should be legally qualified, and indeed the government successfully resisted an opposition amendment that the chairman should be a High Court or Circuit Court judge. This was moved in order to 'guarantee total impartiality' by someone above and beyond the vested interests in a dispute, but was rejected by most of the people who spoke in the debate. Several deputies thought that a member of the judicial branch would be unsuitable because of lack of experience in industrial relations, while the government was of the view that although some judges might have a suitable background in industrial relations, they might not always be available. In the government's view there were other people with the 'right sort of experience for the position' who would be 'seen clearly as being objective, independent and impartial and having sound judgment as well as being reasonably well versed in industrial relations procedures'. In fact the first chairman, Mr Bill Farrell, is a retired civil servant of distinction, having held a senior position in the Department of Labour.

The tribunal can take an application only if a deciding officer and an appeals officer have decided that the applicant is disqualified from receiving unemployment benefit or unemployment assistance because of the trade dispute. This means that the normal claims and adjudication process must be exhausted

---

[12] The material dealt with in this section is to be found mainly in the new section 301B of the 1981 Act, and in the Social Welfare (Social Welfare Tribunal) Regulations 1982 (SI 309/1982).

before the tribunal may assume jurisdiction. The Minister was concerned 'to ensure that the existing machinery would be used as the first resort' and that 'the existing means would be fully utilised before recourse to the tribunal'. It seems remarkable that this procedure should be exhausted even in cases where the disqualification would obviously apply and where an appeal might not otherwise be thought worthwhile. The inevitable cost is unnecessary delay in adjudications being made by the Social Welfare Tribunal. Not surprisingly at least one concerned deputy said that he

should have preferred to see a simpler Bill and one that would short-circuit the system. Problems of this kind are urgent and do not lend themselves to prolonged references to appeals officers, deciding officers and tribunals. The procedure should be speeded up. Nothing hinders the settlement of a dispute as much as delays in the machinery which is available for its settlement. Sometimes that machinery becomes overloaded and cannot deal with the problem as quickly as it might.[13]

The problem of delay is one to which we shall return. In the meantime we may note that an application must be made within twenty-one days of the appeals officer's decision that the trade dispute disqualification applies.[14]

The application must be made on an approved form and must be accompanied by a statement of the facts and contentions on which the applicant intends to rely. On receiving the application the secretary to the tribunal must inform the Minister that an application has been made and must also send the employer concerned a copy of the statement submitted by the applicant. The employer is required within fourteen days of receiving a copy of the applicant's statement to 'enter an appearance to the proceedings by sending to the Secretary to the Tribunal a statement showing to what extent the facts and contentions advanced by the applicant are admitted or disputed'. This places the employer in the rather extraordinary position of having to be a party to the proceedings even though the legal dispute is essentially one between the applicant and the Ministry. The employer has no direct financial interest in the matter yet for all practical purposes appears as the defendant before the tribunal.[15] Although the tribunal appears free to proceed even though the employer fails to enter a notice of appearance, his attendance, and the

[13] 337 *Dáil Debates* 2627–8 (15 July 1982).
[14] The tribunal also has a discretion to accept an application at any time. The tribunal has not yet refused to accept an application which was made outside the 21-day period. In *A 4/84* an application was accepted in November 1984 in respect of a period of disqualification from 1–10 Mar. 1983. The date of the appeals officer's decision is not known. The tribunal accepted jurisdiction 'in the special circumstances of the case', having regard also 'to the fact that the relevant legislation was comparatively new'. *A 3/84* was also accepted out of time, as was *A 1/89*. All three cases involved the extension of earlier adjudications to other workers affected by the same dispute.
[15] In one case the employer's representatives said they wished to advise the tribunal that they would not be assuming the traditional role of employer as adopted at, say, hearings of the Labour Court or the Employment Appeals Tribunal. The company would neither support nor oppose the union's position in relation to śocial welfare benefits. The company was present to answer any questions and to assist the tribunal in its task of making an adjudication (*A 2/82*).

production of any relevant documents, can be compelled. Failure to comply with either of these obligations when required to do so is a criminal offence, with a guilty offender being liable on summary conviction to a fine not exceeding £100.[16] The desirability of involving the employer in this coercive way was, not surprisingly, challenged in the Dáil. Thus, if an application for a tribunal adjudication is made while the dispute still exists, '[a]n employer faced with an industrial dispute may be forced into a confrontation with his or her workforce when the use of conciliation might be more effective. Conversely, if the hearing takes place and the adjudication is made after the dispute has ended, the employer may be obliged to exhume material which in the interests of good industrial relations would be best left buried.'

The procedure at the hearing has been described as 'informality consistent with proper order', with the members of the tribunal and the parties seated around a table. Under the regulations, any party to an application may make an opening statement; call witnesses; cross-examine any witnesses called by the other side; give evidence on his own behalf; and address the tribunal at the close of the evidence. And under the legislation, the tribunal is empowered to take evidence on oath and to administer oaths to persons attending as witnesses, though it has not yet been necessary for this to have been done in any of the cases heard up until the end of 1989. As we have already seen, the primary legislation also gives the tribunal the power to compel the attendance of witnesses and the production of documents. Again, it has not been necessary to use these powers, though reluctant employers have been made aware of them in appropriate cases. Finally, on the procedure at the hearing, the regulations provide expressly that parties summoned to attend a hearing may appear or be heard in person, or may be represented by counsel or a solicitor, or by a representative of a trade union or an employers' association. With the leave of the tribunal parties may be represented by any other person. In practice, legal representation has been rare, having been resorted to only on six occasions (four times by applicants and twice by employers). In practice applicants are represented by full-time union officers and employers by a representative of the Federation of Irish Employers or by a company manager.

Once the tribunal has heard the evidence presented to it and any representations made by the applicant and the employer, it is in a position to 'decide whether the applicant is or was unreasonably deprived of his employment' and, if so, whether he shall 'be qualified to receive unemployment benefit or unemployment assistance and (where appropriate) for what period he shall be so qualified'. An adjudication in favour of the applicant is subject to the proviso

---

[16] There are a few cases where employers have not appeared. In *A 10/83* the employer was not represented at the first of two hearings because of the unavailability of his representative; while in *A 1/89* the employer was not present because he had already given evidence in relation to the dispute which had been the subject of an earlier adjudication. In one interesting case, *A 2/85*, the applicant claimed that he had been laid off because of the unreasonable conduct of the union in calling an all-out strike in support of a group of workers in dispute. The employer was not represented though the union was. The claim failed.

that the other conditions for the receipt of benefit or assistance are satisfied. Under the regulations these decisions may be taken by a majority of the members of the tribunal. The tribunal never discloses whether a decision is unanimous or reached by a majority, however, though it does publish reasons for its decisions despite being under no formal obligation to do so. The only legal obligations on the tribunal are that its decisions be recorded in a document signed by the chairman, which in turn, is entered in a Register of Adjudications, with copies of the decision being sent to the Minister, the applicant, the employer, and to any other interested party. An appeal lies to the High Court on a question of law, despite the fact that adjudications are declared by the Act to be 'final and conclusive'. It is not clear who may lodge an appeal: clearly the applicant and the Minister may do so as parties to the legal dispute, but it is not clear if the employer can. Happily, until now the matter has been academic since no appeals have been lodged. And despite the 'final and conclusive' terms of the Act, cases may also be reconsidered by the tribunal itself in the sense that an interested person (including the Minister) may apply for a review of a decision. If the tribunal is satisfied that a material change has occurred in the circumstances of the stoppage of work or of the trade dispute which caused the stoppage, it may adjudicate on the matter afresh. A review may also take place if new evidence or facts come to light.

IV.   THE ACT IN OPERATION

A. *Introductory*

Between the date of commencement of the Social Welfare (No. 2) Act 1982 and 31 December 1989, forty-seven cases were referred to the tribunal for adjudication.[17] Perhaps their most striking feature is the extent to which the tribunal has not seen fit to develop the jurisdiction beyond the terms of reference set by the government. In the first place, the cases confirm that benefit is 'not payable where industrial action in the traditional sense is taken by employees' despite the wide terms of the Act. The third case dealt with by the tribunal, *A 1/83*, concerned a claim for recognition by ASTMS on behalf of six supervisory and clerical staff at Shamrock Forge & Tool Co. Ltd. The request was rejected initially and the union responded by organizing a sit-in at the premises from 4 October 1982. It appears that the tribunal was called upon to adjudicate on the question of benefit for four workers who took part in the action. The claim was rejected, with the tribunal holding that 'the applicant was, by his own choice, not available for work or willing to work—unless the claim [for recognition] was conceded . . . and there is no evidence to show that the employer concerned unreasonably prevented him from resuming work'. Similarly, in a later case,

---

[17] For a discussion of the tribunal's case-load, see Clark (1985*a*); Kerr and Whyte (1985); and Whyte (1987).

A 11/85, clerical workers organized by the National Engineering and Electrical Trades' Union (NEETU) took industrial action in connection with management's redundancy proposals. A picket line was placed at the company's premises which the applicant craftsmen, also members of NEETU, refused to cross. The tribunal rejected the application, taking the view that the applicants had shown by their action that they were not available or willing to work so long as the strike lasted. Nor was there any evidence to show that the strike was justified by unreasonableness on the part of the employer.

Before proceeding to discuss the cases in which the tribunal has assumed jurisdiction, a few points may be made about the approach it adopts. First, a remarkable feature of the case-law is the tribunal's lack of concern to examine the merits of the dispute, again faithful to the goals set by the government. So in *A 2/87* the tribunal reminded the parties that it was 'not concerned with the merits of the dispute', and only rarely has it departed from this position. One possible example is *A 5/83* where the applicants were held to be entitled to resist new terms imposed by management, the tribunal being influenced by the union's argument that a requirement of 'immediate redundancy' as part of these terms 'contravened the provisions of the Redundancy Payments Act and the Minimum Notice and Terms of Employment Act'. Related to this is a second point, that the principal concern of the tribunal has been with the procedures adopted by the parties—to the exclusion of almost every other consideration. Here the tribunal will determine whether the dispute has arisen because of the employer's failure to consult; because of the employer's failure to consult or negotiate in a reasonable manner; or because of a failure to refer the dispute to independent third parties for adjudication. Also relevant is the conduct of the union, in particular whether the union has been too ready to resort to industrial action without first resorting to dispute procedures. This takes us to the third point, which is perhaps inevitable given this approach, which is that the tribunal approaches each case on its merits, with the doctrine of precedent having no application (to the extent that there is not a single instance of the tribunal in one case referring to an adjudication in another dispute).

In practice the tribunal deals with a small number of potential causes for dispute, most of them relating to employees engaged in some form of defensive action. The main categories dealt with by the tribunal are as follows:

1. Applications by workers laid off for taking industrial action against an employer who is seeking to impose new working practices, introduce new technology, or rationalize production techniques.

2. Applications by workers laid off or locked out for taking various forms of industrial action in support of colleagues who have been disciplined or dismissed.

3. Applications by workers who have been laid off because of someone else's dispute, and who have been disqualified from benefit because they were either

financing the dispute or directly interested in it, or because they were caught by the grade or class provision.[18]

4. Applications by workers in the Comer International type of case. That is to say, from workers who are willing to return after the cause of the original dispute has been removed, but who have been presented with new terms by the employer before work is permitted to restart.

B. *New Working Practices*

Easily the largest number of cases before the tribunal are those arising from management attempts to change working conditions. In determining whether or not benefit is payable in such cases, three major considerations have arisen. The first is whether the employer has tried to negotiate with the workers affected. So in *A 3/87* an agreement was reached between three companies and the ITGWU on a rationalization scheme for the various plants operated by the three companies. The actual details of the new arrangements were to be negotiated at local level for each plant, but at one plant the chief executive of the new company set down new terms and conditions which were not negotiable. When they were rejected by the work-force, the plant was closed, and the staff were laid off until the dispute was resolved some six weeks later. The workers, being disqualified from unemployment benefit, applied to the Social Welfare Tribunal which held in their favour, and in its adjudication made an important statement of principle:

Good industrial relations principles require that employers in seeking to effect signific-ant changes in terms and/or conditions of employment for their employees should ensure that adequate consultation on the proposals takes place with the workers concerned and that, failing agreement, the proposals be processed through accepted procedures, including if necessary a reference to a third party, e.g. the Labour Court, prior to the implementation of the proposed changes.

After considering all the evidence, the tribunal concluded that the employer had failed to adhere to these principles and that the applicants had been unreasonably deprived of their employment.

A second consideration is whether the employer, in seeking to negotiate with the work-force, has done so reasonably. Thus, the tribunal will take into account whether the employer has made his position sufficiently clear, whether he has provided enough information to the union, and enough time for proper collective bargaining to take place. So, in *A 1/85*, the company had decided that if its long-term viability was to be secured, certain changes in relation to its investment, marketing and bonus scheme were essential. A report, with recommendations on the bonus scheme, was received by the company from a body called the Irish Productivity Centre on 1 January 1984, with a summary

---

[18] Both the 'financing' and 'grade or class' limbs of the disqualification were finally repealed in Ireland in 1987: Social Welfare (No. 2) Act 1987, s. 13. For an account of the background to this, see Whyte (1986a: 136).

being furnished to the union on 27 April 1984. Negotiations on the proposals did not begin until June, and as little progress had been made in the initial stages, the company declared its intention of implementing the proposals as from 11 June. When the union refused to co-operate, the company announced that it was closing the factory from 15 June, a decision deferred until 22 June following the unsuccessful intervention of the Labour Court. It was held that in these circumstances the employees had been unreasonably deprived of their employment. This was principally because greater use could have been made of the five-month period of January–June 1984 to process the proposed new bonus scheme through normal industrial relations procedures. The tribunal also pointed out that as a result of this delay in opening formal talks with the union, the negotiations which did take place, including the Labour Court's investigation, were conducted in an atmosphere of crisis. Reference was also made to the fact that the union bore no responsibility for the delay in processing the IPC's proposed scheme.

Apart from the question whether negotiations have taken place and whether they have been conducted in a reasonable way, an additional consideration is whether the employer has sought third-party intervention where negotiations have broken down. In *A 2/83* the employer secured the agreement of one union to introduce some changes to work practices. When the members of another union refused to operate the new procedures they were laid off and not given work until the dispute was resolved a month later. In deciding that benefit should be paid, the tribunal observed that neither the union nor the employer had proposed that the subject-matter of the dispute should be referred to a third party for consideration and recommendation, though such a course would have been consistent with normal procedures for settling disputes. On the question of where responsibility for initiating such a move rested, the tribunal took the view that 'since it was the Company that was seeking to have the new procedures introduced, there was an obligation on Management to ensure that all normal negotiating procedures had been exhausted before the extreme step of lay-off was taken'. This obligation of the employer to bring in a third party to resolve a dispute has been confirmed in a later case. It goes without saying, perhaps, that when a third party such as the Labour Court has been approached, it would be unreasonable for the employer to fail to wait for the Labour Court to conclude its business. Similarly, it has been held to be unreasonable for the employer to fail to comply with a Labour Court recommendation or to seek to enforce such a recommendation where there is a genuine element of doubt as to precisely what the Court did recommend.

C.   *Discipline and Dismissal*

In discipline and dismissal disputes, the role of procedures has also been the crucially determining factor. So the lack of good industrial relations practices on the part of the employer will tend towards an adjudication in favour of applicants. This is illustrated by *A 5/86* (a case involving a non-union shop) where six employees were summarily dismissed. The other workers refused to start work and requested a meeting with the management to discuss the dismissal. This request was refused, but management did meet with the workers to inform them that unless they resumed work they would be dismissed. When the workers refused to do so and renewed their request for a discussion on the dismissals, they were dismissed. The tribunal appeared to have little difficulty in deciding for the applicants:

In the first place, there was a summary dismissal of six employees without prior and full investigation of all the facts concerning the alleged offences, together with, the Tribunal believes, a failure by Management to adhere to basic procedures, dictated by considerations of natural justice and good industrial relations, before a decision to dismiss was taken. Secondly, there was a sustained refusal by Management to accede to repeated requests for a discussion on a matter which clearly had serious implications for the workforce in general. The circumstances surrounding the six dismissals clearly gave the Applicants, in the opinion of the Tribunal, a genuine and legitimate interest in seeking clarification of their terms of employment.

The tribunal continued by pointing out that if management had adhered to the principles of natural justice and good personnel practice in executing the dismissals, and if it had responded to the reasonable requests for discussion, its 'decision in this case would have been different'.

But just as defective procedures on the employer's part may lead to an adjudication in favour of the employees, so bad practice on the part of the employees will lead to a refusal to decide in their favour. The point is illustrated by a number of cases, including *A 2/88*, where a probationary employee of Dunnes Stores was given a week's notice of dismissal for alleged unsatisfactory performance. During the period of the notice a local union official had tried to discuss the dismissal with management which had refused requests for a meeting because the employee concerned was still on probation. When a union request was again refused at the end of the notice period, the staff walked off the job at 2.30 on a Friday afternoon, and were not permitted to return until the dispute was resolved over three weeks later. In these circumstances the tribunal held that although the stoppage of work was 'a direct result of a refusal by the Company to enter into discussions with the Union about the impending dismissal of an employee who was still on probation', it refused the claim for benefit for the first two weeks of the dispute, and allowed it for the third only because of delay on the part of the employer in allowing work to resume. So far as the first two weeks were concerned, the company's conduct did not justify the 'precipitate action' taken by the staff in staging the walk-out without notice while a large number of customers were still in the store. In the view of the tribunal 'such tactics are inconsistent with responsible trade unionism', and could not be condoned.

Nor could the company be expected 'especially having regard to the nature of its business, to tolerate such action by its employees'.

In addition to the tactics and responses of the parties involved, a third consideration in these cases has been whether the matter has already been considered by a third party, such as the Labour Court (or perhaps the Employment Appeals Tribunal). In *A 3/83*, the ITGWU and Alfa Cavan Rubber Manufacturing Ltd. were unable to agree on management proposals relating to pay, manning levels, productivity, and other conditions of employment. The union wrote to the company informing it that the disagreement was being referred to the Labour Court and that it was taking strike action in connection with a claim for the reinstatement of members who had been made redundant eighteen months earlier. The applicant in this case was one of six employees who had been dismissed for operating a go-slow policy, presumably as part of the industrial action to enforce the reinstatement of the redundant staff. In dismissing the application the tribunal held:

In regard to the specific issue relating to the question of re-employing the redundant workers in question, the Tribunal notes that the matter was the subject of an investigation by the Labour Court and that the Court found that the Company had no obligation to re-employ those workers. The Union was, of course, free to reject the Court's finding but clearly, on the other hand, when it (the Union) decides to take strike action in support of that line it must accept responsibility for the consequences of that decision.

So as was shown in the cases dealing with attempts by management to change working conditions, the decisions or recommendations of third parties in the industrial relations field would generally have a strong influence on the decision of the tribunal.

D. *Workers Laid Off because of a Strike*

Apart from the problem presented by those who are unemployed because they are themselves engaged in a trade dispute, a second problem relates to those workers who have been laid off as a result of someone else's dispute. As we saw in Chapter 5, non-participants in a trade dispute may nevertheless be disqualified from unemployment benefit if they have a direct interest in the outcome of the dispute. The same is true in Ireland, with the result that non-participating laid off workers may seek an adjudication from the tribunal. One consideration which has emerged in the cases which have arisen is whether the employer has taken adequate measures to avert the strike and the consequential lay-off. So in *A 10/85* negotiations between the employer and a union of clerical workers broke down on the question of redundancy terms. This led to a strike by the clerical workers and the lay-off of a substantial number of general workers who fell prey to the trade dispute disqualification. The workers who had been laid off were members of different unions, the ITGWU and the ATGWU, both of which had accepted the company's rationalization plans and had agreed redundancy terms. In deciding on behalf of these workers, the tribunal held that when the clerical workers had given their two-week strike notice to the company, 'it would be expected that, in accordance with good industrial relations practices, Management would, during the period of the strike notice, take all reasonable steps open to it to resolve the dispute and avert the stoppage. Such steps would . . . include the reference of the dispute to a third party, such as the Labour Court'. The failure to do so led the tribunal to conclude that the company's approach was 'unfair and unreasonable insofar as those employees are concerned'.

Where the failure by management to avert the stoppage has failed, a second consideration has been whether the employer has managed the lay-off reasonably when faced with industrial action. So in *A 1/84* a strike by ATGWU members at a Nissan Datsun Ltd. plant in Dublin on 15 December 1983 had led to its being occupied by the striking workers. Members of other unions (including the ITGWU) were instructed by management to go home until 4 January 1984, it being agreed that the ITGWU members would be given holiday pay until then. When they returned to work, they were unable to gain admission because the entrance gates had been padlocked and welded by the ATGWU members. In deciding in favour of an application by the ITGWU members, the tribunal said that:

In this situation and as clearly no question of definitive dismissal had arisen, there was an obligation on the Company to make work available to [the applicant] or, if this were not possible in the then existing circumstances, to lay him off. The Company, however, adopted neither of these courses; indeed it appears that it remained totally inactive in the matter, thus leaving [the applicant] and his I.T.G.W.U. colleagues in the unfair position that although being deprived of their employment they were neither dismissed nor laid off. Generally speaking it is expected of an employer to maintain relations where possible.

In the view of the tribunal, a person cannot be said to have been reasonably deprived of his employment unless he '(a) has abandoned the employment (b) was participating in a strike (c) was fairly dismissed on grounds of redundancy or for other reasons or (d) was laid off for good and sufficient cause'. According to the tribunal, none of these criteria applied in this case.

The unreasonable management of the lay-off in *A 1/84* is to be compared with the position in *A 6/83* and *A 8/85* where the applications failed. In these cases the ITGWU was in dispute with Clery & Co. about a claim for recognition and improved terms and conditions of employment. When the union gave five days' strike notice, the company informed the staff, who were members of a different union (the Irish Union of Distributive Workers and Clerks), which appears to have been recognized by the company, that they would be laid off from the beginning of the strike, 24 June 1983. Following their disqualification for unemployment benefit, the staff members of the second union applied to the tribunal, claiming that they were available for work, willing to work, and had been prevented from attending for work without reasonable and adequate consultation. The union had argued that if such consultation had taken place it might have been possible to keep the store open on a partial basis for some time after the strike had started. Although it is difficult in principle to see why workers in this situation should be disqualified, the application nevertheless failed. The tribunal accepted that it would not have been feasible to keep the store open, with as many as 70–80 per cent of the staff being members of the ITGWU and therefore likely to support the strike. A partial operation—by confining business to one floor or to particular departments—was accepted as being neither prudent nor practicable, having regard to major difficulties such as security, supplies and deliveries. The tribunal thus concluded that in the absence of a practicable and reasonable alternative, the lay-off could not justly be construed as unreasonable or unfair treatment. The decision that benefit was thus not payable was nevertheless surprising for it was open to the company to introduce 'an arrangement of lay-off with pay for a short period rather than lay-off without pay after only two days notice'. On the facts the tribunal had indeed accepted that there was 'some merit' in this point and that greater consultation before the lay-off might well have led to such an arrangement being agreed.

E. *Delaying the Return to Work*

This first matter to which the tribunal is directed to have regard in the exercise of its wide discretionary powers appears designed mainly to deal with the Comer International type of situation. Indeed, the Act was amended in Committee to have retrospective effect to give the tribunal jurisdiction to deal with just this dispute. The amendment which was agreed on 22 July 1982, in response to pressure from a number of deputies, provided that a claimant could apply for an adjudication to be made 'in relation to a stoppage of work, or trade dispute, which was or is in existence on or after the 1st day of June, 1982'. In fact the Comer International adjudication was the tribunal's first. It will be recalled that in that case the work-force had participated in an unofficial dispute (as a result of an incident involving a foreman and a shop steward). Although they were ready to return to work on 15 March 1982, and to process their grievance through agreed procedures, they were prevented from doing so because management insisted on an agreement being reached on a large number of highly contentious and unrelated matters before reopening the plant. These included changes in pay, conditions, and industrial relations procedures, and failure to agree to this led to the dispute being prolonged until 30 June. In these circumstances the tribunal held that 'the Company, by including in its pre-conditions for the re-opening of the factory agreement on an entire package of proposals which contained many matters not directly related to issues raised by the unofficial strike, acted in a manner which amounted to unfair treatment of the workers concerned'. The tribunal accepted that the workers were available for work and willing to work as from 15 March 1982, and that they had been unreasonably deprived of their employment from that date.

A similar conclusion was reached in the similar circumstances of the Shelbourne Hotel dispute in the following year. This was again the result of an unofficial dispute, this time following the dismissal of a barman. The strike commenced on 25 August 1983, leading to the closure of the hotel. When the strikers tried to return to work on 1 September 1983, following the intervention of their union, they learnt that they would not be permitted to do so until the union had given a number of undertakings. These related first to disciplinary procedures and other matters arising directly out of the dismissal of the barman, and secondly, to re-organization and restructuring proposals (including redundancies), described by the union as 'major, dramatic and radical', the re-organization plan being 'the most far-reaching ever implemented in the industry' with 'devastating consequences for the workers concerned'. It was not until 28 October 1983 that an agreement was reached on all the outstanding matters, including the re-organization plan and the consequential redundancies. A gradual resumption of work started on 15 November, the hotel reopening on 4 December. In deciding for the complainants, the tribunal concluded that

the Hotel Management's insistence on total agreement being reached on its re-organisation plan before allowing the employees concerned to resume work constituted unfair treatment of those employees. In reaching its conclusion, the Tribunal accepted that the issues involved in the Hotel's re-organisation proposals were not related to and did not arise out of the matter which caused the unofficial stoppage on 24 August 1983 [sic]; it was further accepted that notice of the re-organisation and restructuring plan had not been given to the Union or the workforce prior to 1 September.

Benefit was held to be payable from 14 September.

But although workers in both the Comer International and the Shelbourne Hotel disputes were successful in their applications to the tribunal, it is not always the case that a delayed return will amount to unfair or unjust treatment by the employer even though the employees are available for and willing to work. So in *A 1/86* the applicants were engaged in industrial action on 19 and 20 August 1985 following the breakdown of pay negotiations between their employer, Plessey Office Systems Ltd., and their union AUEW-TASS. When the applicants endeavoured to return on 21 August they were not permitted to do so. The union had made it clear that it was reserving its right to take further industrial action in support of its claim in response to which the employer indicated that a resumption of work would not be allowed unless the union gave an undertaking that there would be no further industrial action. At the same time the company proposed to refer the dispute to the Labour Court and stated that it was prepared to agree in advance to abide by the Court's recommendation. These conditions were unacceptable to the union and the stoppage continued until 18 September when a full resumption of work took place following agreement on the union's claim. Yet despite this success by the union, the applicants failed in their claim for benefit from 21 August. In the view of the tribunal, the company 'did not act unreasonably' in refusing to allow a resumption of work on that date. This was supported on the ground that 'it is difficult to see what other action—apart from increasing its offer beyond what it considered justified—the Company could in the circumstances have taken to protect its business and provide for future employment'. The tribunal was also influenced by the union's failure to agree to refer the matter to the Labour Court. While the right of the union to refuse was not questioned, nevertheless 'it cannot escape certain inevitable and foreseeable consequences that stem from an assertion of that right'.

V. CONCLUSION

When the Bill was passing through the Dáil, there was some concern that its operation should be reviewed shortly after it came into effect. Indeed the Opposition tried unsuccessfully to introduce an amendment whereby it would lapse after six months. In proposing the measure, the Opposition spokesman expressed concern that

the Bill may result in a strike encouragement situation. We would all wish to ensure that that would not happen, but if it occurs and we find that the effect of the tribunal is that we have an encouragement towards the commencement or prolongation of strikes or, on the other hand, an encouragement of employers and employees away from the normal well-tried and established procedures of the Labour Court, then it is important that the House should have a further opportunity of debating the matter.

There was, however, little support for the amendment, which was withdrawn. One deputy pointed out that the legislation had been urgently sought for six months, and if it were to lapse after six months, it would take another six to twelve months to get a replacement. The point was also made that if the amendment was accepted 'we are saying that the Bill is only being introduced for one or two specific cases', whereas there was a general need for such legislation to improve industrial relations and shorten rather than lengthen industrial disputes. For its part, the government suggested that a parliamentary committee could carry out a review after the expiry of the first twelve months, and undertook to amend the Bill 'in the light of experience'.

But as is often the case neither the Act nor its practical operation has had the negative consequences which the Opposition had feared. The work of the tribunal was in fact considered by the Curry Commission on Social Welfare which was set up in August 1983 with wide terms of reference, including 'To review and report on the social welfare system and related social services and to make recommendations for their development having regard to the needs of

Irish society'. In its wide-ranging report of 1986, the Commission referred to the Social Welfare Tribunal and concluded that

There has not been any public expression of dissatisfaction with the operation of the Social Welfare Tribunal or in relation to its effect on industrial relations. It was established to cater for a specific problem, highlighted by a number of industrial disputes in 1982. We are satisfied that it is fulfilling the role for which it was established (Curry 1986: 412).[19]

It may also be significant that although employers were initially opposed to the Bill, there is now no employer resistance to it, nor any pressure from employers for its repeal. Most employers appear to co-operate with the tribunal, the lack of any deep-rooted dissatisfaction being reflected perhaps by the fact that there has not been a single appeal to the High Court. This is a remarkable tribute to a body which does not have a lawyer among its members or its secretariat. The tribunal appears to excite little adverse comment in the press, from which there is no pressure for its removal. Nor is there any concern at high political level for the repeal of the legislation. In fact, despite the Minister's undertaking possibly to amend the legislation in the light of experience, it has been necessary to introduce only one technical amendment. In 1987 the powers of the tribunal to review its earlier decisions were extended. Henceforward this power was no longer confined to cases where there was a material change of circumstances of the stoppage or the trade dispute, but could apply where there is new evidence or new facts which in the opinion of the tribunal could have affected its decision.

The successful operation of the legislation is due in no small measure to the low-key and cautious approach of the tribunal. We have seen how the tribunal does not excite controversy by refusing generally to become involved in an examination of the merits of the dispute, although many of the disputes in which it is engaged may be highly controversial. Similarly, the tribunal has successfully avoided controversy by its refusal to second-guess the work of the industrial relations agencies, even though its jurisdiction would clearly permit it to do so. The point is illustrated by *A 3/83*, discussed above, and perhaps more clearly by *A 2/85*. In that case seven employees were suspended from duty for allegedly refusing to carry out management's instructions, and because they were engaged in key areas, all other employees were laid off and the factory was closed. The employer then imposed a number of conditions for the reopening of the factory, one of which was the resignation of four of the seven suspended workers. When this demand was rejected by the union, the dispute was referred to the Labour Court, which recommended the reinstatement of the four individuals, but noted that the crisis had been precipitated by their conduct and that of the three other workers. In the view of the Labour Court, all seven had rendered themselves liable to suspension or dismissal under the terms of the collective agreement, and it recommended that their

[19] For comment, see Whyte (1986).

conduct should be recorded as a disciplinary warning. The tribunal was greatly influenced by these findings, holding:

In the light of the Labour Court's comments to the effect that the suspended workers concerned were in breach of the Agreement of 26 June, 1984, and had rendered themselves liable to suspension or dismissal by their actions, the Tribunal is satisfied that the Company did not act unreasonably in suspending the seven workers.

But because the Labour Court also found that management had 'erred seriously' by demanding the resignation of four of the suspended workers as a precondition of reopening, the applicants were justified in rejecting this particular condition. Consequently, although the suspensions were initially justified, they were prolonged to an unreasonable extent by management's introduction of an unfair condition for their termination. Benefit was thus payable for part of the period of the dispute.

Apart from the avoidance of any discussion of the merits of the dispute, and the tribunal's apparent willingness to be bound by (rather than to challenge) the industrial relations agencies, the timing of adjudications is another factor which will have helped to deflect potential controversy. It is a remarkable feature of the tribunal's adjudications that they are almost invariably issued after the dispute has ended and work has resumed. In this way the tribunal avoids making a judgment on the employer's conduct which might affect the settlement of the dispute and disturb the work of the conciliation agencies. Yet, paradoxically, although the delay may contribute to the success of the tribunal, it may also be regarded as an Achilles heel in the sense that unemployment benefit is not being paid at a time of need (during the dispute), with the result that the workers involved are not relieved from the pressure to return because of financial burdens, even though the conduct of the employer is largely to blame. There are in fact a number of factors which contribute to delay. The first is that the applicant must exhaust the procedures for unemployment benefit, which means making a claim to the deciding officer and an appeal to the appeals officer. It appears that there is no way of expediting this procedure, even when it is futile to use it. Secondly, there may be delay on the part of the applicants. Although the Regulations require applications to be made within twenty-one days of the appeals officer's decision, the tribunal has never yet refused a late application. In *A 5/85* an application was made by workers some fourteen months after the dispute had ended, the tribunal not explaining what the special circumstances were that induced it to accept jurisdiction. A third cause of delay is practical matters relating to the administration of the tribunal. It is often difficult to assemble the five part-time members of the tribunal at short notice, a problem which is compounded should it be necessary to adjourn the hearing. Although most applications are disposed of after a single hearing, others need more, as in the case of *A 12/85* which required four hearings, held between January and May 1986. And on top of all of this, there is the necessary delay involved in reaching a decision which has to be written up, a process which can only be lengthened by the tribunal's otherwise sensible practice of not having minority decisions. As a result of these different pressures and considerations, it is perhaps not surprising that the problem of delay should be acute.

For a combination of reasons (not all of them unequivocal blessings by any means), the tribunal appears to have been a considerable success and has become an established feature of the social welfare system. The scope for controversy has been deflected still further by the sharp reduction in the number of applications for adjudications made to the tribunal in recent years. The number of cases dealt with by the tribunal has fallen since the peak years of 1984, when 12 adjudications were made, and 1985, when 13 were made. Since then the annual adjudications have been 7 (1986), 3 (1987), 3 (1988), and 2 (1989). The reasons for this decline are not abundantly clear, though it is matched by a parallel decline in the incidence of industrial action generally in Ireland recently (Department of Labour 1989). This is associated with the corporatist Programme for National Recovery (1987) whereby the Social Partners entered into a national agreement on pay restraint for three years, from 1988–90. But given the jurisdiction of the tribunal and the nature of the disputes referred to it, this seems not to be a convincing explanation. The tribunal deals not with disputes where employees are seeking more pay, but with those where employees are seeking to defend themselves against attempts by employers to change terms and conditions of employment. So although the Programme for National Recovery may be relevant, it does not seem likely to provide the whole answer. Other explanations may relate to the possibility that much of the restructuring of Irish industry giving rise to the disputes has now taken place, or to the possibility that some of the people who in the past appeared before the tribunal will now qualify for unemployment benefit because of the liberalization of the trade dispute disqualification in 1987, bringing it into line with the position in Britain. It would be nice but optimistic to suggest that another possible explanation is that employers are gradually changing their industrial relations practices in order to avoid censure by the tribunal. This would be consistent with the government's hope that as the tribunal became more established, fewer cases would emerge because employers would revise their procedures and act reasonably. But whatever the reason for the decline in the number of cases, this feature of the new jurisdiction must at least give rise to a strong presumption (albeit rebuttable) that neither the passing of the 1982 Act nor the work of the tribunal has contributed to an increase in the incidence of industrial action. As a result the main criticism of the 1982 Act is not that it has gone too far, but that it has not gone far enough, a point to which we return in the concluding chapter.

[8]
Conclusion

The legal position of the British worker engaged in a labour dispute is quite remarkable. A strike, for whatever reason, is a breach of contract; any form of industrial action short of a strike can lead to the total loss of pay; those engaged in industrial action may be dismissed with impunity (regardless of the reasons for the industrial action); there is no right to unemployment benefit; and strikers and their families are penalized by social welfare legislation, even when the dispute is the singular fault of the employer. Yet given the new theoretical framework for contemporary labour law, the legal position on this, and on many other issues, is perfectly understandable. The new market efficiency model sees the function of labour law as being designed to reduce or at least lessen the impact of obstacles to the efficient working of the labour market.[1] Given that trade unionism and collective bargaining together constitute one such obstacle, it would make perfect sense to eliminate the strike weapon which forms the power base of collective bargaining. Remember Lord Wright's famous dictum that 'The right of workmen to strike is an essential element in the principle of collective bargaining'.[2] Indeed, if anything, it could be argued that policy on the question under discussion, as in other areas, has been too cautious given the gulf between the paradigm legal framework dictated by the market efficiency model of labour law, and the legal framework of contemporary British labour law.[3] Why, for example, should there be any restrictions on the employer's power of dismissal; and why should strikers' families receive any payment by way of income support? There is no humanity in the market-place.

The fact that the statutory framework inherited by the Thatcher government could be harnessed so easily to the ends of a radical new economic policy speaks volumes about the failure of the previous regime adequately to serve the ends of a much different theoretical model of labour law. This was the social justice model which dominated the post-war period, and was concerned above all to protect workers from the arbitrary use of power in the work-place, and to enable the individual to participate through his union in the process of making and administering the rules which governed working life. A key element in the

---

[1] For an account, see Ewing (1990).
[2] *Crofter Hand Woven Harris Tweed* v. *Veitch* [1942] AC 435, at p. 463.
[3] For an account of this paradigm legal framework, see Epstein (1983); Hanson and Mather (1989).

success of this project was collective bargaining, the promotion of which was an important feature of labour market policy until 1979. 'Closely related to collective bargaining . . . is the freedom to strike'.[4] For if 'workers could not, in the last resort, collectively refuse to work, they could not bargain collectively'.[5] Yet both Grunwick and Wapping are monuments to the failure of the post-war legal regime adequately to promote these values. As such they are not only a symptom of the failure to meet theory with practice, but also a reflection of the obsessive approach to labour law in the pre-1979 era. British labour law policy in general, and on the right to strike in particular, has been concerned almost exclusively to confer wide immunities in contract and tort on trade unions and their officials while neglecting the individual worker for whom the sacrifice of a job may be much greater than the damages which might be visited upon his organization. For a number of reasons it seems unlikely that that mistake will be made again. So given a clean slate, and the likelihood that the freedom to strike will not be unlimited, and that there will be 'a framework of legality', how could the law be used to protect the individual who exercises what would be regarded on the street as a basic human right?

I. THE CONTRACT OF EMPLOYMENT

The starting point of any framework of protection for individual workers is thought to be the contract of employment, and in particular a provision, however expressed, which provides that participation in a lawful strike is not to be regarded as a breach of contract. So we find, for example, that the Labour Party has put behind it the once unanswerable Donovan questions by proposing in its policy review that in the case of 'legitimate industrial action' (a concept yet to be spelled out) 'both the employer's and the employee's contractual duties will be suspended for the duration of any industrial action' (Labour Party 1989: 23). Such a measure would hardly be unprecedented. Under the labour law of France, Italy, and West Germany provision is made for the suspension of the contract of employment during industrial action, though the circumstances in which the doctrine applies varies according to the jurisdiction. And notably, express provisions regulating the contract in such circumstances are known also to common law jurisdictions. The Canadian labour law regimes generally contain a measure of which the following from Alberta is typical. There it is provided that 'No person ceases to be an employee within the meaning of this Act by reason only of his ceasing to work as a result of a lawful lock-out or a lawful strike or by reason only of his dismissal contrary to this Act'.[6]

---

[4] *Reference re Public Service Employee Relations Act, Labour Relations Act and Police Officers Collective Bargaining Act* (1987) 38 DLR (4th) 161, at p. 200 (Dickson, C.J.C.).

[5] At p. 201, quoting Kahn-Freund (1983: 292). Cf. the quite remarkable rhetoric and reasoning in the judgment of Bird C.J. in *County Sanitation District No. 2 of Los Angeles County* v. *Los Angeles County Employees Association, Local 660*, 699 P. 2d 835 (Cal. 1985).

[6] Labour Relations Act 1988, SA, c. L–1.2, s. 87.

An interesting feature of this and other Canadian provisions is that in providing that the contract is not ended, they do not also make provision for the status of the contract during the strike, a reflection perhaps that the matter is not of great practical importance. In one case, however, the Supreme Court of British Columbia stated that the effect of legislation of this kind was that during a strike 'certain incidents of [the contract] were suspended', and that when 'the strike ended, the correlative obligations of the employees and the employer to work and to employ were once more in force'.[7] Yet although the concept of suspension thus seems to be well known,[8] it is doubtful whether it provides an adequate solution to the problem. That is to say, the introduction of the doctrine of suspension *de jure* as opposed to *de facto* may not alone provide the answer. In common with that of many European states, Belgian law distinguishes between lawful and unlawful strikes so that the former is regarded as a breach of the employment contract whereas the latter is regarded as a suspension. It appears, however, that the concept of suspension is not enough to prevent the dismissal of strikers. For while an unlawful strike justifies the instant dismissal of the workers involved, so in a legal strike 'the employer can dismiss workers during the strike by serving them with a proper term of notice' (Blanpain and Engels 1988: 257). It could thus be a mistake to exaggerate the practical value of the concept of suspension or continuance to the individual striker. For the fact is that the contract would be suspended only until such time as the employer chose to terminate. The danger is that at best it would secure a right to be dismissed with notice. It is thus not the concept of suspension which protects strikers as much as statutory restrictions on the employer's power of dismissal.

This is not to deny that a statutory concept of suspension would have some advantages. But these could arise mainly in the law of tort rather than in the law of contract. So while suspension might only require notice before dismissal, rather than prevent dismissal, it would help to ensure that employees could not be restrained by injunction for unlawfully interfering with their employer's business. The concept of suspension would thus nip in the bud any potential liability caused by the decision in *Barretts and Baird (Wholesale) Ltd.* v. *IPCS*.[9] If a strike was regarded as a suspension rather than a termination of the contract, the action of the strikers could not be regarded as unlawful means for the purpose of tortious liability. But it is not only the strikers themselves who would benefit in this way. The concept of suspension would to some extent undermine the economic torts generally, thereby restricting the liability of union officials and trade unions for organizing industrial action. If the strike was deemed only to suspend the contract, those organizing industrial action

---

[7] *United Brotherhood of Carpenters and Joiners of America, Local 1928* v. *Citation Industries Ltd.* (1983) 46 BCLR 129, at p. 135.

[8] It is also known in this country *de jure* (Income Support (General) Regulations, SI 1987/1967, Schedule 1(b)) and *de facto* (Employment Protection (Consolidation) Act 1978, s. 45).

[9] [1987] IRLR 3.

could not be liable for inducing breach of the contract, and as is now well known, it is this which is the principal basis of liability. So while the potential benefits of suspension should not be exaggerated, nor should they be under-estimated, even if paradoxically the benefits do not arise principally in the law of contract. This is not to deny that there would be difficulties. A blanket concept of suspension would go a long way to removing tortious liability which presumably would no longer be politically acceptable. If the doctrine of suspension were to apply to all strikes, it would presumably be necessary to introduce statutory liabilities for those forms of industrial action which are not to be protected, rather than the present approach which is to retain common law liability in such circumstances.[10] A blanket doctrine of suspension would remove a significant portion of common law liability.[11]

II.   THE PAYMENT OF WAGES

The deduction of wages from workers engaged in a dispute raises many complex questions. Under the present common law rules, however, these have been answered in a way which is consistently inequitable. It is difficult to justify a regime which allows the employer to withhold all wages despite substantial performance of the contract by the employee. And while it may be easier to justify deductions from the wages of workers who fail to provide full service, this is less easy when the employer is for all practical purposes permitted unilaterally to determine whether the worker's conduct is in breach of contract, and to decide how much to deduct. In some cases, indeed, the employer may not be entitled under the contract to make the deduction. Yet the uncertainty caused by the open-ended and dynamic nature of the em-ployee's contractual obligations simply reinforces the power of the employer to use the threat of non-payment to impose changes which may not be permitted under the contract. In other cases the employer may be clearly entitled to make a deduction, such being the nature of the employee's contract. But in plucking a figure from thin air as the basis of assessment, the employer would have to err seriously, with an excessive sum, to make it worthwhile for the employee to mount a legal challenge.

One possible response might have been to protect those engaged in industrial action without straying too far from the principles underlying the general law of wages which applies currently. This much could have been done by the simple expedient of repealing section 1(5)(e) of the Wages Act 1986. This would mean that deductions for participating in industrial action would have to be made, if at all, in accordance with the general principles laid down in the

---

[10]   The point is more fully discussed in Ewing (1986).
[11]   Subject to tortious liability for mere interference with the performance of a contract of employment short of breach. See *Torquay Hotel Co. Ltd.* v. *Cousins* [1969] 2 Ch. 106, at p. 138; and Trade Union Act 1984, s. 10(1) (which suggests that direct interference with the performance of a contract of employment short of breach is tortious).

Act. The most important of these are that the employer must have authority under the contract to make the deduction, and that the terms of that authority must be notified to the worker in writing. In a unionized plant, contractual notices about the employer's power to make deductions would almost certainly lead to dispute and negotiation. If there was a dispute about the employer's power, it may not always be easy to argue that deductions are authorized under the contract. And if there was a negotiated agreement, the matter would fall to be governed by section 18(4) of the Trade Union and Labour Relations Act 1974. This would mean that any such collective agreement would have to be in writing, state expressly that its terms shall be incorporated into individual contracts of employment, and be reasonably accessible at the work-place of employees governed by it. In addition, each contract of employment must incorporate (expressly or impliedly) the terms of the agreement. Otherwise the agreement, being designed to 'restrict' the right of workers to strike or engage in other forms of industrial action, would be ineffective as a source of the contract of employment.

Recent developments suggest, however, that this approach may no longer be effective. In the first place cases such as *Wiluszynski*[12] allow the employer to withhold all wages even when faced with partial performance by employees. And decisions of the EAT have held that the Wages Act does not apply to situations of non-payment as opposed to deductions from wages.[13] In that context there is thus a need for a rather more radical form of intervention than the repeal of section 1(5)(e) of the Wages Act 1986. An opportunity to deal with the matter would clearly arise if we were to reverse the policy of deregulation and to legislate on wages in a matter consistent with ILO Convention No. 95. In any event, a minimum framework of protection would have two essential features. First, although employers could rightly refuse to accept partial performance, this would be done only after an industrial tribunal had determined that the workers were in fact acting in breach of contract. Second, if the employer accepted performance from the staff—by allowing work to continue—then he must pay for the services provided. In the case of substantial performance, the obligation would be full payment of wages while in other cases employees would be paid to the extent of their performance. Again, however, some independent agency should stand between the employer and his employees before this power is exercised, as a safeguard against abuse. Before deductions are made, the employer would be required to satisfy a tribunal that the employees were in fact in breach of contract and were failing to provide substantial performance. Having done this, the employer would be obliged to satisfy the tribunal that the amount of any deductions was lawful under the contract and was fair and reasonable.

---

[12] *Wiluszynski* v. *Tower Hamlets LBC* [1989] ICR 493.
[13] See *Barlow* v. *A. J. Whittle* [1990] IRLR 79, and *Alsop* v. *Star Vehicle Contracts Ltd.* [1990] IRLR 83.

III.   UNFAIR DISMISSAL

Perhaps the most pressing concern for a new framework of labour law is to address the great gap exposed by Wapping. Apart from the extraordinary inequity of the current position, and indeed of that in 1978, the matter is all the more pressing for the fact that the lack of protection for individual strikers has been found to be in breach of two international treaties to which Britain is a party. Thus, the legislation has been found to be inconsistent with the (original) European Social Charter which by article 6(4) requires Britain to recognize 'the right for workers and employers to collective action in cases of conflicts of interest, including the right to strike, subject to obligations that might arise out of collective agreements previously entered into' (Council of Europe 1987).[14] More recently, the Committee of Experts of the International Labour Organization found the legislation to be incompatible with article 3 of ILO Convention 87 on Freedom of Association and the Right to Organize (ILO 1989).[15] According to the Committee, it is inconsistent with the right to strike as guaranteed (by implication) by the Convention for an employer to be permitted to refuse to reinstate some or all of his employees at the conclusion of a strike, lock-out, or other industrial action without those employees having the right to challenge the fairness of the dismissal before an independent court or tribunal. Although section 62 of the Employment Protection (Consolidation) Act 1978 (as amended by the Employment Act 1982, section 9 and now the Employment Bill 1990, clause 9) offers an opportunity for the review of the discriminatory dismissal of strikers in some circumstances, this was considered by the Committee not to offer adequate protection (even before the 1990 amendments), partly because it is still open to an employer to dismiss an entire work-force with impunity. The government was asked to introduce real legislative protection for those engaged in strikes or other industrial action.

In moving in this direction, we would again not be braving uncharted waters. All the major European states now have some form of guarantee to protect strikers from dismissal. In Italy, 'recognition of the right to strike' not only implies that the contract is suspended during the strike, but also that 'the employer cannot dismiss the strikers during the strike period' (Treu 1986: 183). Similarly, in France, 'the employer must keep the strikers in his employment. He cannot introduce any sanctions for participating in a strike, much less dismiss the strikers simply for taking part in the strike. If the employer decides to continue to operate and bring in replacements during the strike, he will nevertheless at the end of the strike have to restore the jobs of those who have taken part in the strike' (Despax and Rojot 1987: 299). But such protection is not confined to Europe, and is also known in the common law jurisdictions of North America, most forcefully in Canada where the position typically is now guaranteed expressly by legislation. In Alberta, for

---

[14]   For a full discussion, see Hepple (1988).

[15]   The text of the Committee of Experts' Report is reproduced in Ewing (1989).

example, the Labour Relations Act provides that neither an employer nor anyone acting on behalf of the employer shall refuse to employ, or to continue to employ, any person or discriminate against any person in regard to employment, or any term or condition of employment, because the person has participated in any strike that is permitted by the Act.[16] Indeed some jurisdictions go further, with Manitoba, for example, protecting from dismissal or discipline workers who refuse to perform work which would directly facilitate the operation or business of another employer whose workers are engaged in a lawful strike.[17]

But even without such guidance from the international community, pressure from the trade union movement is such to suggest that an alternative labour law strategy in the future would need to address this question. In 1986 the TUC held a consultative conference on labour law reform with a number of unions submitting written responses. Several of these demonstrated a degree of impatience with the present legal framework. Thus, the APEX submission contended that section 62 was 'a grave mistake', that it should be 'abolished', and that 'Employees dismissed during the course of a strike should have the same right to bring unfair dismissal proceedings as anyone else' (APEX 1986). A rather different proposal was submitted by COHSE. The union argued that dismissal for participating in industrial action should not be permissible, and that dismissal for taking part in a strike should be protected as an unacceptable reason in the same way as dismissal for membership or participation in the activities of a trade union under section 58 of the Employment Protection (Consolidation) Act 1978 (COHSE 1986). Yet another theme was developed by SOGAT 82, which argued that workers who take part in a strike approved by a ballot should be protected from dismissal (SOGAT 82 1986). Support for an initiative in this direction appears to be growing. Indeed, such is the degree of support that even the Labour Party has been brought on board, despite the apparently insuperable obstacles to legislation of this kind which were identified in the past. The party's policy review offers a commitment that 'Workers will no longer be sacked for taking legitimate industrial action', and that 'It will be unlawful to dismiss an employee on the grounds that they have taken such action' (Labour Party 1989: 23). This right would apply regardless of the number of people employed in the enterprise.

This is not to deny that there are hard questions to be answered in drafting the proposed legislation. One such question relates to the fact that presumably not all strikes would be protected from the sanction of dismissal. In other jurisdictions the protection applies typically to lawful strikes only, which may mean only to those preceded by proper notice following a strike vote after the expiry of a collective agreement. Although these restrictions are not necessarily likely to be applied here, the Labour Party policy review does reflect an emerging consensus that the right to strike cannot be unlimited, and that some

---

[16] Labour Relations Act 1988, SA, c. L–1.2, s. 147(a)(vii).
[17] Labour Relations Act, SM 1976, s. 12.

form of restriction will have to be accepted as a price for effective protection of individual strikers in some cases. The form which these restrictions will take will be determined by political circumstances rather than by principle, but what is so far unresolved is the position of workers who take part in a strike which falls outside the scope of legality. Those within it will presumably be protected from dismissal. For those outside there are three options. The first, and least attractive, is to say that such people may be dismissed without redress. The second is to continue to apply section 62 of the EPCA to such people so that the employer can dismiss, but only if everyone who took part in the strike is dismissed, failing which the others may claim for unfair dismissal. The third and final possibility is to permit those dismissed for engaging in strikes outside the framework of 'legitimate industrial action' to claim for unfair dismissal just like anyone else. Although this last option may be the easiest to justify in principle, paradoxically it may not provide as much protection for dismissed workers as the second which would focus the attention of the tribunal on the reason for discrimination rather than the legality of the strike. Perhaps the best solution would be to combine the second and third options and to provide that to avoid liability the employer must dismiss everyone and in the circumstances these dismissals must be fair.

Apart from the scope of the protection, a second question is whether it would ever be possible for a worker to be dismissed while participating in a lawful or a legitimate strike. What would be done about repudiatory conduct —other than participation in the strike—in which the employee might engage? This might include moonlighting for a rival firm, or misconduct, including perhaps damage to property. The question is, however, not difficult to answer. There is no reason in principle why the protection against dismissal should extend beyond the act of participating in the strike to include conduct which would justify dismissal but for the strike. In other jurisdictions, the restrictions on dismissal of strikers typically does not prevent dismissal on account of strike-related misconduct.[18] Of some interest, however, is the fact that in Canada, at least, the employer's right to dismiss in such circumstances may be lost if it is exercised for improper reasons, even in cases of serious violence. So in one case the Alberta Labour Relations Board found evidence of serious damage to company property as well as violence directed at strike-breakers.[19] This led the Board to conclude that the employer was entitled to dismiss the employees for cause. But what the employer was not entitled to do was to reinstate two of the twenty-five who had been dismissed. The two in question were identified as being 'amongst the worst offenders' but were reinstated because 'they had turned on the union'. This led the Board to conclude that the failure to re-engage the other strikers was motivated by an anti-union animus,

---

[18] Note that the Labour Relations Act 1988, SA, c. L–1.2 expressly provides that 'Nothing in this Act detracts from or interferes with the right of an employer to suspend, transfer or lay off employees, or to discharge employees for proper and sufficient cause' (s. 148).

[19] *International Woodworkers of America* v. *Zeidler Forest Industries* [1987] Alta LRBR 31.

with the result that the employer's conduct was unlawful. There is no reason why a similar provision could not also apply here. An employer who dismisses a worker during a strike would be required to convince a tribunal that the reason was misconduct and that the employer acted reasonably in the circumstances. On the facts of the Alberta case just discussed, it would be open to the tribunal to hold the dismissal unfair.

IV.   THE RIGHT TO REINSTATEMENT

The protection of employment status and the prohibition against dismissal are of little consequence if the employer replaces the workers on strike, maintains production, and refuses ever to re-employ the strikers. The difficulty which could thus arise is that although the strikers would still be employees, and could not be dismissed, the employer would deny any obligation to give them work. So although prohibited from using the weapon of termination, the employer could shed workers in dispute by a process of attrition, with sagging morale leading to the gradual drifting away of those on strike. The legal problems are well illustrated by developments in the United States where protection against the dismissal of strikers has been read into the National Labor Relations Act. But so far as reinstatement is concerned, a distinction is drawn between the unfair labor practice striker and the economic striker. In the case of the former the employee has a right to reinstatement, with the employer under an obligation to dismiss if necessary any replacement workers. So far as the latter is concerned, the matter is governed by *NLRB* v. *MacKay Radio and Telegraph Company*[20] where it was held that despite the protection against dismissal in the National Labor Relations Act, an employer has not 'lost the right to protect and continue his business by supplying places left vacant by strikers. And he is not bound to discharge those hired to fill the places of strikers, upon the election of the latter to resume their employment'. This is not to say that the economic striker is completely unprotected, for there are modifications to this basic rule.[21] Yet even when these qualifications are accounted for the bottom line is simply that the employer can hire permanent replacements with the strikers having no right to reinstatement.

The decision in *MacKay Radio* thus suggests that there may be inherent limitations in the preservation of employment status and in the protection against dismissal as guarantees for individual strikers. In order to be effective the courts would have to infer that the right not to be dismissed gives rise to a corollary right to be reinstated (on what terms?) at any time on the election of the employee (even though the strike may not be over). The employer would be under a corresponding duty to accept the strikers and if necessary to dismiss any replacements who have been hired on a temporary or indeed a permanent basis. But more than this, if the right to reinstatement thus inferred was to be

---

[20]   304 US 333 (1937).
[21]   See *NLRB* v. *Fleetwood Trailer Co.*, 389 US 375 (1967).

effective, the courts would have to be prepared to underwrite it with an effective sanction. The only feasible sanction would be unfair dismissal. Here the courts would have to be prepared to say that the refusal to allow the reinstatement of strikers would amount to a constructive dismissal on the basis that the employer's conduct is a breach of contract. Following that the courts would have to be prepared to say that the dismissal was automatically unfair, presumably because it was due to the worker's participation in the strike. It is, however, easy to imagine that the courts might not be prepared to make all the necessary leaps, or indeed that employers might well seek to thwart this nice development. It is not inconceivable, for example, that the employer might argue that the workers have been dismissed not because of their participation in the strike but because there is no work for them to do, either because the operations have closed or because a replacement labour force has been hired. Employer resistance will only be intensified by the threat of unfair dismissal proceedings by the replacement labour should they be terminated to make way for the strikers, a risk which would be more likely were Labour to implement its proposal to abolish the qualifying periods.

The problem is one which might thus need some form of statutory regulation supplementary to the doctrine of deemed contractual continuation, and the right to reinstatement. Possible solutions to the problem are offered by a number of Canadian jurisdictions. In Ontario an employee engaged in a lawful strike is entitled to reinstatement within six months of the beginning of the strike.[22] In Alberta the entitlement is within a period of two years of the beginning of the strike.[23] Rather ominously perhaps, the right to reinstatement in Ontario is 'on such terms as the employer and employee may agree upon', although in offering terms of employment the employer may not discriminate against the employee by reason of his having exercised rights under the Labour Relations Act. Manitoba takes a different approach.[24] If a strike or lock-out is ended without an agreement (for example, if the workers are forced back to work) it is an unfair labour practice for the employer to refuse to reinstate the employee in his employment. This differs in some important respects from the Ontario and Alberta provisions. First, in Manitoba there is no right to reinstatement until the strike ends, whereas in Ontario and Alberta the employee in principle has the right to return while the strike continues. But second, there is no limit on the right to return: if the strike in Manitoba exceeds six months or two years, the statutory right does not expire. On the other hand, one important similarity is that the right to reinstatement in both cases applies only if the work performed by the employee at the time of the dispute continues when the request for reinstatement is made (Ontario), or after the strike or lock-out ends (Manitoba). But the most important similarity of course is that the right of strikers to reinstatement cannot be defeated by the hiring of

---

[22] Labour Relations Act, RSO, c. 228, s. 73.
[23] Labour Relations Act 1988, SA, c. L-1.2, s. 88.
[24] Labour Relations Act, SM 1984-5, c. 21.

permanent replacements, though the employer is free to hire temporary staff to perform the tasks of those in dispute.

But if the reinstatement of strikers is to be considered, a number of hard questions need to be asked. Thus, if the dispute is not settled, for how long does the right to reinstatement survive; what would be the position of any displaced replacement workers; and on what terms would reinstatement take place? Fortunately, these questions do have answers. As to the first, the Alberta model of a right to return within two years from the start of the strike merits careful consideration. If a dispute lasts that long it will be clear to the workers concerned that it is unlikely ever to be resolved on their terms. As to the second of the three questions, a suitable precedent is provided by the law regulating replacements for workers on pregnancy leave.[25] There is no reason why the dismissal of a striker's replacement should not also be regarded as a dismissal for cause, which would be fair if properly executed. So far as the third of these questions is concerned, there would be some justification for rejecting the Ontario and Alberta approaches (which effectively allow the conditions of return to be dictated by the employer) in favour of a right to return to the conditions prevailing at the time the dispute started. The obvious objection to this is that it would unduly tie the hands of the employer in the sense that any imposed variation of contractual terms could be resisted by a striker, with those on strike entitled to reinstatement on the old terms. But the fact is that those on strike in that situation might be entitled to judicial relief where their contractual rights were being violated. There is no reason why their position should be any less secure when they adopt tactics of self-help rather than the expensive and cumbersome process of litigation. In any event the employer is fully protected by the fact that he could still dismiss the workers after the strike, not because of the strike, but because they failed to submit to the new terms.[26] Admittedly this is a matter which will require serious consideration in the future.

The solution proposed here assumes then that the employer would be free to hire temporary replacements to do the work of those on strike. There are, however, some jurisdictions which go further and which seek to protect the security of the striker by hindering or preventing the employer from taking on such replacements. In jurisdictions such as New Jersey, Arkansas, and California, this is done indirectly by making it unlawful for any person to supply labour to a strike-bound employer. There are indeed similar restrictions

---

[25] Employment Protection (Consolidation) Act 1978, s. 61. Quaere whether any right to return in this area need be as rigid or as difficult as the current rules on the right to return after maternity: see *F. W. Woolworths plc* v. *Smith* [1990] ICR 44.

[26] A good example of this being *Robertson* v. *British Gas Corporation* [1983] IRLR 304 where the plaintiff gas meter readers successfully sued to recover bonus payments the employers had unilaterally withheld in breach of contract. They were subsequently dismissed for refusing to agree to a variation of their contracts of employment. The dismissals were held by an industrial tribunal not to be unfair: see *IDS Brief* 282, Aug. 1984, p. 8.

on employment agencies in Britain.[27] But other jurisdictions go even further. In Italy and Spain a strike-bound employer is not permitted to hire even temporary replacements to do the work of those on strike.[28] A similar rule was introduced in Quebec by a 1983 amendment to the Labour Code.[29] This not only prohibits employers from hiring temporary or permanent replacements to do the work of those on strike, but also restricts the power of the employer to transfer strike-bound work to other plants or to transfer other employees to the strike-bound plant.[30] But although this approach has some advocates in Britain,[31] it is questionable whether it would be either desirable or necessary. The Quebec provisions in particular have been highly controversial (allegedly contributing to a flight of capital from that Province[32]) yet not always very effective (with one bitter newspaper dispute in Montreal broken by the use of management personnel). It is true that the freedom to hire temporary replacements gives the employer a great advantage in a dispute. But a ban on even temporary replacements would give the union an even greater advantage. As it is, striking employees would have some security in the fact that they could return to work at any time on the terms in force at the beginning of the dispute, with a more equitable social security system helping to deal with immediate financial needs. It is to a consideration of that question that we now turn.

V.   UNEMPLOYMENT BENEFIT

If the present law on the contract of employment and unfair dismissal is difficult to justify, the same is true of the law relating to the disqualification of strikers from unemployment benefit. For the underlying rationale of the disqualification is no more convincing than the thinking behind the present unfair dismissal rules. The principal argument here is the need to maintain state neutrality which would be compromised by the payment of benefit, an argument which is reinforced by the need to maintain a degree of consistency

[27] The Conduct of Employment Agencies and Employment Businesses Regulations 1976, SI 1976/715, reg. 9(11) which provides that 'A contractor shall not supply workers to a hirer as direct replacements of employees who are in industrial dispute with that hirer to perform the same duties as those normally performed by those employees'. For this purpose a contractor is defined as a person carrying on an employment business which is defined in turn by the Employment Agencies Act 1973 to mean 'the business (whether or not carried on with a view to profit and whether or not carried on in conjunction with any other business) of supplying persons in the employment of the person carrying on the business, to act for, and under the control of, other persons in any capacity'. Note also that although unemployed workers may be directed by the Department of Employment to a strike-bound enterprise, they cannot be forced to accept it. See Labour Exchanges Act 1909, s. 2(2); Employment and Training Act 1948, s. 2(3); Social Security Act 1975, s. 20A(1)(a) (as amended by the social security act 1989). See further, Official Report, Standing Committee F, 9 Feb. 1989, cols. 393–4.

[28] See Treu 1986: 183; Olea and Rodríguez-Sañudo 1988: 146.

[29] An Act to Amend the Labour Code, SQ 1983, c. 22, s. 88, introducing a new s. 109.1 to the Labour Code.

[30] This provision was described by a Canadian labour leader as 'a model for the rest of Canada . . . [which] unfortunately, the rest of the country has yet to follow' (Carr 1987).

[31] See Bercusson (1977); Evans and Lewis (1987).   [32] Globe and Mail, 8 Oct. 1986.

with insurance principles which would be undermined by the payment of benefit to people who were voluntarily unemployed. It has to be said, however, that although these arguments might support the disqualification, they do not dictate that it should take any particular form. British law has always been thought to be consistent with these principles even though it is much more liberal today than when the disqualification was first introduced in 1911. Presumably it would be possible to introduce a further degree of liberalization while arguing convincingly that the law remains faithful to these underlying goals. Certainly it has never been seriously suggested that those American states, in which some (though not all) respects the trade dispute disqualifications are less restrictive than the British, have compromised either state neutrality or insurance principles. The point is then that the underlying policy goals have been used to justify both highly restrictive and relatively liberal regimes. Indeed the recent debate in West Germany about unemployment benefit serves only to illustrate the elastic qualities of the concept of state neutrality. There the statutory obligation of state neutrality was used to justify a court ruling requiring unemployment benefit to be paid to workers laid off by a strike in which they had a direct interest. The concept of neutrality was then used by the legislature as a pretext for restricting this decision.[33]

Apart from the inherently non-prescriptive qualities of the arguments in favour of the disqualification, a second difficulty is that the concept of neutrality is in any event not necessarily persuasive. A large body of American literature has demonstrated convincingly that the non-payment of benefit is not the same as neutrality. Thus, with forceful logic Lesser (1945: 175) has argued that to the extent that payment of benefit would have the unneutral effect of supporting workers and fostering strikes, the denial of benefits would have the unneutral effect of supporting employers and discouraging strikes, and fostering lock-outs. In other words, employees are encouraged to end their action by the non-intervention of the fund. And apart from thus placing the fund behind employers in a dispute, it is also argued that non-payment of benefit aids employers by weakening the strength of the group in dispute. Thus, the holding out of benefit to those who refrain from participation in the dispute 'amounts to considerable pressure to deter workers from combining their economic strength' (Lesser 1945: 175). On this argument non-payment is a form of coercion. But apart from the claim that non-payment is not synonymous with neutrality, the second argument here is that the state should not in any event necessarily be neutral. With equally forceful logic Shadur (1950: 299) argues that some strikers deserve to be financed to the extent that they are attempting to protect rights provided by legislation or by contract. The objection to financing strikers loses its impact, he argues, whenever the shutdown has resulted from clearly unreasonable conduct on the part of the employer. These points, which made a major impact on the Supreme Court of

---

[33] For an account of this, see 'Strike Payments Law Reformed', 148 *European Industrial Relations Review* May 1986, 10–11.

Canada,[34] are as forceful here as they are in the United States, for it is as true here as it is in most American jurisdictions that benefit is not payable to those engaged in a lock-out, or in a strike caused by the unlawful conduct of the employer.

Arguments derived from insurance principles are equally unpersuasive. Fierst and Spector (1940: 464) have pointed out that if we accept the assumption that the fund should not subsidize voluntary unemployment 'we are left with no explanation for the disqualification of workers who are locked out by their employer, or who are not directly involved in the strike which caused their loss of employment'. Yet as we saw in Chapter 5, British law, in common with many other legal systems, has always denied benefit not only to participants, but also to those with an interest in the dispute, albeit the extent of the interest required has generally narrowed over the years. On a slightly different note, Lesser (1945) after questioning the voluntary nature of unemployment caused by a strike in response to an employer's attempt to impose substandard, illegal or other unreasonable conditions, has maintained that even if a strike is considered voluntary, it does not follow that strikers should not be compensated. He draws an analogy to benefit paid to individuals who voluntarily leave with good cause, or who refuse offers of alternative employment without good cause, indicating that the criterion of voluntariness is subordinated to other criteria which, from the social point of view, are considered paramount. If it is socially desirable to pay benefits to workers who with good cause have left employment, or refuse to accept employment, he argues that there is no good social reason, so far as the question of voluntary unemployment is concerned, for denying benefits to workers on strike because of conditions that make the work unsuitable (Lesser 1945: 171). But even more irrational than this is the fact that a worker who voluntarily quits without good cause is disqualified for only a limited period. Until recently the maximum (now twenty-six weeks) was set at six weeks. Yet a worker who voluntarily leaves in concert with others is disqualified for the entire duration of the stoppage even though he would have had just cause if he had acted alone.

It is perhaps paradoxical that the arguments in favour of the trade dispute disqualification in fact require that unemployment benefit should be paid to strikers in some cases. In other words, the underlying policy of disqualification does not permit, but requires, further liberalization of British law. Yet there is nothing intrinsically extraordinary about the payment of benefit to workers on strike. In the United States, in the Railway Labor Act jurisdiction, the disqualification applies only to a worker involved or interested in a 'strike [which] was commenced in violation of the provisions of the Railway Labor Act or in violation of the established rules and practices of a bona fide labor organisation of which he was a member'.[35] Congress apparently 'deemed

---

[34] See *Hills* v. *Attorney General of Canada* (1988) 48 DLR (4th) 193, esp. at pp. 211–13. The case was concerned with the financing limb of the disqualification which still operates in Canada.

[35] 45 US C[ode] A[nnotated], s. 354(a-2)(iii).

continuous, uninterrupted operation of railroads so vital to the public interest that it offered to railroad workers this special dispensation conditional upon their compliance with procedural safeguards plainly designed to defer strikes to the last possible moment'.[36] Although not going quite so far, a number of states pay benefit where the dispute (whether a strike or lock-out) is caused by what appears to be fault on the part of the employer. So in Alaska, Arizona, Montana, and Utah the disqualification does not apply where the dispute is caused by the employer's failure to comply with a state or federal law pertaining to hours, wages or other conditions of work; in the case of Montana this extends to the laws pertaining to collective bargaining. Alaska and Arizona also pay benefit where the dispute is caused by the employer's failure to conform to a collective agreement or contract with employees, while West Virginia pays benefit 'if the employees are required to accept wages, hours or conditions of employment substantially less favorable than those prevailing for similar work in the locality, or if employees are denied the right of collective bargaining under generally prevailing conditions or if an employer shuts down his plant or operation or dismisses his employees in order to force wage reduction, changes in hours or working conditions'. Finally, Utah also pays benefit where the strike has been fomented by the conduct of the employer'.

It is not widely known that these initiatives have parallels in Britain. We saw in Chapter 5 how benefits were payable between 1924 and 1927 to workers on strike as a result of an employer's breach of a collective agreement. And although they no longer reflect modern practice, there are also decisions of the Umpire holding that a dispute provoked by the illegal conduct of the employer was not a trade dispute for the purposes of the disqualification. The first such decision appears to have been issued in 1922, *Case No. 2358*, where employers in the coal-mining industry gave notice to terminate contracts of employment and to re-engage the staff at reduced rates, ostensibly for financial reasons. The miners walked out, but their claim for unemployment benefit was allowed, with the Umpire concluding in his decision:

Further evidence has been submitted by the applicants' association, which appears to show that the proposals made by the employer would have involved, if accepted, a breach of the provisions of the Coal Mines (Minimum Wage) Act 1912. In these circumstances I cannot regard the offer as being effective, and the applicants should not be held to have lost employment by reason of a stoppage of work which was due to a trade dispute.

In so holding, the Umpire rejected a claim by the employer that the 'men could have accepted the proposal and subsequently tested the legality in court'. In fact, the decision became an established exception to the wider terms of the disqualification, having been argued in several subsequent cases, successfully

---

[36] *Brotherhood of Railway and Steamship Clerks, Freight Handlers, Express and Station Employees* v. *Railroad Retirement Board*, 293 F.2d 37 (1956), at pp. 42–3.

so in at least six—all of them in the coal-mining industry. The employers' conduct in these cases involved the breach of a diverse range of statutory provisions: the Coal Mines (Weighing of Minerals) Act 1905; the Coal Mines Regulation Act 1908 (dealing with maximum permitted hours of work underground); the Coal Mines Act 1911 (dealing with ventilation underground); and the Coal Mines Act 1930 (dealing with maximum permitted hours of work underground). It was never fully explained in any of these cases why the disqualification should be restricted in this way—welcome and appropriate though it may well have been.

So exemptions to disqualification have been admitted where the dispute is provoked not only by an employer's breach of a collective agreement, but also by the employer's breach of statutory duty. But what about a breach of contract? Here it seems that in principle the disqualification would apply, with the position being expressed by the Umpire in *Case No. 2461/1928* in the following terms:

The fact that the workmen refuse to treat with an employer who is endeavouring to secure an agreed reduction of wages does not prevent a stoppage of work which subsequently results from being due to a trade dispute (*Decision 1693/25*). The termination of contracts by an employer on the workmen refusing to agree to a reduction of wages is a stoppage of work due to a trade dispute (*Decisions 167/20* and *4035/20*).

There is, however, one exception to this application of the disqualification even where the dispute is caused by the employer acting in breach of contract. In *Case No. 2031/36*, a number of fitters alleged that they had been underpaid, and refused to descend the pit until the balance was made up to them. It was held by the Umpire that they had not lost employment because of a trade dispute, the decision resting on an earlier unreported decision, *Decision 14400/32*, where it was said that 'There was no trouble in these cases about the terms of payment under the contracts of employment or as to what should be the terms of future employment, but whether the claimants had been underpaid or overpaid for work actually done. As the claimants could not induce the employer to pay what the claimants regarded as a debt due to them they refused to continue work'. In the Umpire's view, 'this was not a dispute which was connected with the employment or non-employment, or the terms of employment, or with the conditions of employment, of any persons'. Although there was also authority (*Case No. 282/25*) for the view that 'when the applicant found he was not being paid in accordance with his contract of service he ought instead of leaving to have brought the matter to the notice of his Union representative or have taken proceedings in a Court of Law, so as to try to get his grievance remedied', *Case No. 2031/36* was in fact followed and applied by the National Insurance Commissioner in *R(U) 26/59* where a stoppage was caused when nineteen employees had left their place of work after a foreman had wrongly withheld an income tax rebate from one of the employees involved.[37]

One possibility for the future, then, would be to build upon this Anglo-American experience by adopting a statutory provision whereby benefit would be payable where the dispute was caused by the unlawful conduct of the employer. But although this would be desirable it would not be enough: there is no justification in principle for taking such a narrow view of the matter. If we wish to be faithful to the concept of neutrality and to insurance principles, we would wish to provide for the payment of unemployment benefit to those claimants engaged in a trade dispute within the 'margin of legality', due wholly or mainly to the unlawful or unreasonable conduct of the employer. Where the claimant was disqualified, the ordinary principles of unemployment insurance would dictate that the period of disqualification should not exceed twenty-six weeks (though presumably this will be reduced to six), which as we have seen is the duration of disqualification for individuals who become voluntarily unemployed. (Once again this would not be unprecedented, with the un-employment insurance law in New York providing that disqualification ends after seven weeks even though the dispute may still be in operation.[38]) The twenty-six weeks' disqualification would of course be a maximum with the adjudicating authorities being empowered to impose a lesser penalty where the circumstances so required, or where the dispute was outside the margin of legality but was contributed to in some measure by the provocative action of the employer. So far as adjudication is concerned, no doubt there would be concern that the Department of Social Security should not be drawn into adjudicating the merits of industrial disputes. It is here that the Irish legislation discussed in Chapter 7 has some attractions. Although the substance of the law is too narrow and cautious—why, for example, should benefit be confined to those who have been deprived of their employment because of the employer's fault as opposed to those who have withdrawn their labour because of the fault of the employer?—the idea that disputes should be adjudicated by an independent agency separate from the department administering benefit (and separate from other departments trying to resolve the dispute) is both imaginative and attractive.

VI.   SOCIAL WELFARE BENEFITS

We turn now finally to consider entitlement to social welfare benefits. As we saw in Chapter 6, the present policy has its origins in the decision of the Court

---

[37] It may be noted that in evidence to the Blanesburgh Committee (see Ch. 5) the ISTC submitted evidence proposing that benefit should be paid where the dispute was caused by the employer acting in breach of contract of service: 'We hold the view that it should not be regarded as a trade dispute if either side attempts in an arbitrary manner to impose conditions upon the other party which are clearly a violation of the contract of service existing between the two parties' (Iron and Steel Trades' Confederation 1927).

[38] NY Lab. Law, s. 592. This survived constitutional challenge in *New York Telephone Company* v. *New York State Department of Labor*, 440 US 519 (1979).

of Appeal in 1900. The 1988 amendments are merely the latest modification and hardening of the relevant principles of the *Merthyr Tydfil* case.[39] In determining the continued application of these principles in this area, it is of course true that liberalization of the trade dispute disqualification for unemployment benefit would limit the extent of the problem. Workers who qualified for unemployment benefit would also qualify for income support (or its equivalent) to the extent that the former continued to fall short of the levels provided for by the latter. There would, of course, be cases where strikers on unemployment benefit would not qualify for income support (or its equivalent) because their income from all sources (including savings) would take them above the income support levels. It is to be kept in mind that unemployment benefit is payable because of unemployment, not because of need. Where there is need, however, because of the inadequacy of other sources of income, receipt of unemployment benefit would take the claimant on to income support almost automatically. But while the extent of the problem might thus be limited or narrowed, it would not be eliminated. There would still arise the problem of those workers who are ineligible for unemployment benefit, as well as those engaged in a dispute which, not being caused principally by an event (or series of events) attributed to fault on the employer's part, would not attract unemployment benefit and consequently income support (or its equivalent) if the claimant's requirements fell short of resources.

The central question here is whether workers engaged in a dispute (for whatever reason) should be disqualified from receiving a welfare benefit which is designed to alleviate destitution. If the answer to this question is in the affirmative, it then becomes necessary to consider whether the dependants of those engaged in a dispute should be disqualified from receiving benefit. If the answer to this is in the negative, a further question will need to be considered, namely, on what conditions benefit should be paid to the dependants of those in dispute. For the purposes of this study, however, it may not be necessary to consider the last two questions. Although the prospect of paying welfare benefit to strikers may appear incredible, there may nevertheless be no good reasons for failing to do so. One argument against benefit for strikers challenges the assumption that the function of welfare is to meet need regardless of how it is caused. On this view the function of welfare is to support only those who have need and who are unable to maintain themselves. The effect of this approach is to deny benefit to strikers because their need is self-induced, and because they are free to return to work at any time, albeit not on the terms of their choice. But this argument is deeply flawed because it simply cannot be said that the primary function is to alleviate the need of the deserving poor only. For although there may be great concern in some quarters about the 'undeserving poor', the reality is that, even after ten years of Thatcher-inspired

[39] *Attorney General* v. *Merthyr Tydfil Union* [1900] 1 Ch. 516. The same judicial response has been made more recently with similar rhetoric in other jurisdictions. See *Alden* v. *Gaglardi* (1973) 30 DLR (3d) 760 (Supreme Court of Canada).

reforms, the primary rule of the system is to alleviate need regardless of cause, with only secondary rules operating to punish those who have caused or contributed to their own need. The trade dispute disqualification stands as a major exception to the underlying philosophy of the British welfare system.

The point is most vividly illustrated by rules regulating so-called voluntary unemployment on the part of individual claimants. The primary rule which operates here is that even the voluntarily unemployed are entitled to claim for themselves and their families. This rule has admittedly undergone some modification in recent years, with a secondary rule conflicting with the underlying philosophy being introduced in 1971.[40] Thus, if there is no good cause for the unemployment, the claimant may find that his benefit has been reduced by 40 per cent as a result, though it is to be noted that no reduction is made in respect of the benefit claimed for a partner or for dependant children.[41] The key point, however, is that income support is still payable to meet the needs of the claimant, subject only to a reduction in, rather than a denial of, benefit. Indeed, in some cases (for example, pregnancy or serious illness in the family) the amount of the disqualification is reduced to 20 per cent.[42] The contrast with the striker and his family is thus profound. If their position were to be governed by the underlying principles of the scheme as it applies to everyone else, they would qualify for benefit, subject to a possible reduction of the benefit payable to the striker where there is no good cause for his action. It is not altogether clear why an act by a group of people should be penalized when the voluntary quitting by a single individual would not.[43] Nor is it altogether clear why an act by a group of people should be more heavily penalized than a similar act by an individual. Nor indeed is it altogether clear why the families of strikers should be penalized any more than the family next door voluntarily unemployed on other grounds.

The disqualification of strikers thus cannot be justified as being compatible with the underlying principles of welfare. As a result any alternative rationale for the disqualification would need to be based on fairly compelling and firm grounds, being a rare exception to a well-established principle. One such rationale is state neutrality,[44] an argument we have encountered in the context of unemployment benefit, but which is frequently used to justify the withholding of welfare benefits to strikers. Yet the argument is no more persuasive in this latter context than it was in the former. Again we come back to the question why the state should be neutral by withholding welfare benefits. Clearly there are many instances where, because of the employer's unlawful behaviour, the state ought not to be neutral. It is true that many of the reforms to unemployment benefit already advocated would, as we have seen, mean that

---

[40] Social Security Act 1971, s. 1.

[41] Income Support (General) Regulations 1987, SI 1987/1967, reg. 22.   [42] Ibid.

[43] See also the dissenting judgment of Justice Marshall in *Lyng* v. *International Union, United Automobile, Aerospace and Agricultural Implement Workers of America, UAW*, 99 L.Ed. 380 (1988), at p. 397.

[44] This was accepted by a majority of the US Supreme Court in *Lyng*, ibid.

workers on strike because their employer was at fault would also be entitled to income support. But what about the other cases? If it is accepted that workers may in certain circumstances take industrial action 'the payment of limited benefits preserves a balance between employer and employee which makes the right to strike a possibility for those who would otherwise be denied a way to call attention to their grievances' (Supplementary Benefits Commission 1976: 49–50). These arguments have found some recognition in American courts where in rejecting an attempt to withhold welfare benefits to strikers, it was accepted that 'Labor union membership or activity and the right to strike in proper cases and under proper circumstances is an accepted fact in our industrial community', and that to deny welfare benefits to strikers would be 'to strangle otherwise authorized activity'.[45]

Quite apart from the issue of the state's neutrality is the question whether it is logically possible to secure this neutrality by the simple expedient of withholding welfare benefits to strikers. A convincing answer was given by the New York Court of Appeals which in 1972 was presented with a challenge to the practice of the Commissioner of Social Services of the State of New York to provide assistance to people on strike.[46] Although there was no express statutory authorization for the payments, they were made under the authority of a power which permitted payment to people who were 'unable to maintain themselves'. In dismissing the challenge, the Court rejected the view that the payment of benefit to needy strikers amounted to a violation of the state's policy of neutrality in industrial relations. According to the Court:

It may fairly be said that in cases such as this the policy of governmental neutrality in labor controversies is, in reality, little more than an admirable fiction. Although, on the one hand, the State may not be acting in a strictly neutral fashion if it allows strikers to obtain public assistance, it may not, on the other hand, be seriously maintained that the State adopts a neutral policy if it renders strikers helpless by denying them public assistance or welfare benefits to which they would otherwise be entitled.[47]

The fiction of neutrality becomes mere fantasy when it is considered that while workers are denied benefits to which they would be entitled but for the disqualification, there is no corresponding penalty on employers or disqualification from the 'complex web' of government supports and incentives, ranging from tax benefits, lucrative government contracts, to direct subsidies. This led to Justice Marshall in the US Supreme Court to contend that the denial of welfare to strikers is a one-sided and devastating withdrawal of support which 'amounts to a penalty on strikers, not neutrality'.[48]

The third possible justification for disqualification serves to illustrate the shallowness of the justification built upon state neutrality. This is the state subsidy theory based upon the premiss that the state should not subsidize

---

[45] *Strat-O-Seal Manufacturing Co.* v. *Scott*, 218 NE 2d 227 (1966), at p. 230.
[46] *Lascaris* v. *Wyman*, 292 NE 2d 667 (1972).   [47] Ibid., at pp. 671–2.
[48] *Lyng* v. *International Union, United Automobile, Aerospace and Agricultural Implement Workers of America, UAW*, 99 L.Ed. 380 (1988), at p. 399.

'from public funds actions which are against the public interest' (Supplementary Benefits Commission 1976: 49). This is of course a clear refutation of the state neutrality rationale in the sense that it embraces a clear judgment to withdraw support from activity which is regarded as being socially harmful regardless of its cause. By employing the state subsidy argument to justify the non-payment of benefits to strikers we are implicitly accepting that it is a legitimate use of the welfare system to discourage strikes. For in withholding benefits, the state is not being neutral; rather, it is being deliberately coercive. But be that as it may, the state subsidy theory developed in the early 1970s to explain the changes in the British strike pattern, characterized by 'increases in the frequency, size and duration of strikes' (Durcan and McCarthy 1974: 26). It became part of the 'received wisdom in some quarters' that state subsidies in the form of supplementary benefit and tax rebates 'increase the level of strike activity' (Gennard and Lasko 1975: 346). The theory is based upon an assumed connection 'between strike propensity, strike duration and the loss of income occasioned by strike activity' (Durcan and McCarthy 1974: 27). It assumes that any payments made to workers during a strike would reduce the cost of strike activity and make the workers in question more likely to strike in the first place, and less likely to return to work until their demands have been met. Indeed, one author thought it 'obvious' that 'the provision of public subsidies to strikers may drastically affect the ultimate result produced by the collective bargaining process, since such assistance will reduce the cost of the strike to the employees while simultaneously increasing their capability to continue the strike' (Carney 1973: 534).

Given its simple logical coherence, it is not surprising that this theory should have been influential, having informed both the 1971 and 1980 reforms which reduced benefits to strikers' families. It could of course also justify the long-standing rule whereby strikers themselves do not qualify for benefit, just as it could be used to justify a complete disqualification of strikers and their families for the duration of the dispute. This indeed would be the logical conclusion of the theory. Yet for all its logical simplicity, there is no convincing evidence of any direct correlation between the availability of welfare benefits and the incidence or duration of strikes. A number of studies conducted in the 1970s tend to suggest that this is because there is none. The most important of these, that by Gennard and Lasko (1975), examined strikers' sources of income. They found a wide variety of sources such as arrears of pay, spouse's earnings, casual work, and savings. Indeed, in none of the different groups of strikers studied 'did supplementary benefit make up more than about a fifth of total income' (Gennard and Lasko 1975: 355). The state subsidy provided by supplementary benefit even before the crippling 1980 reforms was thus very limited, a point supported by Durcan and McCarthy (1974: 43–4) who concluded that 'the incidence of state subsidy was so unevenly spread within the average group of strikers' that it was 'implausible to believe that state payments can have been regarded as much more than gratuitous windfalls'.

The same authors contended that 'to the great majority the prospect or receipt of state payments was not sufficiently stable, or at a high enough level, to operate as a decisive factor'. Little wonder they concluded: 'If we are looking for developments which may have exercised a significant or major influence on the growing propensity to strike in the fifties and sixties we must surely look elsewhere.'

The empirical evidence thus suggests that the payment of supplementary benefits under the law operating before 1980 was not a major factor in encouraging people to take strike action. Given that the law has since become much more restrictive, it seems reasonable to assume that the situation will not have changed in the period from 1980 onwards. Yet although there is no evidence to believe that the availability of benefit encourages people to strike action, as Gennard and Lasko (1975: 567) point out, it does not follow that the withdrawal of benefit would not discourage people from taking strike action, though they also suggest that the total removal of benefit would not be a major factor in reducing the incidence of strike activity. There are no data on this question in the 1980s, though it may be pointed out that the new regime did not prevent the miners from participating in a very lengthy strike in 1984/5. Nor did it prevent workers engaged at Wapping by News International from participating in what was also a long and bitter dispute. It does not follow, however, that a new regime which applied the ordinary principles of social welfare to strikers would have the same neutral effect—assuming that this is broadly what the data indicate. The assumption would almost certainly be made that the payment of benefits not only to the families of strikers, but also to the strikers themselves, would inevitably encourage people to take industrial action rather than use other methods for the resolution of their disputes. Yet although assumptions of this kind cannot be disproved in advance of any legislative changes being made, the existing evidence suggests that at best any such reform is likely to make only a marginal, if any, difference in the propensity of people to take strike action.

It is important to bear in mind that the abolition of the trade dispute disqualification in the field of income support would not mean that those on strike would immediately and automatically become eligible for benefit. Those on strike would be subject to the same principles as everyone else, which, so far as strikers are concerned, would have three major consequences. In the first place, in very many cases there will be other income in the household which would have the effect of denying benefit completely, or of reducing it. This would be true, for example, where the spouse of the striker is engaged in full-time employment or where the striker has savings in excess of £3,000, which would go to reduce the amount of benefit or perhaps even remove the entitlement to benefit altogether. Secondly, even where income or capital resources are not sufficient to exclude benefit altogether, it does not follow that the full amount of benefit would be paid. The present income support rules reduce the benefit of those voluntarily unemployed without good cause (though not that of their spouses or children) by up to 40 per cent for up to twenty-six weeks. Although workers involved in a dispute for which unemployment benefit would be payable would be presumed to have good cause for the purposes of income support, provided their resources were such as to render them eligible, there would be no such presumption in the case of workers engaged in any other dispute, and who could thus also suffer a serious financial penalty. But, thirdly, even if there is no penalty, the payment of benefit to strikers will still produce an income which will fall far short of wages and salaries. The cost of striking will remain very high.

VII. PROPOSALS FOR REFORM

It is sensible at this stage to pull together the different proposals which have been made in this chapter. If we accept a social justice theory of labour law as opposed to a market efficiency model, it is necessary to provide some protection of the right to strike. Although we have historically promoted a social justice theory of labour law in Britain, our legal policies on the right to strike have been inadequate, partly because of the failure to address the question of the individual striker and to provide adequate protection against coercion, not only by employers but also by public authorities. A comprehensive package, based on principle, would provide as follows.

1 Participation in a lawful strike would not be regarded as a breach of the contract of employment. Participation in a strike outside the boundaries of legitimate activity would be regarded as a breach of contract, for the purposes of both contractual and tortious liability.

2 Protection from existing common law liability would be provided for workers who take part in industrial action short of a strike.

(a) Although an employer could decline to accept partial performance, this would be only after an industrial tribunal had decided that the workers were in fact in breach. An expedited hearing could be held for this purpose.

(b) Workers permitted to work, despite failing to provide full performance, would be entitled to be paid. If the employer has accepted substantial performance, workers would be entitled to full pay. In other cases employees would be entitled to be paid for the work actually provided.

(c) Although employers would thus be permitted to make deductions for partial performance, this would be permitted only after an industrial tribunal had held that the employees were in fact in breach of contract, and only after the tribunal had assessed the extent of the breach and the amount of the employer's permitted deduction.

3 Employees engaged in a strike, or lock-out, or other industrial action would enjoy adequate protection against unfair dismissal.

(a) It would be automatically unfair to dismiss someone for participating in a strike within the margins of legality. This would not apply to strike-related misconduct.

(b) Employees participating in industrial action outside the margins of legality would be protected either by the ordinary rules of unfair dismissal, or by the retention for this purpose only of the non-discrimination provisions contained in the Employment Protection (Consolidation) Act 1978, section 62 (before the 1982 and 1990 amendments), or by a combination of both.

(c) Although employers would be free to hire temporary replacements to do the work of those in dispute, employees involved in a dispute which falls within the margins of legality would be entitled to return to work at the end of the strike. If the dispute does not end, employees would be entitled to return to work within a period of two years from the day the industrial action started.

4 The rules disqualifying workers from unemployment benefit would be relaxed so that benefit would be payable in a wider range of circumstances than at present. Benefit would be withheld only from those engaged in a trade dispute without just cause.

(a) It would be presumed conclusively that unemployment benefit would be payable where the activating cause of a dispute within the margins of legality leading to unemployment was the unlawful conduct of the employer. This would expressly include conduct in breach of a statutory duty or in breach of contract.

(b) In all other cases benefit would be payable if the activating cause of the trade dispute within the margins of legality was the unreasonable conduct of the employer. This would expressly include conduct in breach of a collective agreement. Where disqualification was imposed, this would not exceed the period of disqualification for the voluntarily unemployed.

(c) There is no reason in principle why these questions should not be resolved by the social security authorities responsible for adjudication. If, however, there are serious objections to this, the Irish Social Welfare Tribunal provides the model for a suitable alternative forum for adjudication. The agency would determine whether the employer acted unlawfully or unreasonably, and would determine the length of any disqualification.

5 The rules disqualifying workers from what is now called income support would be abolished so that workers in dispute would be entitled to benefit if they satisfied the other conditions of eligibility.

(a) Workers in dispute who were eligible for benefit and who were entitled to unemployment benefit under the rules outlined above would also qualify for income support. Workers who were eligible for benefit but who did not satisfy the contribution conditions for unemployment benefit would be entitled to income support as if they did satisfy those conditions.

(b) Workers in dispute who were disqualified from unemployment benefit (or who would be disqualified if they satisfied the contribution conditions), because they were engaged in a strike outside the margin of legality or because there was no just cause for their unemployment, would not be disqualified from income support, but would be treated in the same way as the other categories of voluntarily unemployed claimants. At the time of writing this means that benefit would be cut.

(c) Here, too, claims could be processed by the normal social security authorities. Practical problems would not present insuperable obstacles in this situation since the Irish Social Welfare Tribunal again provides the model for a suitable alternative forum for adjudication. Its task here would be to deal with claims from people who do not satisfy the contribution conditions for unemployment benefit.

All this will no doubt be represented as radical and far-reaching. But they are proposals dictated by principle which are far-reaching only when set against the cautious and conservative approach which dominated labour law thinking in Britain before the election of Mrs Thatcher in 1979.

Appendix 1

*A Note on Litigation Arising out of
the Ambulance Workers' Dispute 1989–90*

28 November 1989	Ambulance workers sought injunction against health authority over wage deductions	Mr Justice Auld refused the injunction saying claim not urgent
10 January 1990	Oxfordshire health authority sought injunction to ban workers setting up alternative service	Mr Justice Judge granted injunction stating that workers could not use vehicles and apparatus
12 January 1990	Oxfordshire returned to court to seek clarification and continuance of injunction	Mr Justice Waller amended injunction to permit workers to use property when carrying out instructions
25 January 1990	Surrey health authority sought injunction to ban workers using vehicles for emergency calls	Mr Justice Hadden granted injunction as requested
7 February 1990	North Western health authority sought injunction to ban workers using NHS property	Mr Justice Steyn granted injunction
18 February 1990	Glamorgan health authority also sought injunction	Injunction granted also preventing workers from entering premises
20 February 1990	Glamorgan sought continuation of injunction	Mr Justice Owen granted extension
20 February 1990	West Yorkshire health authority sought injunction	Health authority then withdrew its request

Source: Labour Research, April 1990.

Appendix 2

Poor Law Guardians and the General Strike

Boards of Guardians
(England and Wales).

Circular 703.

Ministry of Health
Whitehall, S.W.1.
5th May, 1926.

Sir,

I am directed by the Minister of Health to transmit for the consideration of the guardians the following notes and suggestions with reference to the action to be taken in view of the general stoppage of industry.

The position of the guardians now becomes one of great responsibility and importance.

It is to be anticipated that there may be large numbers of applications for relief arising directly or indirectly out of the stoppage, and it will be necessary on the one hand for the guardians to make adequate arrangements for carrying out their statutory duty of relieving destitution and on the other to take all possible steps to conserve their financial resources in face of the demands that may be made upon them, and the possibly prolonged duration of the stoppage. An emergency like the present makes it the plain duty of every board to keep this second consideration always before them in deciding what they can properly do.

With regard to the limits within which relief may be given to persons who are destitute in consequence of a trade dispute, the Minister desires to draw attention to the declaration of the law contained in the judgment of the Court of Appeal in *Attorney General* v. *Merthyr Tydfil Guardians* (1900).

The function of the guardians is the relief of destitution within the limits prescribed by law and they are in no way concerned in the merits of an industrial dispute, even though it results in applications for relief. They cannot, therefore, properly give any weight to their views of such merits in dealing with the applications made to them.

The questions for the consideration of the guardians on any application for relief made by a person who is destitute in consequence of a trade dispute are questions of fact, namely, whether the applicant for relief is or is not a person who is able-bodied and physically capable of work; whether work is or is not available for him and if such work is not available for him, whether it is or is not so unavailable through his own act or consent.

Where the applicant for relief is able-bodied and physically capable of work the grant of relief to him is unlawful if work is available for him or he is thrown on the guardians through his own act or consent, and penalties are provided by law in case of failure to support dependents, though the guardians may lawfully relieve such dependents if they are in fact destitute.

In cases in which the applicant, though ordinarily able-bodied is, as a result of continued unemployment or otherwise, no longer physically able to perform work, relief may be granted, but it is obviously proper that in such a case a full report should be made to the guardians by the relieving officer and ordinarily by a medical officer. As a rule, however, in the event of a man being so reduced by want as is contemplated in the judgment, his necessity would be urgent and should be relieved by the appropriate officer of the guardians on his own responsibility under the powers reserved to him to meet such contingencies.

It will be of special importance for the guardians to scrutinize each individual application with a view to ascertaining that it is a case which they may properly relieve, and that destitution is present before relief is granted. In this connection it should be noted that there have been instances of applications for relief being made by persons immediately on cessation of work, when they would normally have just received at least the wages for the previous week's work.

In the special circumstances likely to arise, it will probably be necessary for the guardians to adopt some defined scale of relief for their guidance, or, where such a scale has already been adopted, to review its provisions and consider whether any modification is desirable.

It is recognised that there will be in every union cases in receipt of relief in respect of which existing arrangements cannot be modified, and it will, of course, be for the guardians to use the discretion in these matters which has been entrusted to them. But the Minister considers that at this moment it is necessary to examine the general situation and in this connection he desires first to draw attention to the scale on which unemployment benefit is paid and to suggest that, as is already the practice in a considerable number of unions, the relief given by the guardians should be so restricted as to be within this scale. The scale is as follows:— 18s. weekly for a man, 5s. for a wife, 2s. for each child.

In cases where, under the Merthyr Tydfil Judgment, relief may not lawfully be given to the man, it may be found necessary to increase the allowances to the women and children above the figures of unemployment benefit but it is thought that such allowances should not exceed the sum of 12s. and 4s. for the woman and each child respectively, these amounts representing what was found reasonable in the emergency of 1921, subject to a reduction corresponding to the fall in the cost of living. Exceptions would naturally be made in this scale, or any other scale that may be adopted by the guardians, in cases in which sickness or other special need was present in the family.

A substantial proportion, not less in any event than one-half of the relief, should invariably be given in kind and the experience of relief given during the dispute of 1921 suggests that the most practicable and successful way of meeting the needs of the distressed areas is by the institution of some form of communal meals. In some districts feeding, especially of children, was organised on a large scale in 1921. There is no legal authority for any bulk payment to another agency by the guardians for the establishment of communal feeding centres, but it is open to them to pay for meals supplied to individual children or adults on the order of a relieving officer or of the guardians, and the Minister hopes that, wherever this is found practicable, the guardians will avail themselves of any facilities that may be provided in their union. He has no doubt that individual guardians will be prominent in the organisation of arrangements of this kind, and that there will be every facility for co-operation between the guardians and the organisations.

The value of any meals so received, and of any other means of subsistence available to the applicant for relief, should, of course, be strictly taken into account in applying any scale of relief which is adopted.

The Minister would add that he attaches particular importance to close co-ordination and exchange of information between the guardians and the local education authority as regards the provision of meals by that authority.

It will be realised, of course, that the powers conferred upon local education authorities by the Education Act, 1921, in regard to the provision of meals are not intended to be so used as to throw the burden of the relief of destitution upon the education rate.

I am, Sir,

Your obedient Servant,

W. A. ROBINSON

Source: Justice of the Peace, 15 May 1926, pp. 299–300.

Bibliography

Alberta Labour (1987), *Labour Legislation Review Committee: Final Report*, Edmonton: Alberta Labour.

Anderman, S. (1985), *The Law of Unfair Dismissal*, 2nd edn., London: Butterworths.

Anon. (1949), 'Eligibility for Unemployment Benefits of Persons Involuntarily Unemployed Because of Labor Disputes', 49 *Columbia Law Review* 550.

Arnot, R. P. (1955), *A History of the Scottish Miners*, London: George Allen and Unwin.

Arthurs, H. W., Carter, D. D., Glasbeek, H. J., and Fudge, J. (1988), 'Canada', in R. Blanpain (ed.), *International Encyclopaedia for Labour Law and Industrial Relations*, Deventer: Kluwer.

APEX (1986), Industrial Relations Legislation: TUC Consultative Document, London [mimeo].

Atleson, J. B. (1983), *Values and Assumptions in American Labor Law*, Amherst, Mass.: University of Massachusetts Press.

Bakels, H. L. (1987), 'The Netherlands', in R. Blanpain (ed.), *International Encyclopaedia for Labour Law and Industrial Relations*, Deventer: Kluwer.

Bates, F. (1986), 'Industrial Action and Unemployment Benefits', 60 *Australian Law Journal* 554.

Bercusson, B. (1976), *The Employment Protection Act 1975*, London: Sweet & Maxwell.

—— (1977), 'One Hundred Years of Conspiracy and Protection of Property: Time for a Change', 40 *Modern Law Review* 268.

—— (1978), *Fair Wages Resolutions*, London: Mansell.

Betten, L. (1985), *The Right to Strike in Community Law*, Amsterdam: Elsevier Science Publishers.

Beveridge, Sir William (1944), *Social Insurance and Allied Services*. Report by Sir William Beveridge, Cmd. 6404, London: HMSO.

Blanc-Jouvain, X. (1972), 'The Effect of Industrial Action on the Status of the Individual Employee', in B. Aaron and K. W. Wedderburn (eds.), *Industrial Conflict: A Comparative Legal Survey*, London: Longman.

Blanesburgh (1927), *Report of the Unemployment Insurance Committee*, Chairman: Lord Blanesburgh, London: HMSO.

Blanpain, R., and Engels, C. (1988), 'Belgium', in R. Blanpain (ed.), *International Encyclopaedia for Labour Law and Industrial Relations*, Deventer: Kluwer.

Booker, G. S. and McPherson, P. (1969), 'Unemployment Compensation and Labor Dispute Disqualification', 20 *Labor Law Journal* 247.

Booth, A. and Smith, R. (1985), 'The Irony of the Iron Fist: Social Security and the Coal Dispute 1984–85', 12 *Journal of Law and Society* 365.

Brooks, A. (1988), 'Myth and Muddle—An Examination of Contracts for the Performance of Work', 11 *University of New South Wales Law Journal* 48.

Brooks, B. T. (1988), 'Australia', in R. Blanpain (ed.), *International Encyclopaedia for Labour Law and Industrial Relations*, Deventer: Kluwer.

Brown, M. V. (1989), 'The Demise of Compensation as a Remedy for Unfair Dismissal in Western Australia: A Casualty of the Robe River Dispute', 19 *University of Western Australia Law Review* 29.

Bruce, M. (1968), *The Coming of the Welfare State*, London: B. T. Batsford.

Buck, T. (1989), 'Actively Seeking Work', 18 *Industrial Law Journal* 258.

Bullitt, S. (1950), 'Unemployment Compensation in Labor Disputes', 25 *Washington Law Review* 50.

Burrows, N. (1988), 'United Kingdom', in A. P. C. M. Jaspers and L. Betten (eds.), *25 Years European Social Charter*, Deventer: Kluwer.

Calvert, H. (1978), *Social Security Law*, 2nd edn., London: Sweet & Maxwell.

Carney, J. T. (1973), 'The Forgotten Man on the Welfare Roll: A Study of Public Subsidies for Strikers', *Washington University Law Review* 469.

Carr, S. (1987), 'Our Strikers Must Be Protected, Too', *Financial Post*, 17 August.

Chief Adjudication Officer (1989), *Adjudication Officers' Guide*, London: HMSO.

Clark, R. (1983), 'The Social Welfare Act 1983. A Commentary', 2 *Journal of the Irish Society for Labour Law* 22.

—— (1985), 'Law and the Unemployed', 32 *Administration* 413.

—— (1985a), 'Towards a "Just" Strike? Social Welfare Payments for Persons Affected by a Trade Dispute in the Republic of Ireland', 48 *Modern Law Review* 659.

Cole, W. J. (1975), 'The Financing of the Individual Striker: A Case Study in the Building Industry', 13 *British Journal of Industrial Relations* 94.

Collins, H. (1982), 'Capitalist Discipline and Corporatist Law', 11 *Industrial Law Journal* 78, 170.

COHSE (1986), Comments on the TUC Document 'Industrial Relations Legislation', London: [mimeo].

Confer, D. R. (1975), 'Pennsylvania's Lockout Exception to the Labor Dispute Disqualification from Unemployment Compensation Benefits', 80 *Dickinson Law Review* 70.

Coote, B. (1982), 'Wages for Workers on Strike', 10 *New Zealand Universities Law Review* 177.

Council of Europe (1987), *Committee of Independent Experts of the European Social Charter. Conclusions X–1*, Strasbourg: Council of Europe.

Creighton, W. B. (1979), 'Judicial Review in Scotland', 8 *Industrial Law Journal* 118.

—— Ford, W. J., and Mitchell, R. J. (1983), *Labour Law Materials and Commentary*, Sydney: Law Book Co.

Curry, J. (1986), *Report of the Commission on Social Welfare*, Pl. 3851, Dublin: Stationery Office.

Davies, P. and Freedland, M. (1984), *Labour Law Text and Materials*, 2nd edn., London: Weidenfeld & Nicolson.

Deakin, S. (1990), 'Equality Under a Market Order: The Employment Act 1989', 19 *Industrial Law Journal* 1.

Denis, P. (1986), *Droit de la Sécurité Sociale*, 5th edn., Brussels: Larcier.

Department of Employment (1989), *Unofficial Action and the Law*, Cm. 821, London: HMSO.

Department of Health and Social Security (1982), *Supplementary Benefits Handbook*, London: HMSO.

—— (1985), *Reform of Social Security*, vol. 1, Cmnd. 9517, London: HMSO.

—— (1988), *A Guide to the Social Fund*, SB 16, London: HMSO.

Department of Labour (1989), *Annual Report 1988*, Dublin: Stationery Office.

Department of Social Security (1985), *Reform of Social Security: Programme for Action*, Cmnd. 9691. London: HMSO.

—— (1989), *A Guide to Income Support*, SB 20, London: HMSO.

—— (1990), *Income Support Manual*, London: HMSO.

Despax, M., and Rojot, J. (1987), 'France', in R. Blanpain (ed.), *International Encyclopaedia for Labour Law and Industrial Relations*, Deventer: Kluwer.

Dickens, L., Jones, M., Weekes, B., and Hart, M. (1985), *Dismissed: A Study of Unfair Dismissal and the Industrial Tribunal System*, Oxford: Blackwell.

Donovan (1968), *Royal Commission on Trade Unions and Employers' Associations 1965–68*, Report, Chairman: Lord Donovan, Cmnd. 3623, London: HMSO.

Drache, D. and Glasbeek, H. (1989), 'The New Fordism in Canada: Capital's Offensive, Labour's Opportunity', 27 *Osgoode Hall Law Journal* 517.

Durcan, J. W. and McCarthy, W. E. J. (1974), 'The State Subsidy Theory of Strikes: An Examination of Statistical Data for the Period 1956–1970', 12 *British Journal of Industrial Relations* 26.

Elias, P. (1982), 'The Structure of the Employment Contract', 35 *Current Legal Problems* 175.

England, G. (1976), 'Loss of Jobs in Strikes—The Position in England and Canada Compared', 25 *International and Comparative Law Quarterly* 583.

—— (1976a), 'The Legal Response to Striking at the Individual Level in the Common Law Jurisdictions of Canada', 3 *Dalhousie Law Journal* 440.

Ephron, S. H. (1986), 'Redefining Neutrality: Alternative Interpretations of the Labor Dispute Disqualification in Unemployment Compensation', 8 *Comparative Labor Law* 89.

Epstein, R. A. (1983), 'A Common Law for Labor Relations: A Critique of the New Deal Labor Legislation', 92 *Yale Law Journal* 1357.

Evans, S. and Lewis, R. (1987), 'Anti-Union Discrimination: Practice Law and Policy', 16 *Industrial Law Journal* 88.

Ewing, K. D. (1981), 'Collective Agreements, Trade Disputes and Unemployment Benefit—The Employer's Breach Exemption', 32 *Northern Ireland Legal Quarterly* 305.

—— (1981a), 'Social Security Act 1980', *Current Law Statutes 1980*, London: Stevens.

—— (1982), 'Industrial Action: Another Step in the "Right" Direction', 11 *Industrial Law Journal* 209.

—— (1986), 'The Right to Strike', 15 *Industrial Law Journal* 143.

—— (1988), 'Il diritto del lavoro negli anni '20: l'esperienza inglese', in G. Vardaro (ed.), *Diritto del lavoro e corporativismi in Europa: ieri e oggi*, Milan: FrancoAngeli.

—— (1988a), 'Trade Unions and the Constitution: The Impact of the New Conservatives', in C. Graham and T. Prosser (eds.), *Waiving the Rules: The Constitution under Thatcherism*, Milton Keynes: Open University Press.

—— (1989), *Britain and the ILO*, London: Institute of Employment Rights.

—— (1989a), 'The Right to Strike in Australia', 2 *Australian Journal of Labour Law* 1.

—— (1989b), 'The Right to Strike in Britain', *Lectures on the Common Law*, Deventer: Kluwer.

—— (1990), 'Economics and Labour Law: Thatcher's Radical Experiment', 28 *Alberta Law Review* 632.

—— and Brodie, D. (1987), 'Social Security Act 1986', *Current Law Statutes*, London: Stevens.

—— and Napier, B. W. (1986), 'The Wapping Dispute and Labour Law', 45 *Cambridge Law Journal* 285.

Fennell, P. (1986), '*Roberts* v. *Hopwood*: The Rule Against Socialism', 13 *Journal of Law and Society* 401.

Fierst, H. A. and Spector, F. (1940), 'Unemployment Compensation in Labor Disputes', 49 *Yale Law Journal* 461.

Flanders, A. (1954), 'Collective Bargaining', in A. Flanders and H. A. Clegg (eds.), *The System of Industrial Relations in Great Britain*, Oxford: Blackwell.

Foster, K. (1973), 'Strike Notice: Section 147', 2 *Industrial Law Journal* 28.

Fraser, D. (1973), *The Evolution of the British Welfare State*, London: Macmillan.

Fredman, S. and Morris, G. (1987), 'The Teachers' Lesson: Collective Bargaining and the Courts', 16 *Industrial Law Journal* 215.

Freedland, M. (1976), *The Contract of Employment*, Oxford: Clarendon Press.

—— (1977), 'The Obligation to Work and to Pay for Work', 30 *Current Legal Problems* 175.

Frick, R. H. (1951), 'Unemployment Compensation—Effect of the Merits of a Labor Dispute on the Right to Benefits', 49 *Michigan Law Review* 886.

Gennard, J. (1977), *Financing Strikers*, London: Macmillan.

—— and Lasko, R. (1974), 'Supplementary Benefits and Strikers', 12 *British Journal of Industrial Relations* 1.

—— —— (1975), 'The Individual and the Strike', 13 *British Journal of Industrial Relations* 346.

Gorman, R. A. (1976), *Labor Law. Basic Text*, St Paul: West Publishing Company.

Gould, W. B. (1982), *A Primer on American Labor Law*, Cambridge, Mass.: MIT Press.

Graham, J. E. (1922), *The Law Relating to the Poor and to Parish Councils*, Edinburgh: William Hodge & Co.

Graulich, B. and Palsterman, P. (1986), *Les droits et obligations du chômeur*, Brussels: Editions Labor.

Greenberg, R. (1967), 'Public Welfare—Striker's Right to Public Assistance', 16 *De Paul Law Review* 516.

Gregory (1932), *Royal Commission on Unemployment Insurance*, Final Report, Chairman: His Hon. Judge H. Gregory KC, Cmd. 4185, London: HMSO.

Haggart, V. J. (1958), 'Unemployment Compensation During Labor Disputes', 37 *Nebraska Law Review* 668.

Hanson, C. G. and Mather, G. (1988), *Striking Out Strikes: Changing Employment Relations in the British Labour Market*, London: Institute of Economic Affairs.

Hasson, R. A. (1987), 'Discipline and Punishment in the Law of Unemployment Insurance—A Critical View of Disqualifications and Disentitlements', 25 *Osgoode Hall Law Journal* 615.

Hendy, J. (1989), *The Conservative Employment Laws: A National and International Assessment*, London: Institute of Employment Rights.

Hepple, B. A. (1986), 'Restructuring Employment Rights', 15 *Industrial Law Journal* 69.

—— (1988), 'Committee of Independent Experts of the European Social Charter. Conclusions X–1', 17 *Industrial Law Journal* 124.

Hickling, M. A. (1975), *Labour Disputes and Unemployment Insurance Benefits in Canada and England*, Don Mills: CCH Canadian.

Hogler, R. L. (1986), 'The Common Law of Public Employee Strikes: A New Rule in California', 37 *Labor Law Journal* 94.

Hughes, J. (1982), 'The Industrial Relations Amendment Act', 10 *New Zealand Universities Law Review* 182.

Hunter, L. C. (1974), 'The State Subsidy Theory of Strikes: A Reconsideration', 12 *British Journal of Industrial Relations* 438.

ILO (1989), Committee of Experts. Convention No. 87. Freedom of Association and Protection of the Right to Organize, 1948. Observations, Geneva [International Labour Organization].

Iron and Steel Trades' Confederation (1927), *Memorandum of Evidence of the ISTC submitted to the Blanesburgh Committee on Unemployment Insurance*, London: HMSO.

Jennings, W. I. (1930), 'Poor Relief in Industrial Disputes', 46 *Law Quarterly Review* 225.

—— (1936), *The Poor Law Code, and the Law of Unemployment Assistance*, 2nd edn., London: Charles Knight & Co.

Jones, D. L. (1956), 'The Conflict Between Collective Bargaining and Unemployment Insurance', 28 *Rocky Mountain Law Review* 185.

Kahn-Freund, O. (1983), *Labour and the Law*, 3rd edn. by P. Davies and M. Freedland, London: Stevens.

—— and Hepple, B. (1972), *Laws Against Strikes*, London: Fabian Research Series 307.

Kerr, A. and Whyte, G. (1985), *Irish Trade Union Law*, Abingdon: Professional Books.

Kidner, R. (1983), *Trade Union Law*, 2nd edn., London: Sweet & Maxwell.

Klare, K. (1982), 'Critical Theory and Labor Relations Law', in D. Kairys (ed.), *The Politics of Law: A Progressive Critique*, New York: Pantheon.

Labour Party (1989), *Meet the Challenge: Make the Change*, Final Report of Labour's Policy Review for the 1990s, London: Labour Party.

Lasko, R. (1975), 'The Payment of Supplementary Benefit for Strikers' Dependants— Misconception and Misrepresentation', 38 *Modern Law Review* 31.

Lesser, L. (1945), 'Labor Disputes and Unemployment Compensation', 55 *Yale Law Journal* 167.

Lewis, R. (1986), 'The Role of Law in Employment Relations', in R. Lewis (ed.), *Labour Law in Britain*, Oxford: Blackwell.

Lewis, W. A. (1962), 'The Law of Unemployment Compensation in Labor Disputes', 13 *Labor Law Journal* 174.

—— (1969), 'The Lockout Exception: A Study in Unemployment Insurance Law and Administrative Neutrality', 6 *California Western Law Review* 89.

Lloyd, C. (1985), 'Street Collections and the Coal Dispute', 12 *Journal of Law and Society* 285.

Lynes, T. (1972), *The Penguin Guide to Supplementary Benefits*, Harmondsworth: Penguin Books.

McCallum, R. (1989), 'Exploring the Common Law: Lay-off, Suspension and the Contract of Employment', 2 *Australian Journal of Labour Law* 211.

McCarry, G. J. (1983), 'No Work, No Pay', 57 *Australian Law Journal* 378.

—— (1987), 'No Work, No Pay: A Replication to Shaw QC and McClelland', 3 *Australian Business Law Review* 174.

—— (1988), *Aspects of Public Sector Employment Law*, Sydney: Law Book Co.

MacFarlane, L. J. (1981), *The Right to Strike*, Harmondsworth, Penguin Books.

Meltzer, B. D. and Sunstein, C. R. (1983), 'Public Employee Strikes, Executive Discretion and the Air Traffic Controllers', 50 *University of Chicago Law Review* 731.

Mesher, J. (1985), *CPAG's Supplementary Benefit and Family Income Supplement: The Legislation.* Commentary by John Mesher, 3rd edn., London: Sweet & Maxwell.

—— (1985a), 'Social Security in the Coal Dispute', 14 *Industrial Law Journal* 191.

—— (1988), *CPAG's Income Support, the Social Fund and Family Credit: The Legislation.* Commentary by John Mesher, 1988 edition, London: Sweet & Maxwell.

—— (1989), *CPAG's Income Support, the Social Fund and Family Credit: The Legislation.* Commentary by John Mesher, 1989 edition, London: Sweet & Maxwell.

—— and Sutcliffe, F. (1986), 'Industrial Action and the Individual', in R. Lewis (ed.), *Labour Law in Britain*, Oxford: Blackwell.

Miners' Federation of Great Britain (1922), *Annual Volume of Proceedings.*

—— (1923), *Annual Volume of Proceedings.*

—— (1924), *Annual Volume of Proceedings.*

—— (1925), *Annual Volume of Proceedings.*

Ministry of Health (1926), 'Poor Law Guardians and the General Strike', Circular 703, *Justice of the Peace*, May 15, pp. 299–300.

Ministry of Social Security (1967), Royal Commission on Trade Unions and Employers' Associations, First Memorandum, History of the Trade Dispute Disqualification for Unemployment Benefit, Minutes of Evidence No. 54, London: HMSO.

—— (1967a), Royal Commission on Trade Unions and Employers' Associations, Second Memorandum, The Objects and Operation of the Trade Dispute Disqualification for Unemployment Benefit, Minutes of Evidence No. 54, London: HMSO.

—— (1967b), Royal Commission on Trade Unions and Employers' Associations, Seventh Memorandum, Trade Dispute Disqualification for Unemployment Benefit: The Grade or Class Provision, Minutes of Evidence No. 54, London: HMSO.

Moore, J. B. (1951), 'Unemployment Benefits and Labor Disputes', 2 *Labor Law Journal* 414.

Morris, G. (1987), 'Deductions from Pay for Industrial Action', 16 *Industrial Law Journal* 185.

Napier, B. W. (1972), 'Working to Rule—A Breach of the Contract of Employment?', 1 *Industrial Law Journal* 125.

—— (1984), 'Aspects of the Wage–Work Bargain', 43 *Cambridge Law Journal* 337.

—— (1987), 'Industrial Action and Payment of Wages', 131 *Solicitors' Journal* 1230.

—— (1987a), 'Strikes and the Individual Worker: Reforming the Law', 46 *Cambridge Law Journal* 288.

National Confederation of Employers' Organizations (1927), Memorandum of Evidence of NCEO submitted to the Blanesburgh Committee on Unemployment Insurance, London: HMSO.

Netter, M. A. (1971), 'Labor Controversies and Unemployment Compensation', 36 *Albany Law Review* 95.

Norris, T. (1985), 'Dissociating from a Trade Dispute, and Claiming Unemployment Benefit', 135 *New Law Journal* 967.

O'Donovan, J. (1976), 'Give up Your Claim or Give up Your Billet: Legal Redress for Victimised Trade Unionists in Australia', 8 *Federal Law Review* 141.

Ogus, A. I. and Barendt, E. (1982), *The Law of Social Security*, 2nd edn., London: Butterworths.

Ogus, A. I. and Barendt, E. (1988), *The Law of Social Security*, 3nd edn., London: Butterworths.

O'Higgins, P. (1973), 'Strike Notices: Another Approach', 2 *Industrial Law Journal* 152.

—— (1976), 'The Right to Strike—Some International Reflections', in J. R. Carby-Hall (ed.), *Studies in Labour Law*, Bradford: MCB Books.

—— (1986), 'International Standards and British Labour Law', in R. Lewis (ed.), *Labour Law in Britain*, Oxford: Blackwell.

Olea, M. A. and Rodríguez-Sañudo, F. (1988), 'Spain', in R. Blanpain (ed.), *International Encyclopaedia for Labour Law and Industrial Relations*, Deventer: Kluwer.

Pittard, M. J. (1988), 'Trade Practices Law and the Mudginberri Dispute', 1 *Australian Journal of Labour Law* 23.

Rains, H. H. (1979), 'Should Strikers Receive Unemployment Insurance Benefits?', 20 *Labor Law Journal* 700.

Rideout, R. W. (1989), *Principles of Labour Law*, 5th edn., London: Sweet & Maxwell.

Ringer, J. M. (1967), 'Effect of Participation in a Labor Dispute Upon Continuation of Unemployment Benefits', 52 *Cornell Law Quarterly* 738.

Rogaly, J. (1977), *Grunwick*, Harmondsworth: Penguin Books.

Rose, M. E. (1972), *The Relief of Poverty 1834–1914*, London: Macmillan.

Rowell, M. S. and Wilton, A. M. (1982), *The Law of Supplementary Benefits*, London: Butterworths.

Rowley, C. K. (1984), 'Toward a Political Economy of British Labor Law', 51 *University of Chicago Law Review* 1135.

Ryan, P. (1976), 'The Poor Law in 1926', in M. Morris (ed.), *The General Strike*, Harmondsworth: Penguin Books.

Saville, J. (1967), 'Trade Unions and Free Labour: The Background to the Taff Vale Decision', in A. Briggs and J. Saville (eds.), *Essays in Labour History*, London: Macmillan.

Scarman, Lord (1977), *Report of a Court of Inquiry under the Rt. Hon. Lord Justice Scarman, OBE, into a Dispute between Grunwick Processing Laboratories Limited and Members of the Association of Professional, Executive, Clerical and Computer Staffs*, Cmnd. 6922, London: HMSO.

Schindler, S. (1938), 'Collective Bargaining and Unemployment Insurance Legislation', 38 *Columbia Law Review* 858.

Scottish Trades' Union Congress (1927), *Annual Report*, Glasgow: Scottish Trades' Union Congress.

Shadur, M. I. (1950), 'Unemployment Benefits and the "Labor Dispute" Disqualification', 17 *University of Chicago Law Review* 294.

Shaw, J. W. and McClelland, R. (1986), 'Selective Work Bans: "No Work No Pay" Revisited', 2 *Australian Bar Review* 250.

Smith, G. F. (1987), *Public Employment Law*, Sydney: Butterworths.

—— (1989), 'Part Work No Pay?', 2 *Australian Journal of Labour Law* 91.

SOGAT 82 (1986), 'The Role of Law in Industrial Relations', London [mimeo].

Supplementary Benefits Commission (1970), *Supplementary Benefits Handbook*, London: HMSO.

—— (1976), *Report of the Supplementary Benefits Commission for the Year Ended 31 December 1975*, Cmnd. 6615, London: HMSO.

—— (1977), *Report of the Supplementary Benefits Commission for the Year Ended 31 December 1976*, Cmnd. 6910, London: HMSO.

—— (1978), *Report of the Supplementary Benefits Commission for the Year Ended 31 December 1977*, Cmnd. 7392, London: HMSO.

—— (1979), *Report of the Supplementary Benefits Commission for the Year Ended 31 December 1978*, Cmnd. 7725, London: HMSO.

—— (1980), *Report of the Supplementary Benefits Commission for the Year Ended 31 December 1979*, Cmnd. 8033, London: HMSO.

—— (1980*a*), *Supplementary Benefits Handbook*, 6th edn., London: HMSO.

—— (1981), *Supplementary Benefits Handbook*, 7th edn., London: HMSO.

Tiley, J. (1981), *Revenue Law*, 3rd edn., London: Butterworths.

TUC (1923), *Annual Report*, London: TUC.

—— (1925), *Annual Report*, London: TUC.

—— (1926), *Annual Report*, London: TUC.

—— (1927), *Annual Report*, London: TUC.

—— (1929), *Annual Report*, London: TUC.

—— (1933), *Annual Report*, London: TUC.

—— (1938), *Annual Report*, London: TUC.

—— (1939), *Annual Report*, London: TUC.

—— (1951), *Annual Report*, London: TUC.

—— (1952), *Annual Report*, London: TUC.

—— (1955), *Annual Report*, London: TUC.

—— (1956), *Annual Report*, London: TUC.

—— (1957), *Annual Report*, London: TUC.

—— (1967), Royal Commission on Trade Unions and Employers' Associations, Minutes of Evidence *No. 61*, London: HMSO.

—— (1971), *Annual Report*, London: TUC.

—— (1973), *Annual Report*, London: TUC.

—— (1977), *Annual Report*, London: TUC.

—— (1978), *Annual Report*, London: TUC.

—— (1978*a*), 'Trade Dispute Disqualification: Supplementary Benefit', London [mimeo].

—— (1979), *Annual Report*, London: TUC.

—— (1986), *Industrial Relations Legislation*, London: TUC.

Treu, T. (1986), 'Italy' in R. Blanpain (ed.), *International Encyclopaedia for Labour Law and Industrial Relations*, Deventer: Kluwer.

Troup, C. (1985), 'Directly Interested in a Trade Dispute', 14 *Industrial Law Journal* 112.

—— (1986), 'Trade Dispute Disqualification', 15 *Industrial Law Journal* 197.

Von Prondzynski, F. (1987), *Freedom of Association and Industrial Relations. A Comparative Study*, London: Mansell.

Vranken, M. (1989), 'Strike and the Individual Employment Contract: The New Zealand Case', 19 *Victoria University of Wellington Law Review* 249.

Wagner, R. H. (1948), 'Unemployment Benefits in Labor Disputes', 53 *Dickinson Law Review* 189.

Wallington, P. (1983), 'The Employment Act 1982: Section 9—A Recipe for Victimisation', 46 *Modern Law Review* 310.

—— (1985), 'The New Politics of Labour Law', in W. E. J. McCarthy (ed.), *Trade Unions*, 2nd edn., Harmondsworth: Penguin Books.

—— (1984), 'Labour Law Now: A Hold and a Nudge', 13 *Industrial Law Journal* 73

Wedderburn of Charlton (1985), 'The New Politics of Labour Law', in W. E. J. McCarthy (ed.), *Trade Unions*, 2nd edn., Harmondsworth: Penguin Books.

—— (1986), *The Worker and the Law*, 3rd edn., Harmondsworth: Penguin Books.

—— (1987), 'Labour Law: From Here to Autonomy', 16 *Industrial Law Journal* 1.

—— (1989), 'Freedom of Association and Philosophies of Labour Law', 18 *Industrial Law Journal* 1.

—— (1990), *The Social Charter, European Company and Employment Rights: An Outline Agenda*. London: Institute of Employment Rights.

Weiss, M. (1987), 'Federal Republic of Germany', in R. Blanpain (ed.), *International Encyclopaedia for Labour Law and Industrial Relations*, Deventer: Kluwer.

Whyte, G. (1986), 'An Evaluation of the Report of the Commission on Social Welfare', 5 *Journal of the Irish Society for Labour Law* 81.

—— (1986a), 'Social Welfare Law. The Year in Review', 5 *Journal of Irish Society for Labour Law* 135.

—— (1987), 'Social Welfare Law 1986/1987. The Year in Review', 6 *Journal of Irish Society for Labour Law* 88.

Wikeley, N. (1989), 'Unemployment Benefit, the State and the Labour Market', 16 *Journal of Law and Society* 291.

Williams, J. S. (1955), 'The Labor Dispute Disqualification—A Primer and Some Problems', 8 *Vanderbilt Law Review* 338.

Index